Border of Death,
Valley of Life

Celebrating Faith
Explorations in Latino Spirituality and Theology
Series Editor: Virgil P. Elizondo

This series will present seminal, insightful, and inspirational works drawing on the experiences of Christians in the Latino traditions. Books in this series will explore topics such as the roots of a Mexican-American understanding of God's presence in the life of the people, the perduring influence of the Guadalupe event, the spirituality of immigrants, and the role of popular religion in teaching and living the faith.

The Way of the Cross: The Passion of Christ in the Americas
  edited by Virgil P. Elizondo
Faith Formation and Popular Religion: Lessons from Tejano Experience
  by Anita De Luna
Border of Death, Valley of Life: An Immigrant Journey of Heart and Spirit
  by Daniel G. Groody
Mexican Spirituality: Its Sources and Mission in the Earliest Guadalupan Sermons
  by Francisco Raymond Schulte
The Virgin of Guadalupe: Theological Reflections of an Anglo-Lutheran Liturgist
  by Maxwell E. Johnson
The Treasure of Guadalupe
  edited by Virgilio Elizondo, Allan Figueroa Deck, and Timothy Matovina
Our Lady of Guadalupe and Saint Juan Diego: The Historical Evidence
  by Eduardo Chávez
La Vida Sacra: Contemporary Hispanic Sacramental Theology
  by James Empereur and Eduardo Fernández

Border of Death, Valley of Life

An Immigrant Journey of Heart and Spirit

Daniel G. Groody

ROWMAN & LITTLEFIELD PUBLISHERS, INC.
Lanham • Boulder • New York • Toronto • Plymouth, UK

ROWMAN & LITTLEFIELD PUBLISHERS, INC.
Published in the United States of America
by Rowman & Littlefield Publishers, Inc.
A wholly owned subsidiary of The Rowman & Littlefield Publishing Group, Inc.
4501 Forbes Boulevard, Suite 200, Lanham, Maryland 20706
www.rowmanlittlefield.com

Estover Road
Plymouth PL6 7PY
United Kingdom

British Library Cataloguing in Publication Information Available

Library of Congress Cataloging-in-Publication Data

The hardback edition of this book was previously cataloged by the Library of
Congress as follows:

Groody, Daniel G., 1964–
   Border of death, valley of life : an immigrant journey of heart and spirit /
Daniel G. Groody.
     p. cm. — (Celebrating faith)
   Includes bibliographical references and index.
   1. Mexican American Catholics—Religious life. I. Title. II. Series.
   BX1407.M48 G76 2002
   248′.089′6872073—dc21   2002003366

   ISBN-13: 978-0-7425-2241-1 (cloth : alk. paper)
   ISBN-10: 0-7425-2241-5 (cloth : alk. paper)
   ISBN-13: 978-0-7425-5890-8 (pbk. : alk. paper)
   ISBN-10: 0-7425-5890-8 (pbk. : alk. paper)

Printed in the United States of America

♾™ The paper used in this publication meets the minimum requirements of
American National Standard for Information Sciences—Permanence of Paper for
Printed Library Materials, ANSI/NISO Z39.48-1992.

In Memory of

William Lewers, csc
And
Joseph Pawlicki, csc

Brothers, teachers, and friends,
who, through countless acts of goodness,
great and small,
sowed the seeds of the Gospel

Our Lady of the Valley Missionary Program

Contents

Foreword

Virgilio P. Elizondo

Some time ago a young man came to me asking for assistance in formulating a fascinating project. As with others who had come to me, it was both an honor and a distinct pleasure to be asked. Little did I suspect at that time what a great influence he would have in my life. Daniel Groody has not only become a close friend and collaborator in the field of Latino theology and spirituality, but also, even more so, one of my great teachers.

One of the things Daniel brings to his scholarship is a passionate love of the people and the material he studies. He sees love as the first principle of Christian thought and action, and he shows how we cannot truly know something unless we really love it. Such love opens the mind to a new level of understanding that reason alone cannot fully grasp. As the great French philosopher Blasé Pascal once said, "The heart has reasons that reason does not know." Nonetheless, love and critical analysis need each other to truly understand. Love without critical reason is incomplete; critical reason without love is empty. In this outstanding work, Daniel combines both critical thinking with a passionate love as he reflects on the profound spirituality of a suffering people.

In *Border of Death, Valley of Life*, Daniel penetrates through the unquestioned negative stereotypes about Mexican immigrants, and he enables us to see their real beauty, dignity, and worth. He allows us to rise above cultural differences and petty political debates that can often obscure our ability to see the things that really matter. Daniel's approach helps us cut through the false allurements of this world and see those values in human life that are truly good and enduring. In doing so, his groundbreaking work demolishes many of the false idols of the world so that the glory of God might flourish.

Because of the intimate relationship between love and spirituality, it is not surprising that the key category of Daniel's work is *corazón*, or heart. He sees the heart as the dynamic center of life and the place of ultimate understanding. In addition, he shows how love has a spiritual power that truly liberates and changes people. By presenting us with a concrete case study, he shows how love transforms not just individuals but an entire people.

Daniel brings to this book a wealth of scholarship and broad experiences in Hispanic cultures and pastoral ministry. For many years he lived in Central and South America and, as a young priest, he went to work with the Mexican people in South Bend, Indiana. But much more than just working among them, he fell in love with them and welcomed every opportunity to enter into their lives and truly become one of them. Gradually, he became incarnated into the culture of the Mexican poor and experienced a gradual transplant of the *corazón Mexicano* into his own body and soul. When Daniel speaks about inculturation in his work, he speaks with authority because he has not just studied it abstractly but lived it personally. From his experience among the people, and his years of study in theology, he reflects critically on what has taken place.

When he sensed that the ordinary ministry of the parish was not meeting the spiritual needs of the Mexicans he worked with, he discovered a program in Coachella, California, which has been specially designed to respond to the needs of the Mexican immigrant workers. He became totally immersed not just in this dynamic program of evangelization, but also in the lives of the people, even visiting their towns of origin in Mexico, taking part in their local rituals, eating their foods and drinking their water and, as a consequence, even getting their diseases, which happened various times in the course of his research.

When it came time for his investigations along the border, he was not content to simply read about immigration, but he wanted to talk personally to immigration officials, *coyote* smugglers, and especially to immigrants in detention facilities and those out in the "field." Based on my experience of him, I have seen how the people welcome him because, in many ways, he has made himself one of them not through a hollow idealism but rather a genuine "pathos" for the people. For the immigrants, he was not just another foreign missionary, but one who had truly taken on their flesh and become one of them, even in their poverty and suffering.

His love for the people and his work among them led him to many unsuspected places and experiences, and with each one, not only did his love for them keep increasing, but also so did the new knowledge and wisdom he was learning from them. Daniel saw beauty, truth, and goodness in them that others had not recognized. He was discovering insights into God, family, values, prayer, spirituality, and church that he had never learned from the excellent courses he had followed in the universities. He saw in these immigrant people a God-infused wisdom and clarity that emerged from the radical simplicity of their lives, their daily suffering, and their dependence on God. In the experiences of these people, Daniel recognized a huge treasury of spiritual knowledge that needed further exploration. As a result, he has written from the voice of the people a message that also challenges, and even offers a word of hope to, those who may find themselves materially comfortable but spiritually empty.

So it is not surprising that Daniel pursued this serious and critical study of the Valley Missionary Program and its people. In the lives of the Mexican immigrants, he found volumes of "living books" that no scholar had yet opened. While others were speaking and writing about such topics as evangelization, inculturation, option for the poor, base communities, popular faith expressions, and other such topics, at Coachella, these topics took on real flesh and spirit for him. For Daniel, Coachella became a living laboratory for studying crucial and contemporary topics, the Church, and other important issues of today.

So, you can imagine my fascination when Daniel came to me asking for assistance. I had just finished, together with Timothy Matovina, a critical study of another fascinating and vibrant Latino community: San Fernando Cathedral in San Antonio. We were dealing with a very ancient and historic congregation, but with Daniel's work there was one very important difference: he was studying newly arrived immigrants in a place they had created for themselves, a place where they would be at home in this new land!

Unfortunately, relatively few such places in the country have a dynamic and truly inculturated evangelization program like that of the Valley Missionary Program. Having visited it myself with Daniel, I see how it is truly a place where Latino immigrants can come to renew their lives in this new and foreign land. Furthermore, this is the first study that deals with Mexican immigration from the perspective of spirituality. No study has looked at the inner trauma they go through in leaving their homes, crossing through the "border of death," and trying to relocate to a totally new and alien land. Yet from this perspective, Daniel asks the important questions that draw out their spirituality. His work offers a critical reflection on what the Gospel offers to the poorest of the poor and the most neglected and exploited people in our country.

Daniel has the unique ability of writing in a way that combines deep emotion, critical thinking, visual discourse, and poetic expression. He carefully and methodically weaves a beautiful mosaic where the ideas, like the vibrant colors in a painting, interpenetrate one another showing the organic unity of his work. He leads the reader into a very personal experience of the lives and struggles of the immigrants. He shows how a genuine encounter with Christ truly heals, liberates, and transforms immigrants, and, in the process, the experience of these immigrants gives new understanding to some of the core doctrines of Christianity.

Another very interesting aspect of this book is the hermeneutic cycle out of which he works. The program he studies is based on theological ideas of Vatican II, Medellín, Puebla, and Santo Domingo, yet it also emerges out of the praxis of the people. The praxis of the program leads to a new understanding of the principles, while the principles give new meaning to the praxis. Such an approach leads to a very creative, sound, and critical theological reflection.

This theological work is clearly the product of a very engaged theologian, one of the trademarks of Hispanic theology in the United States. His profound analysis arises precisely out of his "incarnation" among the people—that is, his deep involvement and identification with the subjects studied. This very original work of this young theologian stands alongside the growing number of great and creative works that systematically engage the particular context from which their theological reflection emerges. His work will not fit easily into the old categories, as new wine will not fit into old wineskins, because he shows us a new way of doing theology that emerges out of the living faith and social reality of a people.

I trust that this book will be as informative, fascinating, and enriching for you as it has been for me. To speak of the reality of God from within the living reality of the undocumented immigrant poor will be a great contribution to our understanding of God, the Church, inculturation, evangelization, and conversion. We are in great debt to Daniel Groody for having brought the faces, bodies, voices, and spirit of the immigrant poor to the important task of theological reflection.

In the voice of the wounded stranger, we hear the voice of God. Daniel has captured that voice and makes it possible for us to likewise hear that voice. His work is a distinctive and original contribution that will enrich the academy, the Church, and many others who may see something of their own life experience in the spirituality of these Mexican immigrants.

—Virgilio Elizondo
Feast of Our Lady of Sorrows

Introduction

M any years ago, while en route to Santiago, Chile, my plane stopped in Mexico City for eight hours. With time to spare, I came up with the idea of visiting the Shrine of Our Lady of Guadalupe. As I waited in line at the airport to confirm my next flight, I approached a middle-aged Mexican woman and her daughter and asked for directions to the Shrine. When I first spoke to them in broken Spanish, they looked at me as if I had just landed from another planet; they had no idea what I was asking. But after repeated attempts, they finally understood me and then rattled off some directions, in machine-gun fashion, that only furthered my total bewilderment and confusion in this new culture. Aware of my struggles and incomprehension, they paused and hesitated. Then, spontaneously, they said, "Let's go. We'll take you to see the shrine and *La Virgen.*" So we got in a taxi, and they took me to the other side of Mexico City, where they showed me all around the plaza and the Shrine of Our Lady, culminating in a visit to the image of Guadalupe.

After a few hours, these two women looked at me and said, "You're coming over to our house for dinner, aren't you?" I said, "I'd love to, but I have a flight at 7:00 P.M." And they said, "That's okay. Just come over to our house and we'll make sure you get to the airport on time." So they took me to yet another part of the city and welcomed me into their community. These gracious people, who hours before were total strangers, introduced me to their neighborhood, their Church, their family, their friends, and even their cow in the back yard! And after a simple feast of *mole and frijoles* they brought me back to airport, and I continued on my travels. Such was my introduction to Mexico!

My experience with this family was the beginning of a love affair with a people, a country, and a culture. Since then, my life has become inextricably intertwined with the Mexican people, and I have become a different person ever since I started living and working with them. Their spontaneity, generosity, hospitality, and deep faith has touched something deep in my life and has led me to reflect more systematically on the treasures of Mexican culture and spirituality. For the past fifteen years, I have worked closely with many Mexican immigrants living in the United States, and their lives have pushed me to probe more deeply their experience of God and the values that emerge from their faith experiences.

Although early on I became attracted to the spirit of many immigrants, I also found myself continually moved by the extent of their suffering. Year after year, many Mexican immigrants shared with me their trials of leaving home, crossing the border, and entering the United States. Through their stories I began to glimpse the inner landscape of the soul of a people. Their eyes often revealed to me the face of Christ; their perseverance revealed to me a spirit of life triumphing over the hurricanes of adversity. When one immigrant woman with fifteen children said to me, "we are poor and it is difficult, but we trust in God and God is faithful," I knew I had to pay attention. Because she spoke with such conviction, even amidst such difficulties, I believed I would learn much simply by seeing how these immigrants experienced, understood, and enacted their spirituality.

The subject of immigration is not new, but the issue is as important now as ever. Especially as the United States grapples with how to fight terrorist threats from foreign fanatics, the pressure to seal off our American borders is tremendous. While there is a legitimate need to control these borders in the interests of national security, my fear is that many people will never hear the other side of the immigration story. This book presents the human face of immigration. The people I write about are not terrorists or drug dealers. Nor are they criminals or enemies. The vast majority of Mexican immigrants who enter the United States illegally are simply hard-working people, willing to work in menial jobs so they can provide for their families back home in Mexico. Mexican immigration presents the United States with terrible ironies: Mexicans are prevented from coming across, yet they are needed to sustain the American economy; they are often denied jobs, yet often they do the work that no one else wants to do; many fear them, yet they can enrich American culture.

While much has been written in recent years about immigration, nothing has been written about Mexican immigrants and their spiritual lives. This book seeks to respond to such a need. Through it I hope to address some of the profound, human, spiritual hungers of immigrants in this country. While many come to the United States with a strong faith, in many places, Mexican immigrants find themselves dying of spiritual famine. They hunger for a deeper spirituality than they find in many of their local Catholic parishes. Even though many Hispanics have cultural roots that lie deep at the heart of Catholicism, many are leaving the Catholic Church. Andrew Greeley estimates that one fifth of the Hispanics who were raised Catholic have left the Church.[1] Because part of this problematic is spiritual in nature, I chose to focus my energies on one place where some important, spiritual movement was happening, in the hopes that this model might serve as a guide for further pastoral development and intellectual reflection.

As I looked around the country to find places where Mexican Hispanics were flourishing in their spirituality, I discovered the Valley Missionary Program. The people of this organization had the most committed spirituality of any community I had ever seen. These immigrants were not simply playing around in their own self-actualization sandbox (in contrast to some spirituality currents in U.S. American society), but they were living out a central value that profoundly transformed their lives and led them to commit themselves to the needs of their neighbors. Because the program enabled many of them to undergo some real changes in the way they understood God, their world, and their very lives, I quickly became intrigued and enamored with the program. One of its compelling features was that the people reached out not only to those who came to Church but also, and especially, to those who had left the Church or had no contact with it at all. In many ways, great and small, the program embodied God's mercy.

A priest of my own religious community, the Congregation of Holy Cross, founded the program. Even within the community, however, the program had received little attention until recent years. One of the reasons for the protracted appreciation was because this priest—as holy, committed and generous as he was—had the reputation of being eccentric, stubborn, and idiosyncratic. For these reasons and a few others, he was sent far away to the forsaken town of Coachella, California, because, it was thought, in the words of a former provincial, that "there he could do the least amount of damage." To everyone's surprise, he started one of the most innovative spiritual renewal programs in the country and became a beloved figure for many of these immigrants. Rejected from the mainstream currents of the Church, this founder became the cornerstone of a great renewal movement in the Church. The program became so successful that these immigrants themselves started bringing it back to many of the villages and cities where they came from in Mexico. Currently, the organization has "associations" or chapters throughout Mexico, and it continues to grow exponentially. I argue that the program thrives because it touches something deep within them; it brings their spirituality to life and it transforms their lives into something new.

At the same time that I developed a pastoral fascination with the program, I also began doctoral studies in Christian spirituality. For five years I was able to carry on a rich dialogue between scholars in Berkeley and these immigrant farm workers in the Coachella Valley. Eventually, I bought the two worlds together in a doctoral dissertation entitled "Corazón y Conversion: The Dynamics of Mexican Immigration, Christian Spirituality, and Human Transformation." This work was my first attempt to understand the spirituality of Mexican immigrants, and it led me to understand better the social location, culture, and spiritual experience of the people. I also wanted to probe how their encounter with Christ in faith led to the restructuring of their core values, beliefs, and priorities. In other words, I wanted to explore how their experience of God led to integral conversion. Since then I have developed this work further and tried to refine my insights into a systematic reflection on the spirituality of these people. This book, then, is the result of sustained reflection over a period of years on the faith experience of a people. It has become an opportunity to weave together the best of scholarship in spirituality with my own insights and experiences of Mexican culture and pastoral ministry.

From an academic perspective, this work in theology is a disciplined reflection on spiritual experience. One of the initial challenges of embarking on such a work in spirituality is that of methodology. By nature, methodology in spirituality is interdisciplinary; it is a bridge discipline. In this particular case, the primary discipline is theology, but this work also draws on sociology and cultural anthropology. Spirituality, as an academic discipline, seeks to weave these different disciplines together into a coherent conversation about the complex experience of human beings in relationship to God.

This work, then, is done at the crossroads of Mexico and the United States, the rich point of intersection between the two countries. It is also a work done at the crossroads between spirituality and theology, culture and theology, fieldwork and theology, sociology and theology, and the grassroots and the academy. Especially for this study, the border has been a fertile place of reflection and inquiry for examining the spirituality of these immigrants.

In the pages that follow, I describe four dimensions of Mexican immigrant spiritual experience: context, revelation, transformation, and interpretation. In chapter 1, I do an extensive description of the immigrant context. The purpose of this description is to bring out the difficulties and struggles of the undocumented immigrant and to name the pains they experience in the process of breaking from Mexico, crossing the border and entering the United States. I argue that we cannot adequately understand a Mexican immigrant spirituality without better understanding their social location, the trials they endure and the wounds they carry as immigrants. In other words, the starting point for this methodology is the concrete life experience of the poor. Chapter 2 begins to unfold the complex process of spiritual encounter that these immigrants experience. More specifically, I look at how one immigrant community experiences Christian revelation and how this revelation corresponds to their wounds and draws forth new possibilities for their lives. In chapter 3, I examine the transformation that flows from their encounter with God. While I look at their process of conversion through the categories of Bernard Lonergan and Donald Gelpi, I also bring out distinctive dimensions of the conversion experience that come out of this particular, cultural context. In the last chapter, I draw on cultural anthropology and recent studies done on the Guadalupe narrative, the *Nican Mopohua*. This story, I argue, functions as a hermeneutic for understanding this immigrant spirituality because it draws together the Mesoamerican story, the Gospel story and the collective stories of these immigrants.

While classical, theological sources provide the undercurrent and foundation for the entire work, the primary sources are the voices of the immigrants themselves. From these voices I try to draw out the hidden presence of Christ and reflect on the liberating truths of the Gospel as revealed through their lives. To do this research, I knew I needed not only to draw from the wells of Christian and Mesoamerican tradition but also to read the "living documents" of the immigrants and others that are involved in their journey. This research led me into various parts of Mexico and various places along the border. Some of my best "libraries" were the immigration detention centers at the border. Many other rich conversations with Border Patrol agents and *coyote* smugglers deepened my understanding as well.

I knew I crossed a new research frontier when one *coyote*-smuggler offered me a "scholarship" so that I could learn about the immigrant journey first hand, in the desert. Instead of charging me the normal $1,600 fees, he offered to take me for free. He said, "the journey will take a couple of days, and it is tiring and exhausting. It is cold in the mountains and the food is so bad you won't even get hungry. But when we walk through the desert, just make sure you have knee-high leather boots, because there are a lot of rattlesnakes out there, and you often run into them by accident. When they bite, however, they usually bite below the knee, but if you have these boots, you should be okay." Needless to say, the journey of the Mexican immigrant is a life-threatening journey that leaves them vulnerable every step of the way. As a result, this work has turned out to be an in-depth look at the crucified people of our own day, and a reflection on God's undying love for them as they struggle to survive.

This book, consequently, deals with spiritual experience on the margins of society. The margins are those places where the poor live, the place from which voices are seldom heard and from which pages are rarely written. From this perspective I have tried to explore the contours of a liberating spirituality. Their lives have pressed me to ask several questions: who is God? What is revelation? What about the Gospel message heals and transforms? How is the face of Christ revealed on the margins of society today? In other words, I ask, in what ways does Christ's presence emerge in the lives in the hungry, the naked, the homeless, the estranged, the sick, and the imprisoned of American society (Matthew 25:31–46)? Because many immigrants, at one time or another, fit all of the above mentioned categories, I felt that their spiritual lives would reveal much about Christian spirituality in general and a Mexican immigrant spirituality in particular.

As I have reflected on this research, I also have drawn from the wells of many great, pioneering theologians. In particular, this book builds on the fine work of Gustavo Gutiérrez, Jon Sobrino, Virgilio Elizondo, Leonardo Boff, Donald Gelpi, Bernard Lonergan, Sandra Schneiders, Alex García-Rivera, and many others. Their penetrating insights into spirituality, theology, and the Church of the poor in South, Central, and North America have deepened my own understanding of God's activity in the world, especially among the economically poor. By describing reality, critically reflecting on it in light of the Gospel and making a constructive interpretation of their spirituality, I have tried to look at one group of Mexican immigrants in particular. My hope is that other groups might also see something of their own spirituality through the experience of these people.

Central to this work is the whole notion of *corazón*, or heart. One of the reasons I choose this symbol is because the heart is central to Christian religion, Mesoamerican religion, and today's

Mexican culture. *Corazón* in Mexican Spanish has a totally different meaning than heart in the English language, where it is often separated from knowledge and reduced to sentimentality. In this study I refer to the heart as a physical organ with a mystical quality. It is the biological-symbolic site of wisdom and knowledge and a metaphor for the whole of one's conscious, intelligent, and free personality.[2] The heart integrates and informs all aspects of a person, including the mind, will, and emotions. The heart, biblically speaking, refers to the core and center of a person and the source of ultimate understanding. In a similar manner, one cannot understand the dynamics of Mexican spirituality without understanding *el corazón*. Spiritual transformation emerges from *el corazón*.

In addition, the whole notion of conversion is central to understanding this Christian, religious, spiritual experience. The word "conversion," however, means different things to different people. In this study, conversion is not about changing from one religion to another or from one religious tradition to another. Rather, conversion in this study is about the intensification of faith in Christ within the Catholic tradition and the transformation of a person through the restructuring of one's core beliefs, values, and priorities. Like the whole notion of *corazón*, conversion is central to understanding this Mexican immigrant spirituality. Likewise, I see spirituality as that force in the world that humanizes and generates life according to the values of the Gospel. I define spirituality as the way a person in community experiences, understands, and enacts a relationship with God in Christ.[3]

The greatest gifts of this book have been the friendships I have made in the course of my research. Above all, this book is richer because of the friends and colleagues who helped to shape it, and my friendships are richer because of this book. I am especially grateful for all who have helped bring it to birth.

I am especially grateful to my parents, Ed Groody and Cathy Groody, and my religious community, the Congregation of Holy Cross, who have done much to awaken and direct a search for God and a hunger for justice. Many of my insights in this work come from my religious brothers Bill Lewers and Joe Pawlicki, who were key mentors and friends before they died in 1997 and 1999 respectively. I would also like to thank Bob Nogosek and John Connor, in particular, who have also been sources of tremendous insight and inspiration in their apostolic zeal and commitment to the people of Coachella. My provincial superiors, Bill Dorwart and Bob Epping, provided me much support in the writing of this book, as did my other brothers in community, especially Tim Scully, Dick Warner, David Burrell, Donald Fetters, John Dunne, Harry Cronin, Bruce Cecil, and Jose Martelli.

Many colleagues gave me very helpful critiques in the course of rewriting this manuscript as well. I would like to thank Allan Deck, Arturo Bañuelas, Michael Downey, John Cavadini, Larry Cunningham, and my teachers and colleagues at the Graduate Theological Union in Berkeley, California, for their helpful feedback and constructive criticisms. I would also like to thank Alex García Rivera, who has taught me much about the universal story of humanity revealed in the little stories of the poor; Tim Matovina, who has inspired me in many ways through his goodness, brilliance, and generosity; Donald Gelpi, who over the years has taught me about the world of nature, the nature of grace, and the grace of friendship; Davíd Carrasco, who has taught me the liberating power of thought and the role of scholarship in liberating the oppressed; and Frank Houdek, who for many years has guided me in the ways of the Spirit and deepened my understanding of God's action in the world. I also want to thank Jim Phalan, George Greiner, Mary Clemency, the Ruvalcaba family, and Janine Siegel for their accompaniment and treasured friendship, near and far, and especially, Virgilio Elizondo, whose life, witness, faith, friendship, and creative scholarship have been endless sources of insight, inspiration, and grace.

I am also indebted to Jim Langford and the staff of Rowman & Littlefield for their help in editing this manuscript. Hoberto and María Serrano backed this project from beginning to end, and many people who helped in many editorial details, especially Hao-Li and Evan Loh, Joy Groody, Anita González, Janie Dillard, Terry Garza, Jennifer Reed, and Edward Cronin.

I am grateful to many (unnamed) immigrants, *coyotes*, and immigration officials, particularly Chief Tom Walker and immigration officers Henry Rolon, Manuel Figueroa, Juan Amaya, Richard López. Rita Vargas Torregrosa from the Mexican consulate in Calexico, California, and Jorge Bustamante from Tiajuana, Mexico, and the University of Notre Dame have also been invaluable resources in helping me understand the complex dimensions of immigration. Fr. Kenneth Boyack from Paulist Press was very helpful in making available the "Catholic Faith Inventory" survey, and David Fajardo assisted with the translation.

My colleagues from the Institute for Latino Studies at the University of Notre Dame also helped fund and support this project, and I would like to thank, in particular, the director of the institute, Gil Cárdenes, as well as Allert Brown-Gort, Maribel Rodriguez, Maria Elena Bessignano, and especially Philip García. I would also like to thank Richard Brown from Washington, D.C., for his help in analyzing and interpreting the results of my survey research.

J. Michael Parker of the *San Antonio Express News* and Mary Rourke of the *Los Angeles Times* were critical in helping me research the newspaper archives for articles on undocumented immigrants. Pamela Ilott provided me a place to reflect and write at Dovehouse, and I am also grateful to Mario and Anita Valencia for their hospitality and friendship and for a home in San Antonio.

While I have changed the names of the immigrants and program members cited in this book, I am grateful to countless members of the Valley Missionary Project whose heart and soul are etched in the pages that follow. I would especially like to thank deacons Cayo Salinas, Fernando Heredia, and Victor González of the Diocese of San Bernardino and the Valley Missionary Program for their unfailing encouragement, dedication, counsel, and guidance in this project. I would also like to thank Juan Peña, Jesus Escobar, Heraculio Aceves, and Juventino Cardona (presidents of the Valley Missionary Program), the executive committee of the program, the English committees, and Rena Bacca for much support and dedication in tasks great and small. This book has been a labor of love to the immigrants of the Valley Missionary Program. It is an act of gratitude for them and a testimony of how they have been special bearers of divine life. May this book speak but the first word of the grace of God revealed through their stories.

—Daniel Groody, csc
Feast of the Triumph of the Cross

NOTES

1. Andrew M. Greeley, "Defection among Hispanics (Updated)." *America*, September 27, 1997, 13.

2. Jean de Fraine and Albert Vanhoye, "Heart," in *Dictionary of Biblical Theology*, ed. Xavier Leon-Defour (Paris: Desclée Company, 1967), 200–202.

3. I am grateful to Simon Hendry, sj, for his insights into this definition.

"The light shines in darkness, and the darkness has not overcome it."

—John 1:5

1

Corazón Destrozado—The Crushed Heart: The Dynamics of Mexican Emigration and Immigration

A HUNGER FOR FREEDOM, A WALL OF SEPARATION

Overwhelming joy went through the Western world as it witnessed the tearing down of the Berlin Wall in 1989. The great Wall had long stood as the symbol of separation between the material abundance of the West and the economic scarcity of the East. It represented the dividing line between freedom and slavery, opportunity and oppression, prosperity and poverty. The crumbling of the Berlin Wall gave a breath of fresh air to the world, and it gave hope for a new era of freedom for humankind. Especially in the United States, the news of the falling of the Wall reinforced the deep U.S. American ideals of life, liberty, and the pursuit of happiness.

Ironically, as the great wall of separation was coming down in Europe, an even greater and more dangerous wall of separation was being fortified along the 1,952-mile border between the United States and Mexico. Though not a wall of concrete, it is a wall of separation between the citizens of the United States and the poor of Latin America. As doors were opening to those who escaped the tyrannies of communism, doors were closing to those who were trying to escape the tyrannies of the unjust economic, political, and social structures of their own countries.

Between 1961 and 1989, in the hope of finding a better life and a more promising future on the other side of the Berlin Wall, eighty people were killed; fifty-nine of them were shot dead by East German guards who protected the border. Between 1995 and 2002, in the hope of finding a better life and a more promising future in the United States, more than 2,000 immigrants have died trying to cross the U.S.–Mexican border.[1] This means that more than one human life has been lost for each mile along the border since 1995. Those who lost their lives attempting to cross from East to West Germany were considered heroes in the United States, yet those who attempted to cross from Latin America to North America are often considered criminals. While many of the deaths along the Berlin Wall were noted internationally, many of the people who die along the U.S.–Mexican border remain unpublicized, unrecognized, unidentified, unburied, and unmourned. In the public eye, the Mexican immigrants who die often seemed like nothing in life, and, in the end, they appear as nothing in death, without even a simple cross to mark their graves.

The newspapers are full of reports of the horrible conditions that undocumented immigrants have to endure in order to cross the border from Mexico into the United States: "At least seven Mexican immigrants died and more than fifty others were rescued in rural San Diego County canyons . . . after a freak spring storm dropped a foot of snow on (the) mountains"[2]; "Six illegal immigrants sleeping on railroad tracks in south Texas, possibly to avoid snakebites, were killed when a Union Pacific freight train ran over them"[3]; "Six suspected illegal immigrants trying to escape Border Patrol agents plunged 120 feet into a ravine near San Diego . . ., leaving one dead"[4]; "Twelve illegal immigrants who crossed the Mexican border perished as they tried to traverse the barren Arizona desert in 115-degree heat and reach a highway. . . ."[5] The dynamics of Mexican immigration are full of stories like these, about people who drown in rivers, freeze in the mountains, dehydrate in the deserts, and get hit by cars or trains. Given all these painful stories of horror, we are forced to ask: What kind of conditions, circumstances, and pressures lead people to take such risks, expose themselves to such dangers, and face the prospect of even torturous deaths?

In order to provide a foundation for understanding the Mexican immigrants' spirituality and their journey, it is important to look more closely at the social, political, cultural, and economic context in order to understand their lives more adequately. Christian spirituality seeks to understand God, human life, and the relationship between the two. As we try to understand the human experience of Mexican immigrants, we must consider why they leave Mexico, what they endure when they cross the border, and what they experience when they come to the United States. Attention to their wounds as well as their aspirations will increase our appreciation for how their spirituality heals and transforms them. On the surface, we will speak about the story of Mexican immigrants, but at the core, their stories touch and dig into some of the most fundamental dynamics of human existence: the will to survive, the desire for connectedness to others, the hunger to make a meaningful contribution to the world, and the search for God in the midst of daily life and its trials. In the particular story of the Mexican immigrants, we discover aspects of the universal human story and the struggle to live with dignity, friendship, and purpose.[6]

BREAKING FROM HOME IN MEXICO

The dynamics of immigration are as old as humanity, but the extraordinary numbers of immigrants today are symptomatic of the ills of our age. Immigration is a global malady that needs to be analyzed in relationship to the political, social, and economic context that precipitates it. Today more than 100 million people are migrating around the world.[7] The effects of globalization on the poor, in particular, increase these numbers daily.[8]

Virtually all immigrants leave their country because of an urgent need, whether social, political, economic, or religious. Chief among these is the widening gap between the rich and the poor of the world. Poverty, hunger, violence, war, the abuse of human rights, religious and racial prejudice, oppressive intellectual conditions, or a deteriorating economic climate all contribute to the flight of people from one country to another.[9] The unequal distribution of wealth and its consequences put enormous stress on poorer countries and provide one of the chief causes of social instability and global migration. Only in the hope of relieving this pressure does one go through the radical experience of separation from one's homeland, roots, language, and customs in order to become an immigrant, a wanderer, a wayfarer, and a stranger in a new and foreign land where, often, a different language is spoken.[10] Migration is a traumatic undertaking. Such a separation leaves an indelible mark on the heart of the immigrant.

The Pressure to Immigrate

The mass exodus of people from Mexico to the United States is indicative of a country in crisis. Many Mexicans emigrate in the hope of relieving some of the intense pressure caused by unemployment, hunger, disease, poverty, and early death. The majority of Mexican immigrants come to the United States primarily for economic reasons.[11] Mexico's 40 percent unemployment rate and low paying jobs, contrasted with the high demand for labor and comparatively high wages of the United States, draws Mexicans into the United States like a magnet.[12] More than 40 million Mexicans live in poverty and dream of making more than the national wage of 35 cents an hour, or 200 pesos (about $20) every two weeks.[13] In brief, foreign debt, a declining Gross Domestic Product (GDP) per capita, and diminishing "real wages" are some of the primary reasons why Mexicans migrate to the United States.[14] In the words of one immigrant named Mario, "I left a wife and three kids at home not because I wanted to get rich but because I wanted us to survive. When we got to the point where we did not have enough to buy even necessary things like tortillas, eggs, and sugar, I had to immigrate."[15] Many are forced to choose between a dehumanizing poverty at home and the perilous crossing of the border into the United States.

People enter or live in the United States illegally when they do not pass through designated border inspection stations, when they present false papers at these stations, or when they enter legally and then overstay their visas. When they do this, they become classified as "illegal aliens." (Because the term "illegal alien" is a dehumanizing term, I will refer to these immigrants as "undocumented" throughout this book.)

Between 6 million and 12 million undocumented immigrants live in the United States, and the majority of these are from Mexico. Every day, some 4,600 immigrants jump fences, swim across canals, and traverse deserts along the U.S–Mexican border.[16] They come in search of low-paying jobs in agriculture, landscaping, construction, and other areas. Statistics show that, despite increasing attempts to control the border, the number of people trying to enter the country illegally is increasing.[17] And while, paradoxically, market liberalization strategies like NAFTA and other free market policies give the impression of a borderless North American economy, U.S. immigration policies and stricter border controls reveal the high walls between the two countries.[18] While new and bold initiatives have been proposed by Mexican President Vicente Fox and have met with some support from President George W. Bush and congressional leaders, the suffering of immigrants will continue in the years ahead, whether immigrants enter with guest visas or enter illegally.

The economic problems that immigrants face affect multiple levels of their identity. Many of those condemned to a life of poverty and destitution often think of themselves as inferior and incompetent. They often begin to blame themselves for their inability to better their lot in life. With fewer opportunities, many people have less incentive to create, innovate, or try new things; they feel quite powerless, even over their own lives. Young people often see no future at all as long as they stay in Mexico. "The most difficult thing," said Jaime, "is feeling the impotence of not being able to do anything."[19] With poor wages, high expenses, unemployment, and underemployment, many immigrate to the United States just so they can support the family. Ironically, the move to come to the United States to support the family often breaks up the family.

Breaking from Family

Mexican immigrants who come to the United States looking for better lives leave behind much of the world they love. While they feel attracted to many of the jobs, opportunities, and material comforts of the United States, the immigration experience exacts a major price on the families and relatives at home. One of the most immediate human costs of immigration is saying goodbye. Only rarely do families emigrate together. Most often, the man is the one who breaks from home, leaving his wife and children behind for eight months, a year, or longer.[20] "The most painful thing," said Juan, "is leaving the family behind, especially the children, but we do it in the hopes that some day we will have something in Mexico."[21]

As the family breaks up, the husband and wife face double burdens. While the husband often faces a future of dangerous border crossings, economic exploitation, and difficult work, the wife suddenly becomes farmer, rancher, parent, provider, and protector of the household. Most Mexicans immigrants do not want to leave home. The majority are not drug dealers. Nor are they terrorists. Often they say that they leave home not because of inordinate ambition but because of the pressing need to survive. "We don't want to steal," said Adán. "We come here to save some money so that later we can return home to take care of our children."[22]

Breaking from the Familiar

Emigrating to the United States also means leaving behind a familiar environment. Because culture permeates every level of a person, Mexicans find it easier to leave Mexico than for Mexico to leave them. Mexicans love Mexico and are extremely proud of their country. It remains their birthplace, their homeland, and their culture: *"Como Mexico, no hay dos"* ("There is no place like Mexico"). Mexico runs through the blood of the Mexicans, and it never leaves them. It remains as much a part of them as their own family. Mexico is a very festive and distinctive place. *Fiestas patrias* (national holidays), *Dias de los santos* (saints' days), and *posadas* (Christmas rituals) shape the psychological and spiritual consciousness of the Mexican, alongside the smell of *tortillas* (bread), *maíz* (corn), *frijoles* (beans), and other aspects of their culture. The relationships, music, drink, dress, and culture all contribute to the life they enjoy in Mexico. However, poverty puts many strains on their lives. Struggling Mexicans spend so much of their energy surviving that many have little leisure time, making it difficult to nurture significant relationships and develop more of their personal lives. Long hours of work and economic scarcity rob many of them of time for intimacy that would allow them to develop more capacities for human connectedness.

Crossing the great border exacts an enormous toll on Mexican immigrants and their families. Leaving home creates many emotional and practical difficulties. In the midst the process of emigration, immigrants often face a terrible irony: they leave Mexico to escape the insecurity of life, only to come to the United States where they experience an even greater insecurity. They give up their homes, their language, and their customs for an uncertain and pre-

carious future. For many immigrants, crossing the border of death means leaving behind much of what ultimately gives meaning, value, and cohesion to their lives.

CROSSING THE U.S.–MEXICAN BORDER

In southern California, there are three main ways of trying to cross the border without passing through designated points of entry: through a fence along the border (those who do so are known as *alambristas*), across the border canals (known as *mojados* or *braveros*), or through the rugged terrain of the desert mountains and valleys. The immigrants make a dangerous crossing with few or no resources. No matter what the method, the three biggest threats come from immigration officials, smugglers (or *coyotes*), and the perils of the natural environment.

Noted journalist John Annerino brings out just how radical and precarious a journey it is for them:

> [The immigrants] will be wearing cheap rubber shower sandals and ill-fitting baseball cleats to protect their feet from rocks, thorns, hot sand, and lava, not form-fitting one hundred dollar hiking boots; they will carry their meager rations of tortillas, beans, sardines, and chilis in flimsy white plastic bags, not freeze-dried gourmet meals cooked over shiny white gas stoves carried in expensive gortex backpacks. And they will sleep on the scorched bare earth in thin cotton t-shirts, not in cozy two hundred dollar, down sleeping bags. They will follow vague routes, passed down from one desperate generation to the next, across a horizonless no-man's land, not well-manicured trails. Their signposts will be sun-bleached bones, empty plastic water jugs, a distant mountain, not hand-painted fluorescent signs with arrows pointing the trail every quarter mile. They will cross a merciless desert for jobs, not for scenic vistas. And nothing will stop these honest people in their quest for a better life, not the killing desert, and not the transformation of the "tortilla curtain" into the Iron Curtain.[23]

The journey across the U.S.–Mexican border means journeying to the very margins of life. Mexican immigrants experience vulnerabilities from every side and dangers every step of the way.

The Border Patrol: *La Migra*

Guarding the door of entry into the United States is the Border Patrol, popularly known as *La Migra*. The Border Patrol, as part of the Immigration and Naturalization Service (INS), is the largest federal police agency in the country with about 10,000 agents.[24] While the United States has had border control policies throughout its history, these policies have become more restrictive in recent years. Since 1986, federal and state legislatures in the United States have sought to control the nation's borders more aggressively through reforms in immigration policy.[25] Currently, the U.S. government spends more than $6 billion dollars employing agents to protect the border.[26] Although the U.S. Border Patrol currently functions to keep out criminals, drug traffickers, and terrorists, it also keeps out other immigrants who come across the border simply to work and provide for their families. These reforms, coupled with anti-immigrant sentiments, have made it both more difficult and inhumane for the illegal Mexican immigrant to enter and stay in the United States.[27]

Beginning in October 1994, the INS launched Operation Gatekeeper near San Diego, California, Operation Safeguard near Nogales, Arizona, and Operation Rio Grande in east Texas and other initiatives near the major urban areas along the border, all of which were directed toward further deterrence of illegal Mexican immigration. Increased federal investment in border control has driven up costs demanded by illegal smugglers, and it forces immigrants, now more than ever, to cross along ever more difficult routes. While the border strategists have adopted a "prevention through deterrence" philosophy to deter immigrants from crossing, there is no indication that immigration flows have diminished in any way; in fact they have actually increased since these reforms were initiated.[28] Restricting the border has not diminished the migration flows; it has merely redirected them and pushed immigrants more and more into dangerous and life-threatening territory.[29] "It's like pressing a plastic bubble," said Richard López of the busy El Centro sector, "if you press one side of the bubble, the air inside simply shifts to the other side."[30] The U.S. policy has dealt more with the symptoms of immigration than the causes, and, until the government implements more comprehensive strategies that deal with the economic, political and social ills of both countries, Mexicans will continue to migrate to the United States.

Shortly after the Border Patrol apprehended Marcos, he said,

Last night was incredibly difficult. After walking so much, my whole body ached, especially my legs, and I was exhausted. You don't get any sleep and the cold penetrates you. We had to sleep for awhile in the mountains, but it was cold, incredibly cold . . . and then we ran out of water. We let ourselves be captured by the immigration officials just so we could get something to drink. It's dangerous and disorienting out there.[31]

For the undocumented immigrant, the perils are greater now than ever.[32]

The stronger the force of the Border Patrol, the greater the risks that the immigrants take. Because many deaths go unreported and undiscovered, the number of those who die trying to cross the border is presumably even more.[33] Until the U.S. dedicates comparable resources to addressing the human costs of migration as it does to the economic costs, many immigrants will continue to die in the process of crossing the U.S.–Mexican border.[34]

Those who do make it across the border still face difficulties as they try to move northward. Shortly after María and Pepe crossed over, they said "our *coyote* (smuggler) told us that we had to hit the ground because an (immigration) helicopter was coming overhead, and we threw ourselves on the desert floor. When we got up, my wife was covered in cactus spines, and for eight days I removed them from her body."[35] In some cases, vigilante groups in Arizona have taken extreme measures to deter immigrants. Some ranchers have even threatened to kill immigrants that trespass on their property.[36]

Some immigrants who are apprehended spend days, weeks, and even years in detention centers and INS facilities. Maria said she was terrified when immigration officials apprehended her: "I spent two months in the detention center feeling traumatized . . . all I wanted to do was come over and see my children and husband, but when they apprehended me, they put my hands and feet in chains, as if I was a criminal or had murdered someone."[37] She is now living in the United States illegally, and she fears leaving her house because she does not want officials to send her back to an immigration detention center.

The presence of the immigration officials extends beyond the border into secondary checkpoints sixty miles north of the national boundary. On highways, at crossroads, and under bridges, Border

Patrol agents use various techniques to detect undocumented immigrants. Such watchfulness leaves many immigrants on a constant state of alert and anxiety. As Guillermo said, "we're tired of living like rats, jumping from one rat hole to another."[38]

The Smuggler: *El Coyote*

In addition to fearing *la migra*, the immigrant also worries about *el coyote*, the smuggler. The term itself has evolved over the years, and people often use it in the negative sense.[39] Generally, the *coyote* belongs to the culture of the immigrant underground railroad, which has an extensive network of people who help immigrants seek safe passage—when they have the money to pay. Sometimes they are called *polleros* or, the most benign, *traficantes de personas*. Most often, the *coyote* smuggles not drugs but people, though in some places they rival, or collaborate with, drug traffickers. According to Rita Vargas of the Mexican Consulate in Calexico, California, *coyotes* work together with a series of guides to help shuttle immigrants across the border.[40] The *coyote* coordinates the overall plan of the immigrant, but the guides are the ones who lead them across the border. Both act as intermediaries in the immigration process, and they know the most about safe passages across the border and the routes which best evade detection by the immigration officials.

Coyote fees are directly proportional to the size of the Border Patrol. The stricter the control at the border, the more immigrants pay for a *coyote*. Currently, a *coyote* costs anywhere from $800 to $1,800, nearly double the cost of one in 1994.[41] The poorest of the poor, however, come across the border alone. They have no money to hire a *coyote* and they are often the ones who get lost and die in the barren desert borderlands.

The immigrants must entrust themselves to the *coyote;* sometimes this is a fatal mistake. Sometimes the *coyote* will lead people over the border only to rob them on the other side. Other times, *coyotes* will leave immigrants stranded in the middle of the desert, to become disoriented and die of dehydration. Still other times, they will have unsuspecting immigrants carry the *coyote's* backpack, which may have drugs in it. If officials apprehend a group, sometimes these same immigrants can be the ones sent to jail. Women are particularly vulnerable, as *coyotes* sometimes demand sex as payment, or take it by force. "In our group," said Jose, "our *coyote* grabbed one of the young women, took her behind one of the mountains and raped her, even though she was screaming and yelling as he abused her."[42] Those immigrants who enter the country illegally face vulnerabilities every step of the way.

The Life-Threatening Elements: *La Muerte*

One of the largest and deadliest areas along the border is the Imperial Valley of Southern California. It is one of the last great, uninhabited areas of the lower forty-eight states. It has a stark and deadly beauty about it. Almost totally uninhabited and uninhabitable, it is home to bobcats, rattlesnakes (sidewinders), raccoons, coyotes, badgers, skunks, rats, scorpions, and illegal immigrants. Temperatures get as high as 120 degrees in the summer, and there are virtually no water sources in the desert north of the border. Many immigrants travel this route as they try to make it into the United States, and it is the area where the most immigrants die each year. On average, an immigrant a day dies trying to cross the border here.[43]

Those who cross the border know they are entering a life-threatening situation. Because of the constant vigilance of the immigration officials, extreme measures are taken to avoid being seen. For those who lack experience, the possibility of death is very real. The canal-crossing method is the most dangerous. People use ropes, inner tubes, rafts, or plastic bags filled with air or they swim the 120-foot body of water. Some who try to cross the canals don't know how to swim—and they drown. Powerful hydroelectric turbines that feed the electric needs of the valley cause strong unexpected currents, which cause many to lose their footing on muddy river floors. For others, the cold water of the canal freezes and cramps their muscles and paralyzes them from making it safely to the other side. Some will seek refuge in a railroad car, a truckload of carrots, or a truck full of flour. In increasing numbers, many are dying in the desert of hyperthermia caused by extreme temperatures. When people die along the barren trails, birds circle the corpses like carrion, animals prey on the carcasses for food, and the cadavers are often left to decompose in the extreme heat of the sun until they slowly disappear in desert sands. These deserts are long, lonely, desolate, and dry. When asked how immigrants felt about crossing the desert, given the fact that many die along the way, Julio said, "We are aware of the dangers, but our need is greater. There's always the risk of dying in the desert, but the desire to survive and keep going is even more important. It's a gamble."[44]

For food, immigrants bring along a can of beans, tuna fish, a few tortillas, and water. Said one *coyote* named Alejandro, "The food is so bad you won't even want to eat it."[45] When they cross the desert floor, many wear knee-high, tough leather boots, so the biting rattlesnakes cannot penetrate them. Some people get blisters or swollen limbs from the physical demands. Some get tired and worn out in the intense journey through the desert, but those who cannot make it, or find themselves too tired to continue, are often left behind. They travel at night so as not to be seen. As food reserves get low, survival becomes an issue. Immigrants often have to suppress and/or repress deep emotions of loss, grief, loneliness, and isolation in order to make it. Many have no time or leisure to reflect on their lives or process their experiences because of the demands of survival.

The desert heat is the second leading cause of death during border crossings. Each year the Border Patrol combs the desert searching for undocumented immigrants. Even though the Border Patrol, the Mexican government, and volunteer organizations like Humane Borders have initiated various search, rescue, and emergency aid initiatives, the number of rescues is arguably low in proportion to the number of immigrants who are crossing. As human rights advocate Claudia Smith noted, "No amount of search and rescue is enough in the vast expanses of hell to which migrants have been rerouted."[46] Others die from various other causes: hypothermia during cold desert nights, suffocation from within confined spaces in trucks and trains, and fatal injuries from vehicle accidents. Put simply, illegal entry across the U.S.–Mexican border is extremely dangerous and potentially fatal.

Some songs in popular culture capture the price that the border crossing exacts on families. The following song is called *Un noble engaño*, "A Noble Deception."[47]

Un noble engaño	*A Noble Deception*
Joaquín tenía quince años	Joaquín was only fifteen
Pedro tenía diez y seis	Pedro was sixteen
venían pa' Estados Unidos	They were coming to the United
salieron de Monterrey	States.

traían grandes ilusiones
de tanto que oían hablar
de llegar a Houston, Texas
y ponerse a trabajar.

A Joaquín se le hizo fácil
el Río Grande cruzar
pero el Río Grande iba lleno
y no lo pudo lograr.
Pedro lloraba el fracaso.
Casi perdió la razón
al ver a su hermano ahogarse
en ese río traidor.

Un año cumple mi hermano
que el cielo lo recogió.
mis pobres padres no saben
que a Houston jamás llegó.
Yo me hago pasar por él
cuando mis padres escribo
no les digo la verdad
ellos piensan que está vivo.

Después de una larga ausencia
yo regreso dispuesto a contarles
todo,
todo lo que
encierro aquí en mi pecho
mi pobre madre llorando me
abrazaba y me besaba
"¡Has vuelto al fin hijo mío!"
Y sus lágrimas rodaban
Y al preguntar por Joaquín,
una sonrisa fingí.
Tuve que seguir fingiendo
Para no verla sufrir.

Yo me hago pasar por él
cuando a mis padres escribo
no les digo la verdad
ellos piensen que está vivo.

They left from Monterrey.
They had great dreams
From hearing so much talk.
They wanted to go to Houston,
Texas,
And begin working there.

Joaquín thought it was easy
To cross the Rio Grande.
But the river was full
And he could not make it.
Pedro cried at the failure
He almost went insane
Upon seeing his brother drown
In that treacherous river.

It was one year since my brother
Was called back to heaven.
My poor parents don't know
He never reached Houston.
I assume my brother's name
When I write my parents.
I don't tell them the truth.
They think he's still alive.

After a long absence
I returned ready to tell all,
All that is
locked up in my heart.
My poor mother crying
Hugged and kissed me.
"You have returned at last, my
son!"
And her tears did fall.
And when she asked for Joaquín
I forced myself to smile.
I had to continue to pretend
So as not to see her suffer.

I pretend I am him
When I write to my parents.
I do not tell them the truth.
They think he is still alive.

ENTERING A FOREIGN LAND

When immigrants cross the U.S.–Mexican border, they enter into a strange and foreign land.[48] They move into unknown territory—socially, culturally, linguistically, economically, politically, legally, and even spiritually. They move from the bottom rung of their home culture in Mexico to the bottom rung of a foreign culture in the United States. They arrive not as tourists but as strangers and outsiders. As a result, immigrants receive a double blow: They are forced to leave the homeland they love and belong to, yet often they feel unwelcome and unwanted when they finally come to the United States.[49] For the undocumented Mexican immigrant, such messages of cultural nonacceptance produce a deep sense of alienation that reaches into every level of the immigrant's life.

Political-Cultural Alienation: Mexican in an American Land

Above all, the immigrants move from a world where they belonged to a world where they are labeled as "illegal aliens." This deepens their sense of estrangement. Even people with green cards are called "resident aliens." They experience acute alienation from home, church, culture, and even themselves. When many Mexican immigrants come to the United States they often experience cultural displacement. The cultural differences often cause immigrants to isolate and insulate themselves from the outside world. Oscar said, "I spent three years alone when I came here, and for the first month I was closed up in my house. I had no friends and I did not want to leave because I thought people were going to look at me as different."[50]

The most immediate experience of alienation is the language. The inability to speak or understand English intensifies their feeling of distance from home. Limited educational backgrounds and illiteracy make it even harder to learn the language. Some cannot communicate about even the most basic aspects of life. "When I was separated from my wife at the border," Miguel said, "I spent weeks worrying about her. I did not even know where she was. She could not even call us because she couldn't read the numbers on the telephone."[51]

For other immigrants, the demands of survival leave little free time to do anything but work. Many labor all day in agricultural jobs, rising sometimes as early as 2:30 A.M. When they arrive home they are often exhausted. In addition, few immigrants have cars, so transportation to classes, even if available, is in many instances very difficult.

Besides language problems, they find it difficult to express the deeper experiences of the heart: fears of being rejected, useless, unimportant, used, abused, mistreated, disregarded, and oppressed. As a result, many immigrants build up high psychological walls between themselves and the outside world: many become strangers even to themselves.

Another form of alienation is cultural. The movement from Mexican culture to an American culture is a dramatic shift. Many Mexicans go through painful moments of disorientation when they enter into U.S. American society. The customs, values, and attitudes are often dramatically different.[52] Even the social geography is quite dissimilar. For example, in Mexico the social life often centers on the town square. More often than not, in suburban United States the center is the shopping mall. The cultural values of the U.S. American and the Mexican are often inverted. As Mexicans enter into the U.S. American world, they often find themselves caught in the crossfire of conflicting value systems. They experience the economic pressures of survival and, at the same time, the constant pressures of a materialistic culture.

When they go back to Mexico, many immigrants often are not accepted in the same way as before they left. Mexicans describe this experience as feeling *ni de aquí, ni de allá* [neither from here (the United States) nor there (Mexico)], and with good reason: it is difficult to survive in one's hometown, yet it is difficult to find a true home in the United States. Living in the United States leaves many Mexican immigrants with the feeling of absolute nonbelonging.[53]

Socio-Economic Alienation: Poor in a Prosperous Land

Virtually all undocumented Mexican immigrants have no security, no benefits, no health care, and no guarantee of long-term work.[54] They pay taxes but get few, if any, benefits. Although undocumented workers pay over $7 billion dollars annually in taxes and social security, many are not eligible for most benefits.[55] They are often abused by their boss (or *contratista*), and, through various types of trickery, sometimes are denied their just wages. Even recent U.S. Supreme Court decisions have decided that federal immigration law takes precedence over labor law, which makes immigrants even more vulnerable. Whereas previous court decisions used to protect immigrant rights and the right to compensation for work rendered, newer legislation has ruled against them, further opening the undocumented immigrant up to labor exploitation.[56]

The Mexican immigrant typically labors in jobs that most U.S. workers do not want. Some are dangerous and precarious. They plow fields in temperatures above 110 degrees, fumigate crops with poisonous chemicals, prune vines amid rattlesnakes and scorpions, pick strawberries with their backs bent over, and tend citrus groves from the break of day. In many ways, the California economy is built on the backs of migrant workers like these. Typically, Mexican immigrants are more willing than U.S.-born workers to take jobs that are boring, dirty, dangerous, and low paying. California's shaky economy in recent years also has created a difficult environment for them. Immigrants are often the scapegoat for social and economic problems. Negative social messages deepen the experience of alienation for these people.

The jobs the immigrants get often are unstable. When workers begin to protest their conditions, they can easily be dismissed. "For every person working in this valley," said Esteban, "there are five more behind them waiting to take your job."[57] Because of the large numbers of immigrants looking for jobs in southern California, there is a super-abundance of unskilled laborers. Corporations maintain the upper hand. This creates conditions in which workers are often exploited and manipulated. "We live in a new era of the plantation-estates," said Mario, "but the only difference is that [our slavery] is more disguised now." Even though he is a college graduate, Mario spends his days working in the agricultural fields of California. "We work like slaves for the multinational corporations, but they have no regard for us. We break our backs in the sun, but for little money."[58] Those who hire the immigrants often see them just as arms and limbs without hearts or souls, unrecognized bodies viewed in terms of their economic usefulness rather then their human and spiritual potential.

Psycho-Spiritual Alienation: Lonely in an Unfamiliar Land

In leaving Mexico, many immigrants enter a world of social poverty and become disconnected from family, culture, and homeland. "The most painful thing is separating from the family and leaving behind your loved ones as you search for a more dignified life," said Gustavo.[59] Loneliness is a heavy burden and one of the most unrecognized aspects of the immigrant's pain.

In the midst of their separation from home, many of these immigrants long to know that they have a place in someone's life, and especially in someone's heart, to know that someone cares, to know that it makes a difference to someone if they are not around. Without the feeling of connectedness, the agony and emptiness can easily give rise to deviant behavior in drugs, sex, gambling, and alcohol, all of which can lead to various psychological and physical sicknesses. Their loneliness becomes all the more acute when they come to the one place they expect to feel at home, namely the Catholic Church. Often, *even there*, they do not feel welcome.

Many Mexican immigrants live in isolated and rural areas. Because their experience of the institutional Church is often limited, some see priests infrequently, so they have little contact with the sacramental life of the Church. They often have a negative or neutral understanding of God and the institutional Church. In general, they are accustomed to few liturgical services, and they often have to pay for those they do request. Many have very limited instruction in catechism as well, except from many of their grandmothers. As a result, many immigrants come with a notion of a punitive God who scrutinizes their behaviors and watches them with a punishing vigilance. Nonetheless, many immigrants have a deep sense of the sacred in their daily lives and a deep sense of the providence of God.

The pressure to work prevents immigrants from addressing their loneliness and other inner pains. After he left his wife in Mexico, Miguel stated, "I would just cover up my pain by working, working, and working."[60] Despite busying himself with constant activity, the loneliness continued to afflict him. He continued, "I used to just try to keep myself busy in the fields because the pain was so intense. It used to drive me crazy, and I used to do almost anything to distract myself so as to numb the pain I was feeling."[61]

Immigrants often feel tremendous longing for their families back in Mexico. Many Mexican children grow up not seeing their father for months or years, lacking even the simplest gestures of touch and affection that are part of a loving relationship.

For those who have no family contacts in the United States, the loneliness is even greater. They have no one to hold or share with on deeper levels. They often experience a deep feeling of rejection. In their isolation and abandonment, they often ask, "Will anyone be there for me?" "Does anyone care?" "Does my life have any significance?" "Can I trust my co-workers?" "Will they call immigration officials?" The fear of being deported is one degree of the immigrant's loneliness, but beneath this is another: The fear that one is nobody to anybody.

Since many of the immigrants leave immediate family behind, they have a deep need to connect to other people. Even when they are around others, however, they often feel incomplete while their family is far away in Mexico. This deep longing to connect is what drives them to take incredibly high risks to return to visit, or to encourage their family to return with them, even with the dangers involved.

For some, their problems worsen as they try to bring their families with them. Jesus Jiménez, a Mexican national who had worked in Fresno, California, is one example. At the age of seventeen, he returned to Mexico to marry the woman he loved. In the perilous crossing over the border, he and his wife hit a snowstorm, and the *coyote* who was guiding them abandoned them to die in the cold. Having been married only two weeks, Jiménez's bride, Osveia Tepec Jiménez, only twenty years old, died in his arms amid the freezing temperatures of the mountains. While recuperating in the hospital, he said, "I've loved her all my life . . . we were going to make a new life here, so much better than the one we had. We had so many dreams, but we will never live them now. It's all my fault for bringing her."[62] Of all the burdens they carry, guilt is one of heaviest.

While some feel noble in their attempts to provide for their families, many experience a burden of culpability, which comes in various forms: the guilt of not being able to return for the funeral of a loved one, the guilt of not being able to raise a family and be a father to one's children, the guilt of infidelity, and even the guilt of not sending enough money home. Amidst this loneliness, the temptations increase. Looking for someone to touch or hold often drives one to search for a prostitute or a passing affair, someone to connect with and alleviate the pain of the loneliness. Afterwards, some immigrants experience a double burden: the burden of loneliness has not lifted, and the burden of guilt remains, a guilt that comes from the feeling of having betrayed the ones they love and have left behind. Some even begin new families on the American border while maintaining a family in Mexico.

Many immigrants experience a complex, overlapping feeling of alienation from home, family, culture, and even God. Drugs and alcohol help alleviate the pain yet drag them into the vicious cycles of poverty, depression, and failure. Loneliness often leads them to shut down emotionally. Many immigrants become all the more in need of love but all the more unable to find it or express it, resulting in a deep feeling of emptiness.

The Immigrant Predicament: A Stranger in a Foreign Land

Some immigrants who come to the United States experience new prosperity and tremendous opportunities. For many, however, their situation gets worse before it gets better. The physical demands of border crossing are arduous enough, but unfortunately they are only the beginning of the difficulties that they experience. While many Mexicans come to the United States looking for a better job, or at least some money to help them survive in Mexico, they often go from bad to worse, from *guate-mala* to *guate-peor,* as some say. Their struggles to survive are as difficult on the U.S. side of the border as on the Mexican side, sometimes more so.

After it is all said and done, after the immigrant has broken from family, gone through the trials of the border crossing, and worked under harsh conditions, many of them ask themselves, "Am I better off now than I was in Mexico?" "Have I really advanced at all?" While they follow the ripening of the crops, many immigrants, humanly speaking, are unable to ripen themselves.[63] Slowly there creeps into the immigrant's consciousness a painful realization that one is in an even more miserable condition than in Mexico.

THE IMMIGRANT JOURNEY AS A WAY OF THE CROSS

For the immigrant, the road across the scorching temperatures of the desert is a devil's highway. In the process of leaving Mexico, crossing the border, and entering into the United States, undocumented Mexican immigrants experience nothing short of a walk across a border of death. Even when they do not die physically, they under go a death culturally, psychologically, socially, and emotionally. Their journey involves an economic sentencing, whereby they have to shoulder the difficult responsibilities of leaving family, home, and culture for an unknown future in the United States and the search for a job with meager wages. The Mexican immigrant experiences an agonizing movement from belonging to nonbelonging, from relational connectedness to family separation, from being to non-being, from life to death. When these immigrants arrive in the United States, they are often tired, burdened, and wounded. Not all Mexican immigrants experience such extremes of the immigration process, but many of them do.

As we look more closely at the lives of these immigrants and the suffering they experience, we see the many forces that affect their lives. The suffering they experience is an important starting point for a discussion about their spirituality. Spirituality pertains to the totality of life, including the social, economic, cultural, political, and economic dimensions that shape it. No serious discussion of the topic can ignore these elements that affect the lives of these immigrants so dramatically. Any credible discussion of a Mexican immigrant spirituality must have reference to the pains and trials of their lives, as well the hopes and desires they have for a better future.

Within the particular stories of their lives, we see echoes of the universal experience of suffering. The poor often bring forth truths that are the most basic to human life. They penetrate the superficialities of a cosmetic culture and reveal the naked truth of human existence. Through them we can glimpse hints of the hidden presence of God who lives with them on the margins of society. These immigrants are willing to descend into the depths of hell in the desert for the people they love so that they may have better lives. Within their particular stories of hunger, thirst, estrangement, nakedness, sickness, and imprisonment we can begin to see the face of a crucified Christ (Matthew 25:31–26:2). In their suffering, the immigrants reveal the hidden mystery of Christ today.

At the same time, the life of Jesus as revealed through the Scriptures gives these immigrants a new way of understanding their own lives. The life, death, and resurrection of Christ are foundational to their spirituality. The naked truth of human life is also revealed in the person of Jesus, who also makes known the truth about God. Like Jesus, many of these immigrants sacrifice their comfort and risk their lives for the good of others (John 15:13). For these immigrants, the life of Jesus reveals the truth about God and the truth about their human experience.

The journey across the border of death is a very real way of the cross for many immigrants, and the entrance to the United States is an experience of crucifixion. Overall, this journey to the United States resembles Jesus' own journey to Jerusalem, a land of great promise but also great suffering. Economically, the undocumented Mexican immigrant experiences a movement from poverty in Mexico to poverty and exploitation in the United States. Politically, they experience oppression. Legally, they are accused of trespassing. Socially, they feel marginalized. Psychologically, they undergo intense loneliness. And spiritually, they experience the agony of separation and displacement. "That's the way it is,"affirmed Carlos, "but it doesn't matter, we still have to keep going."[64] Life in the United States is the place where many Mexican immigrants experience a contemporary Golgotha, but it is also the place where some experience the rising to a new way of life.

NOTES

1. Until recently, accurate statistics for deaths along the border have not been available. While U.S. Border Patrol statistics have differed from those from Mexican authorities, both sides have seen dramatic increases in the number of deaths since 1995. For up to date statistics and information as to why Mexican statistics differ from those of the U.S. Border Patrol, see www.stopgatekeeper.org (accessed June 2002). See also Karl Eschbach and others, "Death at the Border," *International Migration Review* 33 (1999): 430–54. In the Eschbach study, the authors note that while much energy has gone to analyze the economic costs of migration, little effort has gone to a study of the human cost.

2. Ken Ellingwood, H.G. Reza, and James Rainey, "At Least 7 Migrants Perish in Cold," *Los Angeles Times*, April 3, 1999, Sec. A, 1.

3. Times Wire Reports, "Asleep on Tracks, 6 Immigrants Die," *Los Angeles Times*, October 13, 1998, Sec. A, 10.

4. Greg Miller, "6 Fleeing Border Patrol Fall Into Ravine; 1 Killed," *Los Angeles Times*, January 22, 1996, Sec. A, 3.

5. Daniel J. Wakin, "12 Illegal Immigrants Are Found Dead in Desert," *New York Times*, May 24, 2001.

6. Alejandro García-Rivera eloquently develops how the little stories of San Martín de Porres contain the big and universal story of God's love for all of God's creatures. See García-Rivera, Alejandro. *St. Martín De Porres: The "Little Stories" and the Semiotics of Culture* (Maryknoll, N.Y.: Orbis, 1995).

7. Silvano Tomasi, "Pastoral Action and the New Immigrants," *Origins* 21 (1992): 580–84.

8. Among the growing body of literature on globalization, see especially ed. F. Jameson and M. Miyoahi, *The Cultures of Globalization* (Durham, N.C.: Duke University Press, 1998); A.B. King, ed., *Culture, Globalization and the World-System: Contemporary Conditions for the Representation of Identity* (Minneapolis: University of Minnesota Press, 1997); ed. E. Mendieta and S. Castro-Gómez, *Teorías sin disciplina: Latinoamericanismo, poscolonialidad y globalización en debate* (México City: Editorial Porría, 1998).

9. Tomasi, "Pastoral Action and the New Immigrants," 582.

10. Denis Muller, "A Homeland for Transients: Towards an Ethic of Migrations," in *Migrants and Refugees, Concilium 1993/4*, ed. Dietmar Mieth and Lisa Sowle Cahill (Maryknoll, N.Y.: Orbis Books, 1993), 131.

11. A recent study showed that 27.5 percent of Mexican immigrants came to the United States because of the lack of a steady job and a decent wage. CONAPO (Consejo Nacional de Población), COLEF (El Colegio de la Frontera Norte), and STPS (Secretaría del Trabajo y Previsión Social), *Encuesta sobre Migración en la Frontera Norte* (Tijuana: El Colegio de la Frontera Norte, 1994). Other immigrants like Central Americans also have come to the United States because of economic and political instability in their country. For more on this subject, see Leo R. Chávez, Estévan T. Flores, and Marta López Garza, "Migrants and Settlers: A Comparison of Undocumented Mexicans and Central Americans in the United States," *Frontera Norte* 1, no. 1 (1989): 49–75.

12. Jorge Bustamante of El Colegio Frontera del Norte in Mexico claims the wage differential between Mexican and American laborers in blue-collar jobs is ten to one. Others say Mexicans, on the whole, earn about one-fifth to one-fourth of the wages earned by inhabitants of the United States. See John H. Coatsworth, "Commentary on Enrique Dussel Peters' 'Recent Structural Changes in Mexico's Economy: A Preliminary Analysis of Some Sources'," in Marcelo Suárez-Orozco, *Crossings: Mexican Immigration in Interdisciplinary Perspective*. (Cambridge: Harvard University Press, 1998).

13. For a descriptive account of the beauty and poverty of life in Mexico, see John Annerino, *Dead in Their Tracks: Crossing America's Desert Borderlands* (New York: Four Walls Eight Windows, 1999).

14. See Enrique Dussel Peters, 'Recent Structural Changes in Mexico's Economy: A Preliminary Analysis of Some Sources,' in Suárez-Orózco, *Crossings*, 54–74.

15. *Dejé mi esposa y tres niños en México no porque quiero ser rico sino que querría que nosotros sobreviviéramos. Cuando llegó el momento cuando no tuvimos aun dinero para com-*

prar lo más necesario como la tortilla, el huevo y el azúcar, tenía que venir. Interview by author, January 12, 2000, tape recording, El Centro Detention Center, El Centro, Calif.

16. This figure is an estimate and is only an approximate estimate of how many attempt to cross each year. For the number of apprehensions each year, see www.ins.usdoj.gov. For a good, popular overview of the impact of immigrants and Mexican culture on American life, see *Time*, June 11, 2001, special issue "Welcome to America."

17. For up to the date statistics on border apprehensions, see http://www.ins.usdoj.gov/graphics/aboutins/statistics.

18. NAFTA is the North American Free Trade Agreement which, signed on January 1, 1994, seeks the gradual removal of tariffs and other trade barriers between Canada, the United States, and Mexico. In bringing together 365 million consumers among the three countries into an open market, it is now, annually, a $178 billion dollar trade agreement.

19. *Lo más difícil es el sentir la impotencia de no poder hacer nada.* Mexican immigrant, interview by author, January 19, 2000, tape recording, El Centro Detention Center, El Centro, Calif.

20. Eighty-five percent of Mexican immigrants apprehended by U.S. immigration officials are male. U.S. Immigration officers Henry Rolon and Manuel Figueroa, interview by author, January 18, 2000, tape recording, U.S. Immigration offices, El Centro, Calif.

21. *Lo más doloroso es dejar a la familia, principalmente los niños . . . es que uno le duele más . . . pero uno lo hace para el fin de tener algo en México.* Mexican immigrant, interview by author, January 19, 2000, tape recording, El Centro Detention Center, El Centro, Calif.

22. *No queremos robar. Venimos aquí para ahorrar algo y después volver a cuidar nuestros niños.* Mexican immigrant, interview by author, January 19, 2000, tape recording, El Centro Detention Center, El Centro, Calif.

23. Annerino, *Dead in Their Tracks*, 40–42.

24. There are very legitimate reasons for controlling the border that should not be ignored. Kenneth Himes notes, "While generally one might presume that the emigrant is to be accepted it remains possible that a nation may have to regulate immigration in order to meet its obligations to those already within its borders. A nation-state can properly develop policies which protect the common good of the society and this may include limiting immigration when goods such as communal integrity, cultural ideals, and material well-being are threatened by too many immigrants. But . . . claims by governments in this regard are subject to scrutiny." Legal advocates of more open borders and activists like Claudia Smith of San Diego argue that a country's right to control its borders is subject to limitations based on human rights. Border polices that maximize risks and increase the number of immigrant deaths, however, should be vigorously challenged. See Kenneth R. Himes, "The Rights of People Regarding Migration: A Perspective from Catholic Social Teaching," in *Who Are My Sisters and Brothers?* ed. Carleen Reck (Washington, D.C.: United States Catholic Conference, 1996), 28–29 and www.stopgatekeeper.org.

25. The Immigration Reform and Control Act (IRCA) of 1986 targeted illegal immigration. The Immigration Act (IMMACT) of 1990 increased employment-based visas but limited immigration as a whole. California's Proposition 187

threatened to intensify the immigrant's suffering by limiting their access to public services. Susan González Baker and others, "U.S. Immigration Policies and Trends: The Growing Importance of Migration from Mexico," in Suárez-Orozco, *Crossings*, 80–105.

26. See www.ins.usdoj.gov.

27. See www.stopgatekeeper.org.

28. Wayne A Cornelius, "Appearances and Realities: Controlling Illegal Immigration in the United States," in *Temporary Workers or Future Citizens: Japanese and U.S. Migration Policies*, ed. M. Weiner and T. Hanami (London: Macmillan, 1997), 114–44.

29. In Fiscal Year 2001, however, the number of apprehensions actually decreased by 24 percent. It is not clear yet what these figures indicate. Border control advocates argue that this signals the new policies are working because they have diminished the immigration flows. Others think the decline suggests new hope for Mexicans because of the reform policies of Mexican President Fox, who has done much to bring to light the struggles of the immigrant. Still others think that smugglers are remapping their strategies in light of recent policies and simply need time before bringing more immigrants across. Whatever the reason, there are still hundreds of thousands more apprehensions now than in 1994, when the new policies were initiated.

30. U.S. Immigration Officer Richard López, interview by author, January 20, 2000, U.S. Immigration offices, El Centro, Calif. I would like to thank officers Henry Rolon, Manuel Figueroa, Juan Amaya, Richard López, and Chief Tom Walker for these statistics and their generous support in giving me an indepth understanding of life at the border, especially the extensive efforts they have made toward saving immigrant lives when endangered in the border crossing.

31. *La noche fue muy pesada. Con mucho caminar, todo mi cuerpo me duele, lo que es piernas, lo que es cansancio, porque uno no duerme y nos agarró el frío. Tuvimos que dormir un rato allá en las montañas, pero hacía mucho frío, fué un friazo . . . y después se nos terminó el agua, y en la mañana queremos agua y queremos agua, y dejamos que nos agarre la migra para poder tomar agua no más. Se desorienta allá y es muy peligroso. . . .* Mexican immigrant, interview by author, January 19, 2000, tape recording, El Centro Detention Center, El Centro, Calif.

32. Immigration officials and other humanitarian organizations have tried to protect immigrants through programs that try to rescue them as they have become stranded or lost in the perils of the natural environment, although many of these were not initiated until the middle of 1998. While some cases have been reported where Border Patrol agents have sunk a raft carrying illegal immigrants (Associated Press, "Border Patrol Agent Who Sank Raft Carrying People to Resign," *Los Angeles Times*, 12 December 1999, Sec. A, 14), many other documented and undocumented reports speak about how the Border Patrol has rescued immigrants in the midst of life-threatening conditions. Some immigration officials admit to feeling caught between the rock of government policy and the hard place of human suffering and have helped rescue many immigrants. For a descriptive account of desert rescues of immigrants by the Border Patrol, see Annerino, *Dead in Their Tracks*, 82–101, 173–75.

33. While more than 2,000 people died between 1996 and 2002, these figures are arguably very conservative. These are the documented deaths, and the actual figures are much higher, given the fact that these estimates do not include those who die in the deserts and are buried in the sands, those who drown in the canals or rivers and float into the Gulf of Mexico, and those who die on the Mexican side of the border. See www.stopgatekeeper.org.

34. For more information on immigrant deaths along the U.S.–Mexican border, see www.stopgatekeeper.org.

35. *Nuestro coyote nos dijo que tuvimos que tirarnos al suelo porque venía un helicóptero, y nos tiramos al suelo. Cuando nos levantamos, estábamos llenos de las espinas de los cactus. Por ocho días estaba quitando espinas del cuerpo de mi esposa.* Mexican immigrant couple, November 19, 1999, tape recording, Coachella, Calif.

36. Mark Flatten, "Tensions Heat up Along Border," Phoenix: *East Valley Tribune*, May 27, 2000, A–1, A–6.

37. *Duré dos meses en el centro de detención como traumada . . . solamente quería pasar a los Estados Unidos y ver a mis hijos e hijas y esposo, pero cuando me detuvieron, me amararon en cadenas mis brazos y mis pies, como si fuera delincuente o que había matado a alguien.* Female team member, interview by author, January 19, 2000, tape recording, Coachella, Calif.

38. *Estamos cansados de vivir como ratas, brincando de up pozo de ratas a otro.* Mexican immigrant, conversation with Virgilio Elizondo, San Fernando Cathedral, San Antonio, Tex. Date uncertain.

39. According to Juan Amaya of El Centro Border Patrol in El Centro California, the term *coyote* was first used to describe the immigrant, not the smuggler. Those who crossed illegally by the river were called *mojados,* and those who jumped from bush to bush, trying to avoid apprehension by immigration officials, were called *coyotes.* Like the animal, they sought refuge in the wild and tried to reach their objective through clandestine and cunning means. Later, the term *pollos* described the immigrant, who was under the control of the *pollero.* Since the *pollos* are physically in danger by the *coyote,* it came to describe the physical dangers experienced by the immigrant as well.

40. Today the professional *coyote* not only risks his own life but enlists children to function as guides. They find it safer and cheaper to pay a child to usher people across the border. While an adult *coyote* can face a sentence of six to twelve years in prison, minors receive only a brief time at juvenile detention centers, and they are released, at most, after a few months. One fourteen-year-old boy, who makes his living as a *coyote,* crosses the border regularly only to clean windshields on cars on the other side. Associated Press, "Immigrant Smugglers Use Youths as Guides," *San Antonio Express News,* February 2, 1999, Sec. B, 2.

41. *Migration News* indicates that the price of being smuggled to Los Angeles doubled between 1994 and 1996, from $250–300 to $500 or more (*Migration News,* March 1996, February 1997). My own research indicates that in the year 2002 the costs are much higher. Border Control strategists argue that tighter borders will deter immigrants, which subsequently leads to higher smuggling fees. In fact, most of the time families living in the United States help pay for the fees of those trying to enter. See also Peter Andreas, "The U.S. Immigration

Control Offensive: Constructing an Image of Order on the Southwest Border,"
in Suárez-Orozco, *Crossings*, 341–56.

42. *En nuestro grupo el coyote agarró una de las mujeres jóvenes, la llevó detrás de una loma y la violó aunque ella gritaba.* Mexican immigrant, interview by author, November 12, 1999, tape recording, Coachella, Calif.

43. For up to date statistics, see www.stopgatekeeper.org.

44. *Estamos conscientes de los peligros pero la necesidad es más grande. Hay el riesgo de morir en el desierto pero el deseo para sobrevivir y seguir adelante es aún más importante. Uno viene a jugárselo.* Mexican immigrant, interview by author, January 19, 2000, tape recording, El Centro Detention Center, El Centro, Calif.

45. *La comida es tan fea que no quieres comerla.* Mexican *coyote*, interview by author, November 16, 1999, tape recording, Salton City, Calif.

46. See www.stopgatekeeper.org (Accessed July 2001).

47. Nicolás Ochoa and Paul Sandoval, "Un noble engaño," recorded by Los Huracanes del Norte, Luna Records LULP1083 (1982). See Herrera-Sobek, *Northward Bound*, 300–301. Used with permission.

48. California alone receives approximately 40 percent of all *legal* immigrants. In addition, California receives approximately 40–50 percent of the estimated 250,000 illegal immigrants, the majority of which come from Mexico. These numbers point to the fact that California absorbs the burden of the nation's immigrants. While many immigrants pay federal taxes, the majority of the services they require come from state and local budgets. These factors have helped contribute to an anti-immigrant ethos in the California culture, including Proposition 187, which sought to deny public education and even emergency medical care to undocumented immigrants.

49. Tragically, 85 percent of U.S. Americans want immigration flows to stop entirely. For an example of anti-immigrant sentiment, see www.projectusa.com.

50. *Pasé tres años en soledad cuando vine aquí, y estuve un mes encerrado en casa. No tenía amigos y experimenté discriminación. No quería salir por el miedo que la gente me iba a ver diferente.* Mexican immigrant, interview by author, January 21, 2000, tape recording, Coachella, Calif.

51. *Pasé semanas preocupada por ella. No sabia adonde le llevaba. No podía llamarnos porque no sabia como marcar los números en el teléfono.* Mexican immigrant, interview by author, January 21, 2000, tape recording, Coachella, Calif.

52. For more on this subject, see Virgilio P. Elizondo, *Galilean Journey: The Mexican-American Promise* (Maryknoll, N.Y.: Orbis, 1983).

53. For more on this subject, see John Phillip Santos, *Places Left Unfinished at the Time of Creation* (New York: Viking, 1999), Richard Rodriguez, *Hunger of Memory: The Education of Richard Rodriguez: An Autobiography* (Boston, Mass.: D.R. Godine, 1982), and Virgilio P. Elizondo, *The Future Is Mestizo: Life Where Cultures Meet* (Oak Park, Ill.: Meyer-Stone Books, 1988).

54. In large part because of the stress involved in surviving, one of the leading health issues among men and women farm workers is hypertension, and the nation's health clinics are able to serve less than 20 percent of all migrant farm workers. The health problems migrants suffer are more complex than that of the general population. See http://www.ncfh.org/aboutfws/status.htm.

55. Wendy Young, "United States Immigration and Refugee Policy: The Legal Framework," in Reck, *Who Are My Sisters and Brothers?* 45.

56. For details on the *Hoffman Plastics Compounds, Inc., v. National Labor Relations Board,* see http://a257.g.akamaitech.net/7/257/2422/mar20021045/www.supremecourtus.gov/opinions/01pdf/00-1595.pdf (Accessed 29 April 2002).

57. *Por cada persona que está trabajando en este valle hay cinco más que pueden tomar tu trabajo.* Mexican immigrant, interview by author, January 21, 2000, tape recording, Coachella, Calif.

58. *Estamos en la nueva época de la hacienda, pero la única diferencia es que ahora es más disfrazada." Trabajamos como esclavos para las corporaciones multinacionales, pero no nos hacen en cuenta. Nos Quebramos las espaldas, pero por muy poco.* Interview with Mexican Immigrant, January 21, 2000, tape recording, Coachella, Calif. In the context of this interview, *hacienda* refers to a modern version of indentured servitude. In Mexico's colonial period, *haciendas* were large, Spanish-owned estates, focused primarily on agriculture or livestock, which were sustained by indigenous workers. In many cases, *haciendas* flourished at the expense of native communities. Sometimes Indians left their communities to work on the *haciendas.* After having been given wages in advance, wages quickly evaporated, and the Indian laborer went into debt or subsequently was forced into a form of debt servitude. Other *haciendas* provided a share cropping agreement, where the Indian laborer was granted a parcel of land in exchange for a portion of his crops and perhaps other services to the landowner. In other instances *haciendas* were a place where native Indians could temporarily find a job to earn extra money and help pay off the expenses of a tribute tax. For more information, see Janine Gasco and Louise M. Burkhart, "The Colonial Period in Mesoamerica," in *The Legacy of Mesoamerica: History and Culture of a Native American Civilization,* ed. Robert M. Carmack, Janie Gasco, and Garry H. Gossen (Upper Saddle River, N.J.: Prentice Hall, 1996), 154–95.

59. *El dolor principal es la separación familiar y dejar sus seres queridos mientras busco una vida más digna para todos.* Mexican immigrant, interview by author, January 21, 2000, tape recording, Coachella, Calif.

60. *Cubría mi aflicción con trabajar, trabajar, y trabajar.* Mexican immigrant, interview by author, November 14, 1999, tape recording, Coachella, Calif.

61. *Trataba de estar ocupado en los campos porque el dolor era tan fuerte . . . Me volvía loco, y haría cualquier cosa para distraerme para no sentir el dolor.* Mexican immigrant, interview by author, November 14, 1999, tape recording, Coachella, Calif.

62. Anne-Marie O'Connor, "Conditions Turn More Perilous for Border Crossers."

63. I am indebted to Hollywood filmmaker Robert Young, who produced the film *Alambrista,* for this penetrating insight.

64. *Así es, pero, ni modo, tenemos que seguir adelante.* Mexican immigrant, interview by author, January 19, 2000, tape recording, El Centro Border Patrol Detention Center, El Centro, Calif.

2

Corazón Rehabilitado—
The Rehabilitated Heart:
The Dynamics of
Healing and Empowerment

A SPIRITUAL HOME IN A FOREIGN LAND

The Coachella Valley

After crossing the deadly border between Mexico and the United States, many immigrants come to the Coachella Valley in southern California. The Coachella Valley begins about sixty miles north of the border town of Calexico, California, and extends up to the town of Palm Springs. Between the beginning and end of the valley are economic and cultural extremes, ranging from billionaire software executives, who enjoy the world-class golf and tourist industry, to the destitute migrant workers, who sustain much of the resort infrastructure and work in the agricultural fields.

In the lower end of the Coachella Valley is the town of Coachella. It is a small, agriculturally rich but economically poor town of about 20,000 people, most of whom are immigrant Mexicans. In the midst of this poor town is one of the most powerful spiritual renewal centers in the country, which is called the Valley Missionary Program.

The Valley Missionary Program is a Catholic organization that addresses the personal struggles and spiritual aspirations of Mexican immigrants and others who come to them.[1] Having looked closely at the context of the Mexican immigrant, and the wounds

41

that result because of it, in this chapter we will first examine the Valley Missionary Program and the spiritual-cultural setting of these immigrants. Secondly, we will study the process of their spiritual renewal through a four-day retreat called "Missionary Encounter." This retreat has a profound impact on these immigrants and gives us key insights into what brings their spirituality to life. Finally, we will reflect on the theological principles from this retreat that are central to shaping their spirituality. By examining the dynamics of religious encounter through this retreat, we gain greater insight into the spirituality of these Mexican immigrants, which may also provide a basis for additional reflection among other groups.

The Valley Missionary Program

The Valley Missionary Program began in 1973 when Fr. William M. Lewers, csc, then the provincial superior of the Congregation of Holy Cross, sent Fr. Joe Pawlicki, csc, to respond to the needs of immigrant workers in the Coachella Valley. During the years he was in the valley, Fr. Pawlicki worked side by side with César Chávez, Dolores Huerta and the United Farm Workers (UFW), who fought for just wages and better working conditions for migrants.[2] In the process of fighting for justice, Fr. Pawlicki realized that much more work also needed to be done to help renew the spiritual lives of these immigrants. While he recognized they wanted economic, social and political justice, Fr. Pawlicki sensed that they wanted a more vibrant spirituality as well. He also realized that the existing structures of the Catholic Church failed to meet the deep spiritual hungers the immigrants had. He observed that many of the immigrants who came to the Coachella Valley from Mexico did not have any formal connection to the Church. Few came to Mass on a regular basis, and many who did often felt alienated and out of place. Virtually no worship services were offered in Spanish, little attention was paid to their cultural roots, and almost no effort was being made to reach those who lived on the social, geographical, and economic margins of the valley, especially the migrant workers.

To help these immigrants make more of a connection to the church community, Fr. Pawlick created a method of outreach for them. Inspired by the changes of Vatican II, and the episcopal conferences in Medellín, Colombia and later Puebla, Mexico, Fr.

Pawlicki created an evangelization program for these immigrants that was based on a concrete option for the poor and the creation of small, basic, Christian communities.[3] While he began implementing this vision through street preaching and various workshops in parish halls, he later used *Cursillo* retreats as a way of intensifying their spirituality, drawing members into the Christian community and facilitating the process of integral conversion.[4] *Cursillo* was an immensely formative element of Fr. Pawlicki's pastoral strategy, but his vision eventually brought him into conflict with that of *Cursillo*, and he eventually left the movement. In time he developed a new retreat called *Encuentro Misionero* or "Missionary Encounter."[5] This retreat has many of the positive dimensions of the *Cursillo* retreat, but it has been enriched and contextualized to speak especially to Mexican immigrants. In particular, he integrated a theology of fiesta into the rituals of the retreat, making the weekend a profound moment of celebration in Christian community and friendship with God.

While Fr. Pawlicki gave the program its initial direction, he allowed the immigrants themselves to shape the retreat in such a way that it correlated with their own unique life struggles and spiritual desires. He paid attention not only to their suffering but also to their faith. He listened not only to their difficulties but also to their aspirations. He brought not only the presence of Christ to them but also he found it among them. Though the Valley Missionary Program was initiated by a clergyman and shaped by the larger tradition of the Church, it is substantially the fruit and product of the work and insights of these immigrant people. As a result, the program offers a unique window on a Mexican immigrant spirituality.

In an area where Hispanics have been neglected by the Church and society, the Valley Missionary Program has energized the Hispanic immigrants of the region with a real sense of mission and purpose. The Program has thousands of members, and they are often the spiritual lifeblood of many of the parishes of the diocese. Many of those who participate in the program, who previously had little or no connection to the Catholic Church, are now leaders in renewing their local faith communities and active participants in social change throughout the region. They have an extensive program of community outreach, and they send members into hospitals and prisons throughout the area. The vast majority are hard working farm laborers, but the program has also been successful in transforming the lives of gang leaders, drug dealers, and ex-convicts.

Since its beginning, the Valley Missionary Program has created hundreds of base, Christian communities, some of which have been gathering for decades. These communities are key places where much of the spirituality of these immigrants matures and develops. From these retreats and communities, a spirituality emerges that brings out in them a tremendous capacity for sacrifice and commitment. The immigrants who belong to the program sacrifice 10 percent of their income to sustain it. They also take time off work to participate in the retreats—and they even *pay money to work* on the retreat. Though these sacrifices make some recoil, this program has a long waiting list of immigrants who want to make the retreat and work on it. Many say that they make such sacrifices because the retreat speaks profoundly to their hearts and ignites a spirituality that leads to the flourishing of their lives. Although the retreat by no means cures all their pains and afflictions, and although it has limitations that will be elaborated on later, the Missionary Encounter retreat has enabled many immigrants to discover deep spiritual aspirations that lead to the re-creation of their lives. Because of the success the Valley Missionary Program has had in transforming lives, they have been invited around the world to give their retreats, especially to places in Mexico, from which many of them emigrate.

In summary, the Valley Missionary Program is a renewal organization of the Catholic Church that creates small Christian communities that emerge from a four-day "Missionary Encounter" retreat. Through this festive and energetic program, many immigrants have a religious experience, which renews or gives birth to spirituality. This spirituality heals many of their wounds and empowers them to make positive contributions to the world. The combination of healing and empowerment leads to a genuine experience of liberation. It helps them discover a more vibrant relationship with God, and it transforms their lives so that they realize more fully their God-given dignity, human potential, and divine vocation.

The Shrine and the Retreat House

Beyond the immense impact on church and community, one of the most visible fruits of the Valley Missionary Program is the stunning and inspiring shrine and retreat house that these immigrants have built. Drawing from their rich cultural and spiritual heritage, these immigrants have re-created part of their Mexican homeland on American soil. They have mixed into the stucco and mortar of each of the buildings parts of their very own spirits and souls. The people themselves have created the physical setting of the Valley Missionary Program, and these physical structures, in turn, shape the spirituality of the people. Both the shrine and the retreat house are imbued with Mesoamerican, Christian and mestizo symbols that are foundational to their encounter with God.

A large, Aztec-styled, brick courtyard frames the shrine, giving pilgrims ample space to circulate and pray. In the middle of the plaza is a giant pyramid, which is a replica of the pyramids of the pre-Columbian city of Teotihuacán, northeast of Mexico City.[6] On the front of the pyramid are two large bronze sculptures of *Quetzalcoatl*, the beloved god of Mesoamerican cultures. From the center of the pyramid rises a towering cross, which presides over the whole shrine. And beneath the cross, on a bed of flowers, sit bronze sculptures of the Virgin of Guadalupe and Juan Diego.

Surrounded by pools of flowing water and a desert-garden landscape of mesquite, *agave* and cactus plants, the shrine and retreat house are architectural masterpieces of pre-Columbian and Christian cultures. Together, these symbolically rich buildings help form a sacred icon of the mestizo personality of the people; they help form their spiritual and cultural identity.[7] As these immigrants struggle to find their way in a new and foreign land in the United States, the shrine and retreat house become a place where they find a new center, from which their lives are transformed into something new. These buildings are tangible signs, even sacramental manifestations, of what this Christian community has done by living and working together in a spirit of faith and commitment.

The Missionary Encounter Retreat

The Missionary Encounter retreat provides these immigrants a time and space to step back from the busyness of their lives so that they can have an encounter with the living God.[8] More than simply a weekend of pious platitudes and catchy religious slogans that lull immigrants into a spiritual drug trip, the retreat begins to address some of the wounds of the heart and the deeper hopes that these

immigrants have for their lives.[9] Although it does not affect everyone who makes it, the retreat disposes many immigrants to a foundational spiritual experience. Such a core religious event often
marks the beginning of a lifelong walk in the Spirit that leads to the
regeneration and renewal of the totality of their lives (a theme that
we will explore in more detail in chapter 3).

The spirituality of these immigrants becomes clearer as we look
more closely at how the retreat is organized and how they respond
to the retreat. The retreat is a very elaborate and carefully planned
event that requires months of preparation. It lasts four days, beginning on Thursday evening and concluding on Sunday evening.
Three of the main participants in the retreat are the organizational
team, the candidates, and the spiritual directors. Sixty people work
on the retreat as the team members and sixty people participate or
live the retreat as candidates. The majority of both groups are immigrants. Priest and deacon spiritual advisers, as well, guide the
weekend and give some of the talks. The men and women make
their retreats on separate weekends so that men and women can
develop and express their own unique spirituality. Some of these
differences will be noted in the next chapter, but because adequate
treatment of this subject would be a separate work in itself, the majority of this book is dedicated to what the men and women share
in common in their spiritual experiences.[10]

Ritual and Mexican Immigrant Spirituality

Centered on the life and teachings of Christ, the retreat structures
itself around a series of events or interconnected rituals. These rituals are actions that convey meanings, and they are key to understanding how their spirituality works.[11] The spirituality of these
Mexican immigrants is particularly suited to ritual expression.

Some of the retreat rituals involve formal sacramental expressions of Catholic faith like the Eucharist and Reconciliation, and
others consist of more informal rituals that are unique to the retreat. These rituals help liberate and channel the emotional and
spiritual energy that is released on the weekend, and they help in-
tegrate the complex and even contradictory emotions that surface
on the weekend. These rituals create an organized way of facilitating a divine-human encounter and draw forth the rich spiritual po-

tential of each individual. Through an elaborate sequence of rituals of welcome, healing, fellowship, community building, prayer, cultural affirmation, forgiveness, empowerment, and commission the spirituality of these immigrants comes to life.[12] On the one hand, the rituals heal some of the pains and wounds they have suffered; on the other hand, they make concrete some of the essential truths of the Gospel.

A Spirituality of the Heart

The result of this Encounter retreat and its component rituals is that it facilitates a transformation of the heart, or *corazón*. The heart is central to Christian religion, Mesoamerican religion and today's Mexican culture.[13] *Corazón* in Mexican Spanish has a totally different meaning than heart in the English language, where it is often separated from knowledge and reduced to sentimentality. I refer to the heart as a physical organ with a mystical quality. It best symbolizes the innermost mystery of a person, and it is the biblical metaphor that most comprehensively captures the totality of a human person before God.

In addition, the heart is the source of ultimate understanding.[14] The heart integrates and informs all aspects of a person, including the mind, will, and emotions. In the heart, sentiments, memories, thoughts, reasoning, and planning are united; it is the biological-symbolic site of wisdom and knowledge and a metaphor for the whole of one's conscious, intelligent, and free personality. Especially for these immigrants, spiritual understanding and transformation emerges from *el corazón*.

The Missionary Encounter retreat is so effective precisely because it speaks to their *corazones*, the depth of who they are before God. We cannot appreciate the transforming spirituality of these immigrants without understanding the centrality of *corazón* and its role, meaning, and symbolic power in Mexican life. As Pope John Paul II says, "Christ the redeemer of the world is the one who penetrated in a unique, unrepeatable way (the human) 'heart.'"[15]

Each immigrant responds to the retreat in different ways, in part because each comes with different degrees of openness and different degrees of woundedness. While the retreat disposes people to a spiritual experience, such experience cannot be manipulated, coerced, or even predicted. At best, the retreat functions as an invitation to each person. The section that follows presents spiritual transformation not as a rigid, mechanical sequence of events that all experience equally but as a reflection on the overall pattern of the experience of these people.

In this schema, which is a descriptive synthesis of the overall transformative nature of the program, I will highlight key moments of the retreat that many immigrants say are significant for them. For some, they are immediately struck by the welcome they receive. Others, especially those who have been most deeply traumatized, are often not moved until Saturday evening or the closing on Sunday. And still others may leave the retreat unchanged. The contours of spirituality that I describe below are those that emerge from the community as a whole, though individual immigrants express them. As we look at these responses collectively, and highlight those parts of the retreat that these immigrants most remember, we can see the gradual transformation, not simply of individuals, but of the heart of a people. As we will see, the heart is at the core of this Mexican immigrant spirituality.

A RITUAL PROCESS OF SPIRITUAL TRANSFORMATION

Arriving with a Guarded Heart

The Opening Ceremonies. With faces bronzed by the sun and hands calloused by the arduous toil of their daily lives, the immigrants begin their weekend on Thursday night, unaware of what to expect from the retreat. One of the most challenging moments of the retreat happens in its initial hours, during the opening ceremonies, which function as a ritual of welcome. When each immigrant walks through the doors of the retreat house, he or she enters a room with hundreds of new people. Even before anyone knows anything about these immigrants, they are greeted with a flood of spontaneous affection. Team members clap enthusiastically as each person enters, sing loud and spirited songs, and offer to help them get settled in the retreat. In contrast to the experience of being aliens in a foreign country, the retreat team enthusiastically greets them as honored guests. "We make them feel welcomed," said Maria, a team member, "because we too know what it is like to be rejected and experience discrimination."[16]

But this new world makes many uncomfortable. Prior to the retreat, very few have ever received such attention, even within their own families. In a country and even a Church that has grown cold and unaccustomed to their presence, they have often learned to respond to new situations with alertness, skepticism, and mistrust. Having been abused, trampled upon, rejected, raped, and even ridiculed, many approach the setting with a great deal of trepidation. This is the first time many of these people have ever experienced a room full of strangers singing, dancing, and joyfully celebrating their arrival. Beneath their fears is often a deep feeling of unworthiness, which is a theme that surfaces often throughout the weekend. "Because the people seemed so festive and religious when I got there," said Maria Elena, "I was afraid others would reject me because of some bad things I did. I didn't know anything about God, either, and I certainly didn't feel I deserved that kind of attention."[17]

During these opening ceremonies, the candidates show signs of total disorientation and bewilderment, but the spirit of the team attracts them at the same time. "It all seemed kind of crazy to me to see people singing and welcoming me," said Jorge. "I had lost touch with that kind of joy when I left Mexico. But when I saw the joy on their faces, I saw something of friendship that I wanted to discover again."[18]

The Cracking Open of a Stony Heart

The Gifts. One of the most powerful dimensions of the retreat is the bestowing of many surprising and unexpected gifts. One of the first of these gifts is given through the ritual presentation of the *ramilletes de amor* (or spiritual bouquets), which takes place on Friday mid-morning.[19] This ritual begins when the team members give each one of the candidates a package that contains thoughtfully prepared, hand-made cardboard posters that contain pictures of family, friends, and sponsors. These *ramilletes* also contain citations from Scripture, poems, and encouraging words that are personally addressed to the candidates. As these immigrants receive these simple expressions of love and affection, some of the emotional suppression is liberated in them, and many are broken open to the point of tears. Many of the hearts of stone that found it too painful to feel are now overwhelmed by the memory of those who love them. The sharing of simple but symbolically very significant gifts allows them to tangibly realize that the spiritual journey begins with unconditional acceptance. "I'm twenty-nine years old," said Francisco, "and until today, no one has ever given me anything in my life. As a man, it is the first time I have ever learned how to cry."[20]

The Mini-Dramas. The retreat also presents some very effective mini-dramas, called *dinámicas*, which are ritual reenactments of scenarios in daily life. They bring to light daily struggles pertaining to drugs, gangs, alcoholism, family turmoil, abortion, and other themes. One of the mini-dramas deals with a family that lives on the border. The father has a drinking problem, and he ignores his children. Each day the father sends his child into the street to ask for change so he can buy more alcohol. Dressed in tattered clothes and barefoot, the child goes from person to person in the room, begging for change. When he comes back with only a little money, the father yells at the child and forces him to go back and beg for more. Reluctantly, the child goes back to the streets while the father passes out in a drunken stupor. When the child returns, he pounds on the door to be let in, but the father does not hear him. In desperation the child begs to be let inside, only to die outside on the steps of the house in the freezing temperatures. When the father awakens, he finds his child dead on the ground, and he weeps as he recognizes his neglect and abuse of his family.

Such mini-dramas like these bring to light the destructive behavior of many of the immigrants. There are no scolding sermons. There are no staged guilt trips. The partipants are simply presented with a heart-rending story, which indirectly challenges them to review their own painful stories. As they begin to critically reflect on their own lives, they are forced to ask some very challenging questions about themselves and their day-to-day choices. In the process, much of their coarse, self-protective exterior cracks open to a new space of sincerity and openness. For those who see themselves as victims of fate rather than agents in their own destiny, this moment also can be very liberating. Such reflection leads some of them to take more responsibility for their lives. "When I saw this *dinámica*," Julio said, "I saw my whole life played out before me and the problems I've caused my family through my own drinking."[21]

The Healing of a Wounded Heart

The Meals and the Music. Each meal of the retreat is a spirited and energetic celebration. The meals are ritual celebrations of life in which the opportunities for fellowship are created. Every meal begins with a lavish welcome, similar to the one the candidates experienced upon arriving. When the candidates enter the dining room, the band starts playing and team members greet each person individually, shaking their hands, hugging them, and receiving them enthusiastically into the dining room.

Each of the meals has a prescribed theme. The team spends hours beforehand creating a festive atmosphere with streamers, balloons, pictures, and drawings related to the theme. Such themes include a Mexican fiesta, a Valentine's Day celebration, a formal fashion show, a circus, a Hawaiian Luau, a Mexican cattle ranch, and many others.

Even though most of the participants and team members are economically poor, they celebrate with extravagance. The team gives extraordinary attention to detail in the place settings, napkins, centerpieces, and small gifts that the candidates receive at each meal. These details would mean little or nothing by themselves, but, in the context of the retreat, they make the candidates feel honored that such attention has gone into preparing an elaborate meal for them. "The meals made me feel like I was somebody important," said Juan. "I couldn't believe people went to so much trouble just to make me feel at home."[22]

The music intensifies the festive spirit at the meals. Music is the heartbeat of the Encounter, and it motivates the candidates to dance, sing, and celebrate. It penetrates deep into their hearts and souls, and enables them to express a full range of human emotions, some of which they have not expressed in a long time.

When they sit down to eat, the team serves the candidates as much food and drink as they want. For those who have experienced hunger and have often worked as the servants at table, such service touches them in a powerful way. This is especially true for the women. "In Mexican culture it's the women who always serve the meals," said Sara. "To sit down and have someone serve me was overwhelming. I said to myself, 'I'm really a nobody, so why are they doing this for me?' I never expected such attention."[23]

The Creating of a Spiritual Heart

The Base Communities.[24] One of the retreat's primary goals is to create base, Christian communities.[25] These communities begin on the first night of the retreat, but many continue to meet for the months and years that follow.[26] These communities have rituals of prayer and reflection that help create friendships that are grounded on the spiritual life. They are the places where these immigrants read the Word of God, talk about their struggles, and seek to respond more fully to the Christian message. They also conduct simple assimilation exercises that help them appropriate and internalize the messages of the retreat talks, making them active participants in the process of learning rather than just passive recipients of a doctrinal message. For those who are accustomed to simply going through the motions in formal religious practices, the dynamics of base communities are a new way of approaching God.

In time, the base communities help these immigrants realize that they have people they can turn to when they run into difficulties. These communities of faith also allow them to develop a network of relationships and a sense of belonging. Here they are no longer strangers and aliens but friends of God and each other. "It surprised me how powerfully we began to connect with each other," said Raul. "As we began sharing our lives and listening to each others stories, I felt as if I had known these people for a long time."[27]

The Talks. The retreat has a series of thirteen talks, each of which follows a prescribed ritual. The talks begin with a song, followed by an introduction of the speaker, then the talk itself, and finally the discussion questions. These talks convey the basic doctrine of Christian faith, and they are accentuated by personal stories of the speakers. So that each person's talk might be efficacious, two people are designated to pray in the chapel during the speaker's presentation. The team members who give the talks are mostly immigrants themselves, who live and work in similar conditions as the candidates.[28]

The first talk is on God the Father, who is presented as a loving and merciful Father. The core teaching is that of the Lost Son (Luke 15:11–32). This talk frames the whole retreat because it highlights the totally gracious love of God and the unconditional nature of God's offer of friendship and mercy. It emphasizes that sinners are joyfully invited into the Kingdom of God. On the second day of the retreat, the talks focus on Jesus as the Son of God, who is referred to as *Jesús Amigo*. The candidates are introduced to the notions of sin, salvation, redemption, the Cross, and the role of the base communities in the life of the Church. The primary purpose of this day is to draw the candidates into a deeper personal and communal relationship with Christ so that they come to know God as a close, personal friend. Saturday is dedicated to the Holy Spirit, who is presented as the source of empowerment for those who believe. The talks deal with community, matrimony, the call of the laity, the spiritual life, sin and reconciliation. On this day, the candidates also have a chance to renew their faith through the Sacrament of Reconciliation and Eucharist. The fourth and final day focuses on renewing the world through Christian missionary activity. Here the talks deal with the Kingdom of God and the call to invite others into the same love they have experienced. While simple and basic in their message, these talks help give the candidates a basic framework for the Christian faith and a basic orientation of who they are before God. Overall these talks provide an introduction to central truths about human beings in relationship to God.[29] Many immigrants said that these talks enabled them to hear for the first time that God loves them. "What most filled me with joy," said Juanita, "was the talk that said we are *diocitos* ("little gods," or, in context, "sons and daughters of God."). It amazed me to think that God looks at us that way."[30]

The Touching of God's Heart

El Santísimo (The Blessed Sacrament). As the retreat moves on, spiritual friendship begins to develop in the base communities. As important as these friendships are, however, these immigrants also know in the back of their minds that all human beings fail. Pressures of life, personal limitations, unavailability or distance of friends still leave unopened spaces in the hearts of these immigrants who need the civilizing and humanizing experience of an enduring friendship.

On Saturday noon, the candidates are told that a very important and committed friend has been with them on the retreat, though they have not yet met him face to face. They have already experienced many surprises up until this point, so the sense of anticipation builds. They are not told who this friend is; they are simply told that they are going to meet someone important who loves them very much and has been sacrificing for them since they got there. As they begin discussing who this person is, they are invited to line up, single file, putting their arms on the shoulders of the person in front of them. They are led to the chapel where they are told that the friend who has been waiting for them is Jesus himself, who is present to them in the exposition of the *El Santísimo*, or the Blessed Sacrament.[31] "When I visited *El Santísimo*," said Josefina, "I felt I met someone who was interested in me for the first time."[32]

As they kneel before *El Santísimo*, with simple, meditative music playing in the background, they are invited to talk personally to Christ, as one close friend talks to another. On their knees, many immigrants begin praying to God by pouring out great emotions of hurt, loss, confusion, shame, and guilt. Noticeably less guarded, they speak sincerely and freely about the pains and burdens they have been carrying for weeks, months, or even years. Some pray for friends or relatives who are sick or have died; others pray for guidance, forgiveness, and strength. Some pray for a closer relationship with God; others ask that God touch the hearts of family members and friends. For more than a half an hour, their time before *El Santísimo* is a profound moment of unburdening, a releasing of the pressures and troubles that have oppressed them. Many immigrants find this ritual most revealed the heart of God to them. "From the time I entered, I felt a peace and a tranquility," said Jasmine. "In seeing Christ in the *El Santísimo*, I felt more confidence to ask him for things and unburden the things that weighed on my heart. It was like I encountered Christ for the first time."[33]

The Cross. One of the most central and enduring symbols of the retreat is the Cross; it is always present to them. When they arrive at the retreat, they are given a leather cross to put around their necks. At meals, a large cross stands in the front of the room. In the middle of the shrine, a large cross rises above the plaza. On Friday afternoon, they see a movie about Jesus' death on the cross. And on Friday before dusk, they walk the Stations of the Cross. More than simply a decorative piece of jewelry, the cross shapes the spirituality of these immigrants and gives many of them a new way of reframing their suffering. "The cross means to me that Christ conquered death," said Jose. "Practically, this means to me that all the things we suffer will not conquer us because we believe in Him."[34]

The Stations of the Cross are a ritual way of entering into Christ's sufferings and appropriating its meaning more personally into their own lives. In light of Jesus' own sufferings, they begin to reinterpret their experiences of breaking from home, crossing the border, and living in the United States. For the first time, many begin to make the connections between Jesus' sufferings and their own. "The cross means that Christ is alive and has not forgotten about us," said Juana. "To see the cross means that our struggles, though many, will not conquer us."[35]

The Ennobling of the Mexican Heart

The Mexican Fiesta. Earlier we talked about the importance of the meals and the role they play in bringing about a divine-human encounter. One meal in particular is significant because it links them with their Mexican cultural heritage. At Saturday's lunch, the candidates are invited to an elaborate Mexican fiesta. Those who often have had to deny their culture and feel ashamed of their Mexican heritage are welcomed to a feast where their homeland is affirmed and celebrated. More than a gimmick or technique, this meal is a ritual ennobling of the Mexican heart, a means of affirming the beauty and goodness of Mexican culture, and a way of eliciting pride in their cultural legacy and personal histories. "When I walked through the door," said Mario, "I immediately felt like I was at home, like I was in a place where I could be myself again."[36]

When the candidates enter the dining room for lunch, they are overcome by a tidal wave of Mexican culture. The decorations, dress, and music are all decidedly Mexican. The men wear *guayaveras* shirts, *huarache* shoes, and Mexican bandanas, and the women put on indigenous dresses, headbands, and native jewelry. The walls are an avalanche of green, white, and red balloons and streamers, symbols of Mexican pride and patriotism. Down to the place settings and napkins, everything is Mexican. Even the priests dress in the Mexican cowboy (*charro*) suits and sing poplar Mexican ballads to the candidates. The clothing, decorations, and music all reinforce and affirm the distinctive beauty of the Mexican culture. "Over time, you tend to forget about where you come from," said Alberto, "and this meal brought my culture back to life for me again"[37]

At the end of the meal, the candidates take helium-filled balloons from the dining room and walk out to the shrine. On a small sheet of paper, they write down special prayers and tie them to strings on their balloons. When everyone is ready, they release their green, white, and red balloons to the heavens, painting a Mexican flag in the sky. Symbolizing in part their own hopes that have arisen to the surface, they discover a new pride in their heritage and a new appreciation of God's activity within their own culture and their own lives. "It was like I was finally in a place that understood where I had come from," said Patricia. "For a moment, I felt I wasn't a foreigner anymore."[38]

Our Lady of Guadalupe. Central to the Mexican cultural and spiritual identity is Our Lady of Guadalupe, in whom Mexicans take great pride. For them, Guadalupe is a pivotal historical event, a special source of pride to Mexicans because it took place on Mexican soil. (This subject will be treated in detail in chapter 4, and for a full text of the encounter, see the Guadalupe account as told in the *Nican Mopohua* in the appendix.) Briefly, Our Lady of Guadalupe appeared in 1531 to a poor, Indian Mexican named Juan Diego. After a series of apparitions, and a commission to deliver a message to the bishop, her image miraculously was impressed on Juan Diego's cloak, where it remains today in Mexico City. To this day Our Lady of Guadalupe gives great hope and spiritual aspiration to all people, especially the Mexican poor. As evidenced by her prominent place in the shrine, she plays a very significant role in the lives of these immigrants as well.

As a powerful mother figure, Our Lady of Guadalupe is a great source of strength, especially for those who often feel disconnected from family. They look to her for tenderness, understanding, and providence. She is present at many different times during the retreat, on holy cards, in prayer books, in movies, on shirts, and many other places. She comes through in various rituals of the retreat. They invoke her at times of formal prayers, they speak about her during the retreat talks in an evening session. In various ways throughout the retreat, Guadalupe plays an influential role in forming the spiritual consciousness of these people.

The Cleansing of a Sinful Heart

The Sacrament of Reconciliation. Two rituals of the retreat that help them discover God's forgiveness are the Sacrament of Reconciliation and a foot washing service. Up until this point in the retreat, they have recalled God's blessings to them in their families and friends through the spiritual bouquets. They have been treated as honored guests and friends at the meals. They have meditated on the depth of love that God has for them through formal talks, informal discussions, and various prayer services. They have recalled their rich cultural and spiritual heritage as Mexicans. Now comes the hard part: They must look soberly at themselves and face their own errors. This sacrament gives them time to think about how they have offended their friends, their families, their neighbors, themselves, and God. When many faced the pain of their own destructive choices, they felt deep feelings of remorse. "I just recoiled in shame to think of all the horrible things I had done," said one male candidate. "One of the reasons why I distanced myself from the Church was because I didn't think I could be forgiven."[39]

The ritual of the sacrament consists of writing down their sins on a piece of paper and bringing them to a priest who discusses it with them. (Those who cannot read or write have a private session with the priest.) Each immigrant brings to this moment his or her own sense of personal darkness: unfaithfulness, lying, cheating, stealing, drugs and alcohol abuse, abortion, gang violence, betrayal, and even more serious sins. When they are done, the priest puts his hands on his or her head, prays the prayers of absolution, and instructs the candidate to put his or her confession papers in a box beside him. Then everyone gathers outside in a circle, usually just as the sun begins to set. In the context of their own fears of God's rejection, the group watches as the priest further ritualizes the forgiveness process. He does this by burning each confession paper in a large fire pit, until all the papers are engulfed in flames. As darkness settles over the valley, the only light in the area is the giant flame burning in their midst. "When I saw my sins go up in flames,"

said Irma, "something inside me leaped for joy, like my whole being was liberated."[40]

The Footwashing. In addition to the encounter with Christ in the
Sacrament of Reconciliation, many immigrants also experience
God's forgiveness through a foot washing ritual on Saturday
evening. Set in the context of an agape meal, this ritual deepens
their sense of hospitality and fellowship as experienced at earlier
meals, but it is even more significant because, fundamentally, it is
about an intimate meal with God.

At the beginning of the ritual, the candidates are led to a room
where they expect to have a simple prayer service. In actuality, the
team has prepared a very elaborate reenactment of the Scriptures
that further intensifies their experience of a personal encounter
with Jesus. The room is completely dark, except for small votive
candles. In the middle of the room is a table, shaped in the form of
a cross. In front of the cross are standing thirteen team members,
fully dressed as Jesus and the twelve apostles.

After the candidates are seated, they listen to a reading from John
13:1–15. In this passage, Jesus has a Passover meal with his disciples. At the end of the meal, Jesus revels to his disciples the meaning of his upcoming death and gives them an example of service. He
does this by getting up from table, putting a towel around his waist,
getting down on the ground and washing the feet of Peter.

Step by step, the team reenacts this passage before the eyes of the
candidates. A team member who is dressed as Jesus gets up from
table, wraps a towel around his waist, gets down on his knees, gen-
tly takes the feet of a candidate, washes them with water, dries them
and then kisses them respectfully, tenderly. "At that moment, I felt
so unworthy of what was happening to me," said Beatriz. "I felt I
had abandoned God, but here God was coming to me!"[41] The ritual
makes tangibly real their encounter with Christ. Like other moments of the retreat, this unmerited, symbolic act of God's humility
heals many of them and overwhelms many to the point of tears.

The Awakening of a Joyful Heart

Las Mañanitas. Borrowing from deep within Mexican culture, the
retreat also uses the ritual of *Mañanitas* to help bring to life the spirituality of these immigrants. *Las Mañanitas* (translated as "the little

tomorrows") are a traditional ritual where friends, relatives, and musicians gather early in the morning to sing the praises of a people on their birthdays.[42]

Las Mañanitas begin at 4:30 A.M., when the candidates are abruptly awakened from their sleep. They are given no time to shower, comb their hair, put on makeup, or prepare themselves. Many simply throw a blanket over their nightclothes, wrap a towel over their head and put on slippers. With sleep still in their faces, they are rushed into a dark room, confused as to why they have to get up so early. When they turn on the lights, they are greeted with the sound of spirited, *mariachi* music. As they open their eyes, they are ushered through a human labyrinth, lined by hundreds of people who have come to sing joyfully and vociferously *to them!* These people are family members, sponsors, and other members of the program who have prayed for them throughout the weekend. Some of the guests traveled hundreds of miles to see them in the early hours of the morning!

As the candidates walk past hundreds of people, they are given dozens of flowers, some from people they do not even know. Such flowers have rich symbolic value, and even men are happy to hold them in their hands as they walk through the maze of people. "When someone gave me a dozen roses, I felt like it was me that was flowering. Those roses represented a love that brought me back to life."[43]

Even with their forlorn hair, morning face, and pajamas, they cannot turn back. While some feel embarrassed at first, those who come to see them communicate in many ways that they are not interested in their appearances: they are interested in who they are before God. Through this ritual of *mañanitas*, they are invited into a family who loves them beyond their appearances down to the depths of their being, where God dwells.

"It was like I awoke to a new kind of life and a new world," said Conchita, "which filled me with a peace and tranquility which I had never known before."[44] The shock of seeing so many loved ones is overpowering: "To have people receive me with such joy and love made me feel like I died and went to heaven."[45]

The Empowering of a Loving Heart

Commissioning Blessing. After the highpoint of the *mañanitas*, the tenor of breakfast takes a dramatic turn. Having lived the retreat for three days now, the candidates have become quite accustomed to the routine of being served by the team members and enjoying elaborate meals in a festive atmosphere. When the candidates enter the room for Sunday breakfast, they encounter yet another surprise. The atmosphere is a Mexican cattle ranch. The team is dressed in ten-gallon hats, faded jeans, and cowboy boots. But there is a twist: the team suddenly announces a strike! There is no music. No food. No service. Compared to the overflowing banquets of previous meals, the dining room is an atmosphere of contrasts. Instead of serving the candidates, the team demands to be served.

While initially confusing, this ritual challenges those candidates who are tempted to see Christian life more in terms of personal benefits rather than committed service. The theme of the day is to be a missionary, and the first aspect of missionary life is learning how to be a servant. Some candidates pick up on the challenge immediately, and they begin by offering a team member a seat at table, some serving the meals, and others playing the musical instruments. Throughout the day, the candidates are given the message that, having received, it is now their turn to give. "It was like I realized it was now my turn to serve, like it was an indirect challenge to begin to treat others the way the team treated me."[46] After this initial, humorous protest of the team, however, they revert to their original role of serving the candidates and continuing the festive meal together. In this way the experience of Christian faith becomes a gift and a challenge.

The call to service, however, continues to be emphasized at Sunday's lunch, and the theme is that of a Hawaiian luau. When the candidates walk through the door of the dining room, they slowly follow each other down a maze of colored streamers until they reach a large picture of Jesus and kneel down in front of him. Then the spiritual director puts his hand over each one of them and says, "You are a missionary of Jesus Christ. Go forth and proclaim the good news." This ritual commissions them to share with others the love that they have received themselves. "It was like I was being prodded to go out into the world to share what I've experienced. For me it was no longer about a God who punishes but about serving a Lord who loves me and sends me forth."[47]

The Witnessing of a Grateful Heart

The Closing Ceremonies. The four-day retreat ends with a *clausura* or closing ceremony, which brings together the candidates, the team, and many other people who have lived their Missionary Encounter retreat. The *clausura* is a confirmation ritual. It is a structured way through which the candidates describe their experiences on the retreat and reaffirm a new commitment to their faith. It also introduces them to other members of the Valley Missionary Program, some of whom have belonged for decades. "I really didn't want to see such a beautiful weekend come to an end," said Rolando, "But at the same time, I felt like I had been given wings to fly."[48]

During the *clausura* testimonials, people express gratitude to their sponsors, the team and, most of all, to God for the gift of the weekend. Various members of the team get the spotlight, especially the kitchen crew, who worked behind the scenes most of the time. For many, it is the first time they have ever spoken publicly to a large group of people, and it can be a very emotional experience for many of them. Beyond the words people say, much more is communicated through their facial expressions, tears, and embraces. In the midst of their painful life, the joy of the weekend provides a taste of new possibilities for connectedness and community. The joy and liberation shows in their facial expressions, which reflect a total flowering of new life. For some, their words reflect a healing and empowerment that leads them to a sense of freedom and dignity:

> Before the retreat I felt inferior because I came from such a poor family. We had to pay for *coyotes* and came over as wetbacks, and I didn't have many opportunities to accomplish the things I wanted to like get an education. I felt others were worth more because they had more. But the retreat helped me realize that we are all the same, that we are all children of God, that I matter to God, and that God has called me to something important.[49]

Many immigrants expressed that the Encounter weekend marked the beginning of a spiritual journey with God and a new commitment to serve others.

A CONTEXTUAL THEOLOGY OF ENCOUNTER

Before looking more specifically at the impact that the retreat has on the lives of these immigrants, we will look at some of the founder's theological intuitions, upon which the program is based. In addition, I will add the theological insights I have discovered in observing the dynamics of the retreat and listening to the stories of the people. Fr. Pawlicki's intuitions and my insights help clarify the theological and spiritual foundations of the program.

One of the strengths of the retreat is that it translates solid Christian doctrines of tradition into simple rituals and presentations. The theological depth of these retreat rituals becomes all the more significant as we look at them in light of the immigrant experience. While this work will not treat each of these themes in detail, it is important to highlight some of them and comment on their significance to the immigrants. These theological principles enable us to gain a better understanding of the dynamics of this religious encounter and the spirituality that emerges from this retreat.

The Kingdom of God. The *Encuentro Misionero* retreat is based solidly on God's in-breaking into history through the person of Jesus Christ, who inaugurates the kingdom of God. This kingdom, as Edward Schillebeeckx notes, is about God's presence and action in the world, which becomes visible as human beings care for one another.[50] One central aspect of the kingdom is that everyone is invited without exception. Because of this inclusive dimension, the retreat makes hospitality the foundation of everything else. In contrast to the discrimination that many immigrants experience, the ritual of welcome enables the candidates to enter an alternative world, a world where they experience acceptance in place of discrimination. The team welcomes these immigrants because they believe that in welcoming them they welcome Christ. The underlying theology behind the team's actions is a christological one. The team puts into practice the words of Jesus as expressed in Matthew, "I was hungry and you gave me food . . . thirsty and you gave me something to drink . . . a stranger and you welcomed me." (Matthew 25:35). In clapping upon their arrival, lavishly celebrating their presence, and making them feel at home, these strangers are treated as treasured friends and bearers of divine life. This first ritual communicates to these immigrants one of the most fundamental dimensions of the Gospel: God's universal welcome to all, especially to the marginalized, rejected, and poor of society.

The Unmerited Nature of Grace. The retreat is also designed to bring out in concrete ways the gratuitous love of God. Grace, in the context of the retreat, deals with God's free offer of Himself to His people. As Karl Rahner points out, grace is first and foremost about God's self-communication and presence to human beings.[51] This means that grace is fundamentally about relationships, the foremost of which is one's relationship with God. Such grace comes through the Scriptures, the sacraments, the community, and—especially—the friendships that are created on the weekend. The generous outpouring of God reaches them through the service of the team, the gifts given at meals, and rituals like the *ramilletes*. In the face of feelings of inadequacy and personal inferiority, the *ramilletes* helps these immigrants realize that they are valued for more than their functional and economic contributions to society. They are loved because God *is* love, and this love is communicated to them concretely through the team and the important people that are part of their lives. The recognition of such unmerited love helps these immigrants recover some of their fundamental human dignity and self worth. Through such simple gifts at meals, and the generous offer of the team's time and energy, they receive tangible manifestations of an inward reality: the unmerited nature of Grace. Multiplying gift upon gift at each meal communicates in a concrete way God's infinite, personal concern for them. The experience of finding a community that loves them, even though they have done nothing for them, leads many of them to discover a "pearl of great price" (Matthew 13:46). Such an experience motivates many of them to give even the little they have so they can make it their own.

A Pedagogy of Parables. Jesus did not teach through doctrinal statements but through parables that invited people to reflect and discover the divine message through human examples. These examples correlated with the life experience of Jesus' hearers and were spoken by him in an idiom and language that the people could understand. The retreat communicates some of the most important messages of the Gospel not simply through abstract, rational concepts but through teachings that engage the imagination of the immigrants through every day examples from their own lives. In many respects, these mini-dramas or *dinámicas* function as contemporary parables. As John Donahue notes, the parables give a glimpse of the "Gospel in miniature" and at the same time give shape, direction, and meaning to the Gospels in which they are found. In a similar way, the *dinámicas* are like parables that give shape, meaning, and direction to the retreat.[52] Like those of Jesus, they summon people to a new way of thinking and acting. They also make their religious and ethical messages more accessible to their hearers by grounding them in a setting that is familiar to them (Matthew 13:44, Matthew 18:12–14, Luke 10:30–37, Luke 14:15–24, Luke 16:19–31, and others). The twists in the story lines challenge them to a *metanoia*, a profound change of heart and behavior and a new way of thinking about reality in a way that is consistent with the demands of discipleship.

The Inclusive Nature of the Table Fellowship. In the life and ministry of Jesus, meals were simple but effective ways through which Jesus inaugurated the new creation of God's reign. While the energetic meals of the retreat help convey much of the festive theology that underlies the retreat, they also function as a contemporary expression of the table fellowship of Jesus in the Gospels. Norman Perrin notes that Jesus' table fellowship with tax collectors and sinners is "not a proclamation in words at all, but an acted parable."[53] Such table fellowship makes concrete God's offer of salvation and the promises of God's reign. These festive meals also underscore the fact that something important is happening in their midst and that all are invited, regardless of their class or social standing. To those who pick much of the fruit and vegetables of the nation, yet have little money to dine at fancy restaurants or indulge in rich foods, the meals are an extravagant feast. Such joyful, festive, and abundant meals give these immigrants a foretaste of the kingdom of God and a tangible expression of the Paschal banquet (Matthew 8:11, Luke 13:29, Revelation 19:9).

The Church as a Community of Disciples. Vatican II reintroduced the original notion of the Church primarily as a community. The Church, as the people of God, is also a very important element of the entire retreat. The base communities are instrumental in helping these immigrants gain a new understanding of what it means to be a people of God. More than anything else, these base communities enable them to form friendships based on a common spiritual experience. In contrast to a cold and impersonal experience of Church, these communities enable them to discover the Church as family. In doing so, they resemble the earliest Christian communities (Acts 2), bring out some of the core teachings of Vatican II (*Lumen Gentium*) and highlight some of the central insights of the episcopal conference at *Puebla,* which noted that such an ecclesial perspective "speaks to the hearts of Latin Americans, who highly esteem family values and who are anxiously looking for some way to salvage those values amid the growing cold-bloodedness of the modern world."[54] Through these communities, they begin to see God and the Church not simply in terms of institutional structures but in terms of relationships.

The Relational Nature of Divine Revelation. The talks also help inform much of what these immigrants experience on retreat, and they lay the groundwork for a solid understanding of Christian faith. Nonetheless, beyond simply understanding God in terms of a doctrinal deposit of ethical exhortations, Church obligations, the Creed, the Ten Commandments, heaven and hell, they come to see revelation as God's offer of friendship.[55] For these immigrants, the spiritual life is about the joyful discovery of this friendship with God and the living out of this relationship in communion with others. The revelation of God's love becomes real to them when the Scriptures are explained in the context of a community who love and accept them. As noted in the Vatican II document *Dei Verbum,* through this revelation, God calls people to a profound relationship of friendship.[56] In this respect, revelation, fundamentally, is about God's gift of self to the people God has chosen.[57] To these immigrants, revelation means developing a relationship with God through Jesus, who makes accessible the inner life of God.

The Real Presence of Christ in the Eucharist. The real presence of Christ in the Eucharist and the Blessed Sacrament is an all-important aspect of the retreat and very powerful in the spirituality of the Mexican people. It is through the Eucharist that Christ becomes real to them in the flesh. St. Thomas Aquinas saw the Eucharist as a sign that affects what it signifies and in which the Lord is present in a unique way. For these immigrants, one particular way in which the Eucharist takes on special meaning is through the Blessed Sacrament. Though devotion to the Blessed Sacrament in recent years has often been less emphasized in order to bring out the real presence of Christ in the Christian community, it is clear that the theological foundation of this retreat still rests solidly on this Eucharistic principle. Because these immigrants often feel they are no one to anyone, the

Blessed Sacrament speaks to them as a special moment of the revelation of God's friendship with them. Through it they discover in this moment a new dignity based on their realization that they are children of God. More than simply fieldworkers and servants, they begin to see themselves as companions of Christ who invites them to abide with him in love (John 15:15). The founder's intention here was to help them discover a relationship with *Jesus Amigo*, that is, God's faithfulness in friendship (Matthew 28:20). Unlike the *coyotes* who rob, kill, and destroy, the Eucharist speaks of a God who gives Himself to His people and even lays down his life for them (John 10:1–18).

The Undying Commitment of God. The cross is the most emblematic symbol of the retreat because it summaries the totality of the Christian message.[58] In the midst of the multiple levels of suffering they experience, the cross names their pain, helps them reinterpret their affliction, and gives them confidence that the God of life working in them will help them overcome any of the difficulties they face. Some immigrants see the cross as a badge of courage, a symbol of discipleship, and a call to love as God loves. They also see in the cross not simply the pain and suffering of Jesus but the undying love of God. As Jon Sobrino describes it,

> On the cross of Jesus God himself is crucified. The Father suffers the death of the Son and takes upon himself all the pain and suffering of history. In this ultimate solidarity with humanity he reveals himself as the God of love, who opens up a hope and a future through the most negative side of history. Thus, Christian existence is nothing else but a process of participating in this same process whereby God loves the world, and hence is the very life of God.[59]

The cross enables them to see a love that nothing can destroy. It gives them strength that transforms their seemingly meaningless sufferings into a new capacity for hope, not because God wills their suffering but because Christ's passion has overcome it.

The Inculturation of the Gospel Message. The retreat bases itself on the premise that the Gospel does not come to destroy a culture but to enrich it. This inculturation happens as the deepest truths of the Gospel are gradually expressed through the language, customs, heritage, and symbols of a people. This cultural-spiritual dynamic comes out during the Mexican fiesta and when these immigrants sing their songs, eat their foods, and practice some of their cherished customs. For those immigrants who often feel they leave behind much of what they value and treasure when they come to the United States, the Mexican fiesta ritual is a moment of profound cultural celebration. Such inculturation enables them to see Christ working through their culture, celebrating it, elevating it, and transforming it. Spirituality, in other words, emerges from a culture that is evangelized. Pope Paul VI brings this out in the document *Evangelii Nuntiandi*, "What matters is to evangelize . . . cultures . . . not in a purely decorative way, as it were, by applying a thin veneer, but in a vital way, in depth and right to their very roots."[60] As the retreat brings out the best of the Mexican heritage, these immigrants discover that spirituality does not destroy their culture but affirms it and ennobles it, even while it challenges it and purifies it.

The Healing Power of Reconciliation and Foot Washing. The Sacrament of Reconciliation and foot washing restore broken or damaged relationships with God and others and function as important moments of healing and purification. The retreat, in this respect, speaks to those immigrants who experience not only physical difficulties but guilt on many levels. The Sacrament of Reconciliation is an important moment of healing that gives many immigrants the confidence to begin a new chapter in their lives. Through forgiveness it also opens them up to an experience of divine human friendship. Coupled by the experience of foot washing, these rituals mark new moments of human wholeness for these immigrants. They deepen their sense of God's acceptance of them and often give them a hunger to become better human beings in the future. By design, the ritual burning of the confession papers at nighttime symbolizes what they experience internally: a light that shines in the darkness, a darkness that has not overcome the light (John 1:5). The foot washing, as well, becomes an intimate purification ritual through which God restores spiritual vitality to their broken lives, and it models how Jesus thinks, acts, and lives in the world.

The Experiential Dimension of Resurrection. Resurrection marks the entry into a new life in Christ and serves as the foundation of Christian faith. On the retreat, the immigrants come to understand the resurrection not only conceptually but also experientially.

Beyond merely a cognitive and rational ascent to the resurrection of Christ, the retreat is designed so as to help them experience it in the flesh. Above all, the flowers and songs at *mañanitas* help them awaken to the immense amount of love that is present in their lives and the liberating Spirit of God who lives among them. During the rituals of *mañanitas*, immigrants who once threw themselves on the desert floor at the sound of helicopters now ascend to new dignity at the sound of music. Those who took refuge in spiny cactuses now find affirmation through the gift of flowers. Those who recoiled at the sight of the immigration officials now joyfully greet strangers, who welcome them as brothers and sisters in Christ (Ephesians 2:19). As they walk through a human labyrinth lined by hundreds of friends, relatives, and sponsors, this ritual of *mañanitas* transforms the immigrant's way of the cross into a path of life! The face of God becomes real to these immigrants through the people that love them. They awaken to a new life in the Spirit that generates a genuine rebirth of the soul, a genuine resurrection experience.

The Vocation to Mission. As the Vatican II document *Ad Gentes* states, the nature of the Church is missionary.[61] It states that all Christians are called to move out beyond themselves to proclaim the Good News of Jesus Christ and serve the needs of all people. In this light, the retreat brings to the forefront of their spirituality the vocation to mission.[62] They discover that mission is not simply about words but about attracting others through the compelling witness of love for each other. The knowledge that Jesus as God humbled himself (Philippians 2:5–11) and served others (John 13) so that the world might have life (John 20:31) helps them redefine who they are in relationship to their work. For those who labor in dangerous jobs and meaningless work, the ritual of commissioning helps them rediscover their human dignity and God-given vocations. From their relationship to Christ and their belief in being children of God—and not from debasing servitude or the lack of economic or educational opportunities—they take on the position of serving others. The retreat deliberately treats them as kings and queens so that they might discover more fully their human dignity. Rediscovering their own inner value is central to how they begin to understand the theological concept of redemption.

The Call to Gratefulness. Lastly, in the midst of all the problems that they face as immigrants, the closing ritual allows them to live in gratitude with God. The retreat is designed to help them celebrate, even though their needs and wants are many. While their difficulties often challenge their own happiness, their spirituality enables them to see God at work in the world, even amidst their limitations. The closing ritual is designed to help these immigrants share with others the love and joy they have received, what they have heard, what they have seen with their eyes, and what they have touched with their hands (1 John 1:1). Such experiences enable many immigrants to say of Jesus, "My Lord and my God!" (John 20:28), not because of any external expectation but because they have begun to appropriate the liberating truths of the Gospel into their own hearts and minds. As immigrants who have crossed canals and barren deserts, the retreat is a powerful weekend that enables them to discover God's abiding presence with them, who calls them and brings light out of their own experience of darkness.

A NEW WORLD AND A NEW WAY OF LIFE: A SACRAMENTAL AND INCARNATIONAL SPIRITUALITY

In summary, the spirituality of the Missionary Encounter retreat is profoundly incarnational and sacramental in nature. For these immigrants, the rituals of the retreat are the primary ways through which God touches their lives and becomes human to them. Through the offer of a cup of coffee, a letter from a friend, a sincere *abrazo*, the washing of feet, the gift of a flower, a gesture of welcome, a passage from scripture, the sacraments of the Church, a sincere testimony, an inspired song, and many other ways, the grace of God and the presence of Jesus becomes real and visible to them. They see, touch, smell, feel, and taste God through the team and the various rituals that form the backbone of their encounter with God. As words and actions are intermingled together into these graced ritual events, the heart of the Christian message unfolds before them.

In other words, the retreat offers a structured, ritual presentation of the Gospel message that makes present the mystery of salvation.

These rituals invite the immigrants to friendship, celebration, reconciliation, sincere sharing, fiesta, honesty, promise, purpose, dignity,
hospitality, generosity, service, recognition, care, spontaneity, and
love. The retreat brings out how the revelation of God is related to the
totality of their lives and includes, but is not limited to, formal liturgical moments of encounter with God. These retreat rituals, then, root
their spirituality in daily life; they help them discover, authenticate,
claim, appreciate, and develop profound human and spiritual poten-
tials within each of them; they make visible an invisible God. Such rituals, in essence, are "spi-ritual": in other words, through ritual, the
spirit of God works. These rituals touch the hearts of these immigrants and bring forth their deepest, human hungers for life, inviting
them to surrender in trust to the reality of God through the Life of
Jesus.

Their spiritual experience reveals the cracking open of a stony
heart, the healing of a wounded heart, the creating of a spiritual heart,
the touching of God's heart, the ennobling of a Mexican heart, the
cleansing of a sinful heart, the awakening of a joyful heart, the empowering of a loving heart, and the witnessing of a grateful heart.
Like a cactus in a barren desert after a summer rain, these immigrants
begin to flower in beautiful and unexpected ways. Their experience
of God's love empowers them to realize that they are "no longer
strangers and aliens," in the words of St. Paul, "but citizens with the
saints and also members of the household of God" (Ephesians 2:19).

The retreat is not simply a moment when they have "accepted Jesus" as a personal Lord and Savior. Rather, it is a moment when
they have discovered that Jesus has accepted them, which is at the
heart of the Encounter retreat. This foundational, spiritual experience re-creates many of their lives through gracious love and allows them to unfold into something new through a gradual process
of conversion.

NOTES

1. Sociologists sometimes refer to such organizations as "identity transformation organizations" (ITOs). Arthur L. Greil and David R. Rudy describe an identity transformation organization as follows: "Many organizations, including new
religious movements, radical political movements, 'deprogramming' enterprises,
Alcoholics Anonymous, therapeutic drug communities, and programs for con-
trolled weight loss, have as an implicit or explicit goal the transformation of the

personal identities of their members. Such identity transformation organizations encourage their members to reorganize their behavior, offer them new social roles to play, socialize them to new values, and foster in them new modes of self-conception. . . . Whether we call it conversion, resocialization, deprogramming, or achieving sobriety, the identity transformation process sponsored by such organizations is essentially one." See Arthur L. Greil and David R. Rudy, "Social Cocoons: Encapsulation and Identity Transformation Organizations," *Sociological Inquiry* 54 (1984): 260–78.

2. For more on Cesar Chavez, see Richard Griswold del Castillo and Richard A. Garcia, *César Chávez: A Triumph of Spirit, The Oklahoma Western Biographies; V. 2.* (Norman Okla.: University of Oklahoma Press, 1995), Jacques E. Levy and Cesar Chavez, *Cesar Chavez: Autobiography of La Causa.* 1st ed. (New York: Norton, 1975); Jean-Marie Muller and Jean Kalman, *César Chavez: Un Combat Non-Violent* (Paris: Fayard/Le Cerf, 1977).

3. For more on the theology of liberation and option for the poor, see Leonardo Boff, *Jesus Christ Liberator* (Maryknoll, N.Y.: Orbis, 1978); Virgilio P. Elizondo, *Galilean Journey: The Mexican-American Promise* (Maryknoll, N.Y.: Orbis, 1983); Gustavo Gutierrez, *A Theology of Liberation: History, Politics and Salvation* (Maryknoll, N.Y.: Orbis, 1973); Jon Sobrino, *Christology at the Crossroads* (Maryknoll, N.Y.: Orbis, 1994). See also *Conferencia General del Episcopado Latinoamericano* (Medellín, Columbia: CELAM II, 1968). *Medellín Conference—Final Document. The Church in the Present-Day Transformation of Latin America in Light of the Council.* 2 vols. (Bogotá: General Secretariat of CELAM, 1970–1973) and *Conferencia General del Episcopado Latinoamericano* (Puebla, Mexico: CELAM III, 1979). *Puebla Conference—Final Document. Visión Pastoral De America Latina: Equipo De Reflexión, Departamentos Y Secciones De Celam* (Bogotá: Consejo Episcopal Latinoamericano, 1978.)

4. Beginning in the 1950s, the Cursillo movement has been a major source of renewal for the Church, and it has been a source of empowerment for lay people and clergy around the world. In many ways, the Cursillo movement is the parent of many other lay movements, such as Marriage Encounter, Youth Encounters and many other renewal movements. For more on Cursillo, see Juan Hervas Benet, *Los Cursillos De Cristiandad: Instrumento De Renovación Cristiana*, 6. ed., Madrid: Euramerica, 1965; Marcene Marcoux. *Cursillo, Anatomy of a Movement: The Experience of Spiritual Renewal*, (New York: Lambeth Press, 1982); Jose Diego Martinez O'-Connor, *Cursillos Y Circulos De Estudios De Accion Catolica* (Almeria: Talleres de Graficas Guia, 1972.)

5. The program has an administrative body composed of an executive committee, a spiritual director, a president, vice president, a secretary, and a treasurer. In addition it has presidents and vice presidents of fourteen standing committees. One of the unique features of the electoral process is that presidents and chairpersons can serve only two years. One of the reasons for this policy is to avoid a leadership monopoly by only a few people. Each spring, the program holds a special congress in order to elect new leaders.

6. According to the ancestral stories of ancient Mexico, Teotihuacán was the place where "one becomes deified," where one becomes godly. Miguel León-Portilla describes the myth of Teotihuacán in the following way: "In a tale laced with moral lessons, the Nahua informants described how two gods stepped

forward to offer themselves. The first one was the arrogant Tecuciztecatl (lord of the conch shells), the second was the modest Nanahuatzin (purulent or pustuled one). Both prepared themselves by doing the kind of penance that would permit them to cast themselves into a huge fire and to emerge from it transformed into the sun. Tecuciztecatl, who keenly desired to become the sun, was the first to make his offerings to propitiate a favorable result. Although the expected ritual offerings consisted of fir tree branches and balls of pine moss, on which were to be placed the maguey needles used by the penitent to pierce himself, the ostentatious Tecueciztecatl offered golden balls with spines made of precious stones and quetzal feathers instead of fir branches. And rather than piercing himself and sacrificing his own blood, he was content with presenting spines made of coral. On the other hand, Nanahuatzin bled himself profusely and offered authentic fir branches and sharp maguey needles. Tecuciztecatl was the first to make an attempt when the moment for the sacrifice arrived and the two gods were ready to throw themselves into the fires. But the arrogant god tried four times and each time was afraid; thus, having failed to cremate himself, Tecuciztecatl lost the opportunity of becoming the sun. Then when the turn of the humble Nanahuatzin came, all the gods gathered in Teotihuacán anxiously watched the scene. Because his destiny was to be transformed into the sun of this fifth age, Nanahuatzin, closing his eyes, hurled himself into the fire and was quickly consumed. Desperate, Tecuciztecatl then also threw himself into the fire, but since he did this so belatedly his fate was to be changed only into the pale moon. Because the belief in a necessary reciprocity with the gods for their original sacrifice was fundamental to the ancient Nahuas, vestiges of this concern can be found among their contemporary descendants. Bloody self-sacrifice is engaged in today by those who, in a new form of *tlamahcehualiztli* (act of deserving), take part in exhausting pilgrimages to Christian sanctuaries. These often entail painful penances, such as self-flagellation and the wearing of crowns of thorns. What is perhaps most striking is that accounts have also been recorded that reflect a memory of the ancient tale of the original sacrifice of the gods, who, to restore life on earth, were said to have cast themselves into the divine hearth that had been set ablaze in Teotihuacán." See Miguel León-Portilla, *The Aztec Image of Self and Society: An Introduction to Nahua Culture*, ed. J. Jorge Klor de Alva (Salt Lake City, Utah: University of Utah Press, 1992), 15–16.

7. Though most of these immigrants earn between $4,500 and $15,000 a year, they sacrificed their time, money and talents to build and maintain the Shrine and retreat house. For two and a half years, hundreds of members from the Program volunteered their weekends and worked in the hot desert sun, with temperatures sometimes as high as 120 degrees, in order to create this spiritual home.

8. The *Encuentro Misionero* is open to men and women ages twenty-one and older, although for various reasons the men and women make the retreat on separate weekends. For Hispanic, feminist theological perspectives see M.P. Aquino, *Nuestro Clamor Por La Vida* (San Jose: DEI, 1992), and Ada María Isasi-Díaz and Yolanda Tarango, *Hispanic Women: Prophetic Voice in the Church* (San Francisco: Harper and Row, 1988). For a scholarly perspective on conversion experiences among men and women, see Susan Juster, "'In a Different Voice:' Male and Female

Narratives of Religious Conversion in Post-Revolutionary America," *American Quarterly* 41 (1989): 34–62.

9. In the most extreme forms, some scholars argue that religious transformation is simply a matter of brain washing. See Flo Conway and Jim Siegelman, *Snapping: America's Epidemic of Sudden Personality Change* (Philadelphia: J.B. Lippincott, 1978). Others speak about "drift models" of transformation, which speak about the developmental and voluntary aspects of the process. See Gordon, "Dying to Self" and Theodore E. Long and Jeffrey K. Hadden, "Religious Conversion and the Concept of Socialization: Integrating the Brainwashing and Drift Models," *Journal for the Scientific Study of Religion* 22 (1983): 1–14.

10. Machismo is still a major social problem in Mexico; because of it, Mexican women often say they do not feel comfortable talking about some of their deeper personal issues when men are around. In this light, the segregation of men from women helps them develop more openly and spontaneously. Some of the differences can be determined more through qualitative research than quantitative, that is, more through interviews than surveys. While chapters 2 and 3 will detail some of the differences between men and women based on interviews, extensive survey research did not reveal any major differences in terms of "transformation" or "conversion" indicators. In other words, my quantitative data did not indicate that there were substantial differences in whether men changed more than women as a result of the retreat.

11. James White notes, "Sacramental worship is distinguished by its use of sign-acts, i.e., actions that convey meaning. Sacraments are signs that involve actions, words, and (usually) objects." See James White, *Introduction to Christian Worship* (Nashville, Tenn.: Abingdon, 1980), 145.

12. These dynamics of liberating the heart are slow and gradual, though they are noticeable. They also give a framework for understanding future personal and spiritual development. While not all follow a chronological path of transformation as I have described them, I highlight these responses in the candidates that help illumine the rich texture of their conversion process and spirituality.

13. In many ways the biblical notion of heart better corresponds to the Mexican understanding of the heart. In Mexico, dating back to indigenous sources, the heart is seen as the place of equilibrium and harmony, the place where the biological and the spiritual are united. In the Nahuatl, the ancient Mexican language, the word for heart is *teyolia*, coming from two indigenous words, *yolia* meaning "the one who animates" and *yol* meaning "life." See especially Miguel León-Portilla, *Aztec Thought and Culture: A Study of the Ancient Nahuatl Mind*, trans. Jack Emory Davis (Norman: University of Oklahoma Press, 1963).

14. Jean de Fraine and Albert Vanhoye, "Heart," in *Dictionary of Biblical Theology*, ed. Xavier Leon-Defour (Paris: Desclée Company, 1967), 200–202.

15. John Paul II, *Redemptor Hominis*, March 24, 1979, no 8, p. 24.

16. *Les ayudamos sentir bienvenidos porque nosotros también hemos experimentado rechazo y discriminación.* Female team member, interview by author, 15 July 2001, tape recording, Coachella, Calif.

17. *Al llegar, la gente parecía muy alegre y religiosa. Tenia miedo que me iban a rechazar por las cosas malas que había hecho. No sabía nada de Dios, y seguramente no*

sentía que merecía ese tipo de atención. Female team member, interview by author, 15 July 2001, tape recording, Coachella, Calif.

18. *Me parecía cosa loca ver tanta gente cantando y dándome la bienvenida. Había perdido el sentido de alegría cuando salí de México. Pero al ver la alegría en sus rostros, vi algo de amistad que yo querría volver a descubrir.* Male candidate, interview by author, 15 July 2001, tape recording, Coachella, Calif.

19. The phrase *ramilletes de amor* comes from the Spanish words *ramo* meaning "bouquet" and *amor,* which means "love." A *ramillo* is a bunch of flowers pulled together into a small bouquet. The words "spiritual bouquet" have also been used through the centuries when speaking about spirituality. See St. Francis de Sales, *Introduction to the Devout Life,* trans. John K. Ryan (New York: Bantam Doubleday Dell, 1989).

20. *Tengo 29 años y hasta hoy dia, nadie me ha dado nada. Como hombre, es la primera vez que he aprendido como llorar.* Testimony of Mexican immigrant, 22 October 1999.

21. *Cuando vi esta dinámica, es como vi mi vida entera frente de mí y todos los problemas que le había causado a mi familia por causa de mi tomada.* Male team member, interview by author, 15 July 2001, tape recording, Coachella, Calif.

22. *Las comidas me hicieron sentir alguien importante. Nunca pensé que gente haría tanto para hacerme sentir en casa.* Male team member, interview by author, 15 July 2001, tape recording, Coachella, Calif.

23. *En la cultura Mexicana siempre es la mujer la que sirve las comidas. Sentarme y que otros me sirvieron fue algo increíble. Me dije a mi misma, "no soy nadie—¿porque hacen todo esto por me?" Nunca esperaba tanta atención.* Female team member, interview by author, 15 July 2001, tape recording, Coachella, Calif.

24. For an overview of Base communities, see Margaret Hebblethwaite, *Base Communities: An Introduction* (Mahwah, N.J.: Paulist, 1994); Jose Marins, Teolide Trevisan. *CEBs: La Iglesia En Pequeño* (Santiago: Paulinas, 1996); Thomas Kleissier, *Small Christian Communities: A Vision of Hope for the 21st Century* (New York: Paulist Press, 1997); Robert Wuthnow, *"I Come Away Stronger:" How Small Groups Are Shaping American Religion* (Grand Rapids, Mich.: Eerdmans, 1994).

25. In contrast to other groups like Cursillo, which tried to bring about renewal in the Church through the formation of lay leaders, the primary focus of the Valley Missionary Program and the Missionary Encounter retreat is the creation and formation of base communities. Outside of the retreat, anyone can participate in the basic communities, and they do not have to have participated in a Missionary Encounter retreat before they can come to community.

26. The names of each community are usually very biblical in nature, such as "The Lost Sheep," "Christ the King," "The Apostles of Jesus" and others.

27. *Me sorprendió como empezamos a conocernos en una manera tan fuerte uno con el otro. Al compartir nuestras historias y escucharnos era como que nos conocíamos desde hace mucho tiempo.* Male team member, interview by author, 15 July 2001, tape recording, Coachella, Calif.

28. This allows for a peer-to-peer evangelization, as encouraged by the Vatican document, *Apostolicam Actuositatem:* "In this area the laity can exercise the apostolate of like toward like. It is here that they complement the testimony of life with the testimony of the word." Walter M. Abbott, ed. The Apostolate of the Laity *(Apostolicam Actuositatem).* The Documents of Vatican II, no. 9 (Piscataway, N.J.:

New Century Publishers, Inc., 1966). For online access to The Documents of Vatican II, see http://abbey.apana.org.au/councils/vatican2/v2laity.htm.

29. Walter M. Abbott, ed. *Gaudium Et Spes*, The Documents of Vatican II (Piscataway, N.J.: New Century Publishers, Inc., 1966), nos. 21–22, 40–44.

30. *Lo que más me llenó de felicidad fue la charla que dijo que somos 'diositos.' Me sorprendió pensar que Dios nos vea en esa manera.* Female team member, interview by author, 15 July 2001, tape recording, Coachella, Calif.

31. In recent years, perhaps as a way of emphasizing the real presence of Christ in the assembly and the Scriptures, liturgists have de-emphasized the real presence of Christ in the Blessed Sacrament. This is not to say that liturgists have denied the real presence, only that it has received less attention. Rituals like adoration of the Blessed Sacrament and other such devotional practices have been less promoted and sometimes disdained. Yet in the experience of the people, this ritual is another real turning point for a lot of candidates on the retreat.

32. *Cuando visité el Santísimo, conocí a alguien que estaba interesada en mi por la primera vez.* Male team member, interview by author, 15 July 2001, tape recording, Coachella, Calif.

33. *Desde el momento que entré, sentí paz y tranquilidad. Viendo a Cristo en el Santísimo, sentí mas confianza para pedirle cosas y dejar las cosas que pesaban en mi corazón. Fue como si hubiera encontrado a Cristo por primera vez.* Female team member, interview by author, 15 July 2001, tape recording, Coachella, Calif.

34. *La cruz significa para mí que Cristo venció a la muerte. Prácticamente esto me dice que las cosas que sufrimos no nos va a conquistar porque creemos en Él.* Female team member, interview by author, 15 July 2001, tape recording, Coachella, Calif.

35. *La cruz significa que Cristo vive y que no ha olvidado de nosotros. Cuando veo la cruz significa para mí que nuestras luchas, aunque son muchas, no nos va a conquistar.* Male team member, interview by author, 15 July 2001, tape recording, Coachella, Calif.

36. *Cuando entré por la puerta, inmediatamente me sentí en casa, como en un lugar donde podía ser yo mismo otra vez.* Male candidate, interview by author, 16 July 2001, tape recording, Coachella, Calif.

37. *A través del tiempo, sin pensar, se olvida uno de donde viene, y la comida me recordó de mi cultura otra vez más.* Male team member, interview by author, 15 July 2001, tape recording, Coachella, Calif.

38. *Fue como que si finalmente estaba en un lugar que comprendía de donde venia. Por un momento, me sentía que ya no era extranjera en los Estados Unidos.* Female team member, interview by author, 15 July 2001, tape recording, Coachella, Calif.

39. *Me sentí vergüenza al pensar de las cosas horribles que había hecho. Una de las razones por lo cual me distancie de la iglesia fue porque pensaba que no seria perdonado.* Male team member, interview by author, 23 March 2000, tape recording, Coachella, Calif.

40. *Cuando vi a mis pecados en el fuego, algo dentro de me saltó de alegría, como que si todo me ser fue liberado.* Female team member, interview by author, 15 July 2001, tape recording, Coachella, Calif.

41. *Me sentí como si había abandonado a Dios, pero aquí era Dios acercándome a mí.* Female team member, interview by author, 15 July 2001, tape recording, Coachella, Calif.

42. The ritual, emerging from the Nahua tradition, celebrates that a people are one step closer to their final awakening in death.

43. *Cuando alguien me dio una docena de rosas, sentí como que era yo que florecía. Esas rosas representaban un amor que me devolvía la vida.* Female team member, interview by author, 15 July 2001, tape recording, Coachella, Calif.

44. *Fue como despertar a una vida nueva y un mundo nuevo que me llenó con una paz y tranquilidad que no conocía antes.* Female team member, interview by author, 15 July 2001, tape recording, Coachella, Calif.

45. *Al tener mucha gente recibirme con tanto amor y alegría me hizo sentir que había muerto y subido al cielo.* Female team member, interview by author, 15 July 2001, tape recording, Coachella, Calif.

46. *Es como realicé que ahora me tocaba a mi servir, como un desafió indirecto de empezar a tratar a otros como ellos me trataron a mí.* Male team member, interview by author, 15 July 2001, tape recording, Coachella, Calif.

47. *Fue como si me empujaron a salir al mundo para compartir mi experiencia. Para mí, ya no era de un Dios que castigaba sino de servirle al Señor que me quiere y me manda adelante.* Male team member, interview by author, 15 July 2001, tape recording, Coachella, Calif.

48. *En verdad no querría que terminara el fin de semana tan bonita, pero al mismo tiempo, sentí que me habían dado alas para volar.* Male team member, interview by author, 15 July 2001, tape recording, Coachella, Calif.

49. *Antes del Encuentro, me sentía inferior a los demás por la situación económica de mi familia. Tuvimos que pagar por coyotes y cruzar como mojados y no tuve muchas oportunidades de realizar las cosas que yo querría como educación. Sentía que otros eran más importantes porque tenían más. Pero el retiro me ayudó realizar que todos somos iguales, que todos somos hijos de Dios, que soy importante a Dios, y que Dios me ha llamado hacer algo importante.* Female team member, interview by author, 15 July 2001, tape recording, Coachella, Calif.

50. Edward Schillebeeckx, *Jesus: An Experiment in Christology* (New York: Crossroad, 1981).

51. Karl Rahner, *Foundations of Christian Faith: An Introduction to the Idea of Christianity* (New York: Crossroad, 1982).

52. For more on parables, see John R. Donahue, *The Gospel in Parable: Metaphor, Narrative, and Theology in the Synoptic Gospels* (Philadelphia: Fortress Press, 1988); J. Jeremias, *The Parables of Jesus* (New York: Scribner's, 1963); D. O. Via, *The Parables: Their Literary and Existentialist Dimension* (Philadelphia: Fortress, 1967); J. Lambrecht, *Once More Astonished: The Parables of Jesus Christ* (New York: Crossroads, 1981).

53. This aspect of Jesus' ministry, in Perrin's words, "must have been most meaningful to his followers and most offensive to his critics." At this table Jesus brought together scribe, tax collector, fisherman, and zealot, and he challenged them to a new kind of relationship that was not based on status but upon a common hope for coming of God's kingdom (Matthew 8:11; 11:16–19). The meals help them appreciate God's invitation to fellowship and are a symbol for a new way of understanding relationships (Matthew 9:9–10; Mark 14:1–9; Luke 7:36–50; Luke 19:1–6; John 2:1–11; John 12:1–8). The early Christians put great emphasis, even to the point of excess, on continuing the Jesus tradition of festive table fellowship—

a table fellowship to which all were invited, especially the poor and disenfranchised. As it was in the time of Jesus, the scandal of the retreat is that these poor and marginalized immigrants are the ones welcomed to feast at table (Mark 2:16). See Norman Perrin, *Rediscovering the Teaching of Jesus* (San Francisco: Harper & Row, 1976), 102.

54. *Puebla Conference—Final Document, no. 239.* This also comes out in the recent document, *Ecclesia in America*, which speaks of the Church in terms of conversion, communion and solidarity. See John Paul II, *Ecclesia in America*, (Washington, D.C.: United States Catholic Conference, 1999).

55. For more on revelation, see Ignace de La Potterie, "Le christ, comme figure de révélation d'apres S. Jean," in *Revelation de Dieu et langage des hommes* (Paris: Les Éditions du Cerf, 1972), 51–76, Leonardo Boff, *Jesus Christ Liberator* (Maryknoll, N.Y.: Orbis, 1978), 185–87, 251–53, and Virgilio P. Elizondo, *Galilean Journey: The Mexican-American Promise* (Maryknoll, N.Y.: Orbis, 1983), 50–52.

56. See Walter M. Abbott, ed. *Dei Verbum, The Documents of Vatican II* (Piscataway, N.J.: New Century Publishers, 1966).

57. For more on revelation and relationships, see Sandra Marie Schneiders, *Written That You May Believe: Encountering Jesus in the Fourth Gospel* (New York: Crossroad Publishers, 1999).

58. For more on this subject, see Elizabeth A. Dreyer, *The Cross in Christian Tradition: From Paul to Bonaventure* (New York: Paulist Press, 2001).

59. Jon Sobrino, *Christology at the Crossroads* (Maryknoll, N.Y.: Orbis, 1994), 224.

60. Paul VI, *Evangelii Nuntiandi: On Evangelization in the Modern World* (Washington, D.C.: United States Catholic Conference, 1976), no. 20.

61. Walter M. Abbott, ed. *Ad Gentes, The Documents of Vatican II* (Piscataway, N.J.: New Century Publishers, 1966).

62. For more on mission, see Donald Senior and Carroll Stuhlmueller, *The Biblical Foundations for Mission* (Maryknoll, N.Y.: Orbis, 1983), and ed. James A. Scherer and Stephen B. Bevans, *New Directions in Mission and Evangelization 3: Faith and Culture* (Maryknoll, N.Y.: Orbis, 1999).

3

Corazón Animado—
The Animated Heart:
The Dynamics of Conversion
and Transformation

A FOUNDATION FOR CONVERSION

"When I first crossed the border," said one immigrant from Jalisco, "I didn't have a problem. I jumped over the fence and made a run for it, and the Border Patrol didn't catch me. My brother was with me, but he was not so lucky; they apprehended him soon after he got over. Then I was alone. And I didn't know what to do, so I figured I would call my family and let them know what was happening. But I didn't have any money, so I begged some people on the streets for some change. And this is the worst part. Each person I asked on the streets turned away from me, rejected me, called me names, and even threatened to call the Border Patrol on me, and all I wanted to do was contact my family! I mean, I know what it is like to go three days without food. I know what it is like to hide myself as a stowaway in the lower baggage compartment of a bus. I know what it is like to endure the freezing temperatures of the mountains. But the worst kind of suffering is to experience these kinds of rejections, when people treated me like I was dirt, like I was only a dog. It made me feel so totally humiliated, like I wasn't worth anything. I felt about as low as any human being can feel on the earth . . . and I have felt like this many times since I've lived here in the United States. . . . But when I came here on this retreat, my whole view of life changed. I had never been treated so well in my life, anywhere. I felt like a king! I began to realize something I never knew before: that I was worth something, that I am valuable, that I have a purpose in life, that I really am

79

somebody to God, that other people really do care, that I am not alone and that I have a mission in life."[1]

The story of this Mexican immigrant resembles that of many others who live the Missionary Encounter retreat. The undocumented Mexican immigrants often experience multiple levels of rejection and alienation: linguistic, cultural, economic, political, personal, and religious. They experience great trials, especially in the indignities they have to undergo in breaking from home, crossing the border, and entering the United States.

In contrast, the community of the Valley Missionary Program provides an oasis of acceptance in a desert of rejection. This oasis becomes the means through which many discover a new center for their lives from which a new self-identity develops. While the retreat does not solve all their problems, nor cause them to experience overnight changes in personality, it does often initiate many profound changes in their lives during and after the weekend. Some said the weekend marked a new beginning, a *metanoia*, a change of heart and direction in their lives.

For many immigrants, the weekend lays the groundwork for a new foundation, upon which they build a new life. In other words, the weekend initiates a conversion process through which they experience an intensification of faith in Christ, which leads to the transformation of their core beliefs, values, and priorities. This means restructuring and repatterning their attitudes, their emotions, and the way they relate to others. In order to do this, they often need to address the pains and wounds of the past to become freed from their narrow agendas, excessive emotional baggage, negative self-images, relational conflicts, communication difficulties, ignorance, rugged individualism, inadequacy, anger, sin, guilt, and a sense of failure in many areas of their lives. In a word, conversion is liberating for these immigrants when it means freedom from all those things that oppress their lives so that they can be free to be simply who they are before God.[2]

This conversion process is key to understanding their spirituality. In this light I refer to spirituality as the way a person, in community, experiences, understands, and enacts a relationship with God.[3] Many say the retreat has enabled them to feel again a range of emotions in their lives. Some participants mention how their experience has transformed the way they live out many of their relationships (especially with the Church), and they describe how they have become more free, more intimate, and ultimately more loving. Still other immigrants talk about the new insight they have gained into themselves and new perspectives that have helped them re-interpret their experiences. Some also talk about changes in the way they make decisions on a daily basis, especially in their responsibility to their families and communities. And lastly, and most of all, most express that they have come to a new awareness of the presence of God, who has invited them into a profound and personal friendship through the person of Jesus.

As a result of the retreat, immigrants undergo changes that illuminate different dimensions of the conversion process.* Drawing on the immigrant's commentaries about the retreat as well as the works of Bernard Lonergan and Donald Gelpi, I have differentiated the conversion process into five areas: affective, social, intellectual, moral, and religious.[4] These categories provide a helpful framework from which to listen to the voices of the immigrants themselves, even though these classifications come out of a North American cognitive and cultural framework. While these categories have limitations in their application to the Hispanic context, they are helpful in differentiating the complex process of change. At the same time, the spiritual experience of these immigrants and their process of integral conversion add new dimensions to these categories. Not only do these categories help outline some of the ways conversion happens, but also these same categories acquire new meaning through the experience of the conversion of the poor. In addition, these categories help bring the voices of these immigrants into dialogue with the wider panorama of spiritual experience and the dynamics of conversion that emerge from other parts of the world.

---

*While much of my research relies heavily on qualitative data such as interviews, I also conducted extensive surveys in which I tried to measure the change that the retreat makes in their lives. I did this by giving the same 120-question survey to candidates and team members, and then I compared the results. Although such data is not the primary focus of this book, the results are shown in figure 3.1.

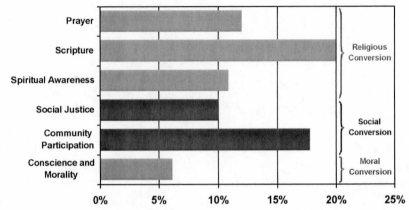

Figure 3.1.   Transformation Indicators for Missionary Encounter Retreat: Percent Differentials between Candidates and Team.
Source: Based on Catholic Faith Inventory survey. Survey used with permission from Paulist Press.

AFFECTIVE CONVERSION THROUGH
THE EXPERIENCE OF THE BEAUTIFUL

As noted above, when they come to the United States, many immigrants work day, night and often on weekends simply to earn enough money to survive. Not surprisingly, the immigration experience and their cultural isolation in the United States cause many immigrants to shut down emotionally and suppress many feelings, desires, and aspirations. The retreat experience, however, enables many to experience a tremendous liberation. Many who make the Encounter retreat claim, without hesitation, that it is the most powerful and beautiful experience they have ever had. Words like "strong" (*fuerte*), "powerful" (*poderoso*), and "incredible" (*increíble*) are some of the ways they begin to describe the intense emotional reaction to the retreat: "It was simply the most beautiful experience of my life," said Guillermo from Michoacán.[5]

The retreat draws forth intense emotional responses of joy, sorrow, gratitude, pain, and love, and it also initiates a process of affective transformation in the lives of these people. They talk as if a flame has begun to burn away the deadwood of loneliness and emotional fatigue, changing the pain of the past into a new energy and capacity for love and service. The retreat marks the beginning of an important movement from guardedness to openness, from negative stereotypes to a more positive self-identity, and from guilt to forgiveness.

From Guardedness to Openness

Many arrive at the retreat with a guarded and cautious heart. For many immigrants, trust comes only with great difficulty. Years of abuse and exploitation that stems from a life in poverty, compounded by mistreatment from *coyote* smugglers and oppressive bosses, have led many to be wary of people who try to help them. Many have difficulty believing they are loved and valued. Cloaked in shame, fear, doubt, anxiety, and sometimes illiteracy, many have learned to hide from the pain of their own unworthiness and the feelings of their own inadequacy. Behind their sometimes tough exterior, the inner beauty of many of these immigrants remains hidden in a shell of self-protectiveness. Some commented that the retreat experience cracked open this isolating shell and enabled them to suddenly discover the profound depth of their inner lives. Each aspect of the retreat, especially the talks, the meals, and the surprises, encourages the candidates to reflect on the way they are living and how they are relating to themselves, their families, their co-workers, and God. Some mentioned how the foot washing ritual and the agape meal, in particular, helped break down the walls of the immigrant's self-protectiveness and open them to a new revelation of the beauty of God and others.

The beauty of the retreat experience helps many immigrants to begin to transform the negative energy of their destructive emotions into more constructive patterns of living. Though some spoke about how the retreat brought to light the negative sides of their personalities and some painful experiences in their lives, many discovered a beauty within them they never suspected and never realized they possessed, which heightens their experience of affective conversion.

Through the surprises, the candidates go through a powerful range of emotions, from the serious and solemn prayer in the *Santísimo* to the wild and uproarious laughter and singing at meals. As the walls and barriers begin to break down, and each begins to step out of the primary role that defines them as husband, wife, mother, son, brother, or sister, they start to experience new dimensions of their lives. Many who have been emotionally shut down begin to experience a new awakening of self, a self that is richer, fuller, and more alive than before they came to the retreat. Such openness led some to an emotional "remapping" of their lives, which enabled them to have a greater capacity for compassion. As these immigrants begin to risk opening themselves up to others in the context of a caring community, new life begins to dawn in them. Change happens as they let the love of other people enter and reorient their lives and lead them in a new direction.

From Negative Stereotypes to a More Positive Self-Identity

The retreat helps redirect the emotional contours of their lives by facilitating a shift from negative stereotypes to a healthier self-identity. Deeply ingrained within many of them is the pattern of self-loathing and self-deprecation, and often it is difficult for them to find the path that leads to self-acceptance. The retreat marks an important step toward greater self-reflection and enables many of these immigrants to step back and take a critical look at their lives. Often, little time exists to reflect on the traumas of the past and their effect on their personal lives. Most do not have the money to go to counseling to process the impact of their experiences on their identity and relationships. Few have ever tried to analyze their own psycho-spiritual matrix through which they interpret the world and the events they experience.

The retreat, however, enables them to come to a greater knowledge about themselves. The Encounter mirrors back to the candidates the type of lives they are living while at the same time, it calls them to a new way of life. Prior to the retreat, rather than mirroring upwards toward God or inward toward themselves, they mirror outward toward the social norms and status quo. In so doing, many Mexican immigrants begin to internalize their own sense of social inferiority. Most of them begin to believe the degrading stereotypes that mainstream U.S. society has attached to them: that they are worthless, inferior, unworthy, ignorant, and dispensable, no more than a pair of money-yielding arms without a heart or a soul, without face or feeling. These negative social messages often contribute to negative self-images, which, in turn, produce much anxiety and turmoil within their souls. Since they do not know how to express themselves, these emotional conflicts often result in hostility, aggressiveness, and violence toward their own family, friends, and co-workers.

Affective conversion as "emotional repatterning" entails the rehabilitation of their damaged self-image that leads to the realization of their own inner beauty. As a result of the retreat, many immigrants expressed that they began to rediscover treasures within their own homes, their own families, and their own lives. As Isabel said, "Before the Encounter I didn't think I was worth anything, and at times I was afraid of other people. In the Encounter, I realized that God was near to my heart, which gave me the confidence in myself and enabled me to reach out to other people."[6] At various moments, the revelation of their own inner beauty, and the beauty of others they meet on the retreat, helps them to appreciate in a new way the beauty of God expressed in the life of Christ. This is affective conversion.

From Guilt to Forgiveness

As candidates face their own guilt and inner disorder, they discover a new horizon of forgiveness. Many are drawn toward repentance not because of humiliating sermons but because of their encounter with goodness. In light of the experience of love, beauty, and caring people, they began to see their own errors more clearly. Some spoke about the guilt they felt just by living far from the family: "Sometimes you forget to send money to your family in Mexico," said Mario, "and then you begin to realize what you're doing and who you are neglecting."[7]

Some candidates also realized their failure as parents or as friends. Still other immigrants experienced a tremendous inner healing through the ritual confession of their sins in the Sacrament of Reconciliation. One construction worker said, "I went to confession for the first time in thirty-five years . . . and it broke me down into a mound of jelly. I just sort of figured that a lot of the stuff I had done could not be forgiven, but after confession I felt like a tremendous burden was lifted off my shoulders."[8] Many said that the experience of accepting God's unconditional offer of mercy was the means through which they experienced a new lease on life. One farm worker said, "after the Sacrament of Reconciliation, I left a new person . . . this hard heart of mine was not so callused anymore. I felt God's forgiveness and God's love in a very concrete way. After this, I felt a tremendous joy, which empowered me to love others."[9] Many others said that this experience of love and acceptance laid the groundwork for a life of prayer.

The retreat initiates a long process of restructuring the emotional patterns of the candidates' lives. Some of the immigrants spoke about how the retreat helped them begin to order their emotions in such a way that they became more capable of perceiving the gifts that are present in their lives. Years after living his retreat, Emilio said, "I feel like now I am more sensitive to the beauty that surrounds me, but I am also more sensitive to the suffering of others and the way we abuse the world in which we live."[10] The inspired beauty that leads these immigrants to affective awakenings and the reshaping of their emotional landscape also led them to want to lead better lives, not out of coercion or force but through the inner draw of love. The process of affective conversion for these immigrants reveals the heart's desire for beauty, a beauty that heals, liberates, and makes a person into a new creation.

SOCIAL CONVERSION THROUGH
THE EXPERIENCE OF LOVE

As we have already noted, after arriving in the United States, many of the immigrants in the Coachella Valley feel various levels of cultural displacement, inner alienation, and personal loneliness. This feeling of estrangement only deepens when they realize that many of their relatives and friends live in Mexico. Seeing them is particularly difficult, if not impossible, because of the lack of proper documentation, the dangers involved in multiple border crossings and the costs involved in returning home to visit them.

While living in the United States, many also feel pressure to deny their cultural roots in Mexico, which only increases their sense of inferiority and shame about their identity and their cultural roots. Most of them feel they need to suppress their socio-cultural heritage in order to move ahead within the dominant culture in the United States (even though, little by little, the dominant culture in the United States is becoming more and more Latino!). In brief, they often feel displaced and disconnected, far from their home. In contrast, the retreat initiates important movements from cultural denial to cultural affirmation, from indifference to care and from a family of blood to a family of the Spirit.

From Cultural Denial to Cultural Affirmation

The retreat helps many of these immigrants move from a place of cultural denial to a place of cultural affirmation. For four days, they experience an alternative world that allows them to feel proud of their Mexican heritage and more connected to the significant people in their lives and the new people they meet on the retreat. The retreat's message often reaches them through the medium of familiar cultural expressions in the music, decorations, dancing, food, jokes, rituals, devotions, and architecture. The creation of such an environment enables many of them to feel at home for the first time since they left Mexico. Attention to their socio-cultural context affirms their identity and history and, ultimately, their humanity. As these people discover the beauty and dignity within their Mexican culture within a spiritual context, they come to see that the Church does not want to destroy their culture or Europeanize it, but to draw forth from it the deepest truths about the human experience. As their cultural identity becomes more connected to their personal identity and their spiritual journey, a social conversion enables them to redefine their relationship to their culture and celebrate it as they seek to live within mainstream American culture.

The Mexican past gives some important clues to the present spirituality of these immigrants, though much more study needs to be done with respect to the relationship of Christian spirituality to the Mesoamerican ancestral culture. As these immigrants are educated about their cultural history in a positive way, they come to value themselves more and appreciate the richness of their cultural heritage. Such affirmation also makes them more open to the Gospel message. In contrast to evangelization approaches at the time of the Spanish conquest in the early sixteenth century, which more often than not destroyed the indigenous culture rather than ennobled it, this approach to evangelization respects the culture of the people and works within it, while at the same time promotes a social transformation.[11]

Such retrieval of the ancestral cultural and religion is not a matter of developing a sentimental, romantic notion of the religious

past and then idolizing it. Neither is it a matter of blending of the
ancestral religious symbols and blindly grafting them with the
symbols of Christianity. This approach leads not toward a syn-
cretism of the pagan past with the Christian present but a deeper
and richer synthesis of the action of God throughout the totality of
their history. Evangelization in this case begins with immersion
into the culture and a profound respect for it. Many immigrants
said that they could appropriate the liberating truths of the Gospel
precisely because the message correlated with the experience of
their lives and attentiveness to their collective histories and present
struggles.

Here we find the seeds of social conversion. "During the meal
(with the Mexican theme)," said Janina, "I began to think about my
roots and my culture. This helped me be open to the message (that
was being communicated) . . . I realized that although we grew up
very poor, economically speaking, we had a tremendous wealth in
our togetherness as a family and our history as Mexicans."[12] As
these immigrants felt understood and appreciated, they began to
see God's activity not only within the history of Christianity within
Mexico but also within the indigenous religions that preceded it.
This is a sharp departure as well from the mainline U.S. understanding of conversion (Protestant and Catholic), which often sees
the conversion process as a turning away from native cultural and
religious ethos and adopting a totally different religion.

The Second Vatican Council in *Nostra Aetate* supports such a
process,

> The Catholic Church rejects nothing that is true and holy in these re-
> ligions. She regards with sincere reverence those ways of conduct
> and of life, those precepts and teachings which, though differing in
> many aspects from the ones she holds and sets forth, nonetheless of-
> ten reflect a ray of that Truth which enlightens all. . . .[13]

Because inculturation is important in the process of spiritual
transformation, conversion to Christ must not be equated with conversion to North American culture.

This rich yet complex revelatory structure of the Valley Missionary Program is also embedded in the central architecture of the retreat center. The shrine synthesizes and integrates various levels of
the revelation of God throughout their history and culture. The

Mesoamerican Pyramid, on top of which is a statue of Guadalupe, and above which rises a cross, symbolizes this rich revelatory character of the program. It also allows immigrants to approach the sacred with the confidence that God understands where they have come from and what they struggle with on a daily basis.

The Aztec-Pyramid, Guadalupe figures and cross function symbolically in such a way as to structure a cultural-spiritual revelation of God's presence in history and today. These symbols reveal a profound exchange between the past and the present, between the Aztec and the Christian and between the individual and the community. These symbols also give expression to the way the Gospel works within culture and transcends it at the same time. Together, these symbols are interdependent and mutually enriching. Each builds upon the previous one without destroying the other. They interact with each other in a symbolic unity and create the context through which the divine is experienced, communicated, and received by the immigrants. Such a structure leads these Mexican immigrants to feel at home, even if they only remotely recognize the connections to the ancestral culture. This *mestizo* shrine also allows many immigrants to flourish in a new, harmonious, spiritual identity and affirm that, as Anita did, "this is where peace walks."[14]

Not only do the candidates gradually discover the power of God's revelation in their collective histories, but they also discover God's presence to them in their own personal histories. By reflecting on their own lives, they begin to see how God is intimately a part of their own personal history and human development. Without these moments, many said they would wander more aimlessly in life, and, without roots, they would be living without any purpose, goal or sense of contribution to the world.

This rootedness leads to a sense of cultural acceptance and personal acceptance, and this personal acceptance leads them to a sense of God's acceptance of the totality of their lives. This affirmation of culture connects the immigrants with their roots and brings meaning to their personal histories. The entire retreat experience, in the context of a festive, very Mexican cultural-religious atmosphere, gives them not only a deep sense of a very positive self-worth but also a deep appreciation of their *mexicanidad*. This is an essential feature of the social conversion process.

From Indifference to Care

Because of the harsh economic conditions, long working hours, and the constant struggle to survive, many immigrant parents find little time for leisure, conversation, tenderness, and other humanizing activities. Although among Mexicans there is often a strong emphasis on family, sometimes there is equally an experience of harshness and alienation within the family itself.[15] Often family life is taken for granted and, in many cases, abused or neglected. Especially for many of these immigrants, perhaps no area of life needs more transformation than that of family life.

The effects of the Encounter retreat are most palpably felt in the home. Many immigrants mentioned that the retreat enabled them to express a greater care within their own family. Teresa, who works as a maid at a nearby resort hotel, said "[The Encounter] helped me change the way I treat my children. In place of nagging discipline and harsh words, I became more capable of speaking to them in a loving and caring way."[16] Some realized how they need to begin the long process of restructuring their ways of relating to their children or their spouses, and others spoke about learning to love and show affection for the first time. Through this process social conversion begins to emerge.

Many struggle with communication. Husbands and wives agree that they have trouble understanding each other, as do children and parents. While the weekend in no way solves all of the communication conflicts they experience, it does give many a new freedom to be more honest about their lives and more able to realize some of the fundamental needs for connectedness. As Sandra said, "In my family I get along better with my parents and there is more communication between us now. Before we were a bit divided, but after the Encounter, we grew closer to God and each other as a family."[17]

From Family of Blood to Family of the Spirit

The movement from indifference to care manifests itself concretely when these immigrants move beyond a sense of a family of blood and develop a sense of a family of spirit. Because some have felt totally alone, discarded by society, and marginalized from any sense of meaningful belonging, they often come alive socially when they sense someone cares about them and welcomes them. No matter whether they are single, married, divorced, gay or straight, whether their family still lives in Mexico or in the U.S., whether they have a solid family or a dysfunctional one, many people, through the retreat and the base communities, experience a new sense of family. They begin to experience a certain bondedness, companionship, and *amistad* (friendship) beyond anything they have experienced in other significant relationships in their lives, and such relationships begin to redefine the way they understand what it means to be "Church." "What most impressed me," said Timoteo, "was hearing the talk about the friendship love, that is, love that we encounter in community . . . it is what has most stayed with me and has made me understand what Church is really about."[18] Through this newly discovered sense of family, even when they still feel the absence of family relationships in Mexico, some become even more aware of a deep spiritual unity that goes beyond the limitations of geographical space. "Not even in our own families have we experienced such love," said Eduardo.[19]

Other immigrants talked about how the retreat helped them develop new attitudes toward their work and new relationships with their co-workers. Felipe said the retreat helped him redefine his relationship with his neighbor, which previously had been more competitive than cooperative. "If my neighbor planted flowers," he said. "I would plant better ones. No matter what he did, I would try to do better, whether it be with his house, his family, or his own personal life."[20] Now, he said, if his neighbor has no flowers, he gives him some. If he needs some assistance, he offers it. When he is in trouble, he helps him.

Some immigrants shared how the retreat helped them discover the meaning of friendship: "To live the Encounter [retreat] helped me tremendously," said Esteban, "I came to know many people who lent a helping hand and loved me even without knowing me . . . it made me think about many things. I think the more one has suffered the more this experience hits them."[21]

For these immigrants, one converts to a set of relationships, to a community, to a network of friends that helps shape and form their identity and meet their need for connectedness to others.[22] Social conversion in the case of these people begins on the inside and ripples outwards toward other relationships. As the program grows and develops, however, more attention needs to be given to how structural injustices contribute to their suffering and how more effort needs to be dedicated to changing these unjust structures.

Nonetheless, these immigrants discover through the retreat that social conversion means discovering a profound sense of belonging,
which is one of the deepest desires of the human heart.

INTELLECTUAL CONVERSION
THROUGH THE EXPERIENCE OF THE TRUTH

Some of the talks on the retreats deal specifically with gender in-
equalities, corruption, lying, and many other deep-rooted social
problems that permeate the culture. Many of the destructive elements within individuals and their cultural histories are identified
and challenged in light of the Gospel. The transformation process
here entails the conversion of oppressive cultural dynamics as a
means of deepening the humanizing potential of the culture. A new
moment in their lives begins to dawn when many of these immigrants move from being *machos* to *hombres verdaderos* (from studs to
authentic men), from *viejas* to *mujeres dignas* (from old maids to dignified women) and from functional illiteracy to internalized wisdom.

From *Machos* to *Hombres de Verdad*
(From Studs to Authentic Men)

According to some immigrants, the retreat transforms people's sexual self-understanding. One of the more dramatic changes in men
happens when they begin to be self-critical of their *machismo* attitudes and redefine what it means to be a real man (*un hombre ver-
dadero*). *Machismo* lies deep in the psyche of the Mexican male, and,
simply defined, it is an attitude of male superiority and masculine
primacy. It takes the notion that the male is the head of the household to an extreme and results in sexist attitudes and oppressive relationships between men and women. In general, machismo manifests itself in a domineering and controlling personality that gets
much of its strength from bossing women around. Not all men who
come to the retreat have such macho attitudes, but many do, which
creates problems in many relationships.[23]

    Machismo is particularly pronounced in the culture of economic
poverty. Other cultures share oppressive masculine traits, but

machismo tends to be more pronounced the lower one descends on the socioeconomic scale. Among the poor in Mexico, machismo is part of the masculine socialization process, and it is the model that many follow.[24] In the case of the Mexican immigrant, often the decision to immigrate is the man's prerogative, and not infrequently, the woman is merely informed, rather than consulted, about the decision and its implications for the family as a whole. When the men make their retreat, the team presents new models of masculinity that affect those with a machismo mentality. The team leaders often show themselves as being capable of listening, caring, loving, and serving.

Ramiro said,

> Before the Encounter I was one of those guys who only wanted to be the boss of the family. I wanted to give orders, I wanted to do everything and control my wife and tell her what she could do and could not do. This caused a lot of fights and we would get angry at each other, resulting in much bitterness between us. We were not happy . . . and we had times when we just wanted to separate. The Encounter helped me turn around my life and helped me ask for forgiveness. Even so, my macho side didn't suddenly disappear. Sometimes my macho character comes back into play and I revert to old patterns.[25]

A significant shift transpires in the way a man understands his masculinity. Some gradually discover that the true man is one with a human heart who can cry, feel, and listen. Some become more aware of how machismo attitudes have negatively affected their relationship with their family and eroded, if not destroyed, the bonds of trust and communication in the home.

Several factors on the retreat contribute to the breaking of the exterior shell of machismo: seeing capable men live out their maleness with confident humanness, being receptive to love expressed by other men, observing the service-oriented nature of the men on the team, and listening to the moving testimonies of the speakers, during which some of the men cry and openly express emotion. In the process of social conversion, some of the men said that the retreat helped them redefine their masculinity: "I feel like I am just beginning to learn what it means to really be a man," said Tomás, "and to know the difference between being macho and being a real human being."[26]

From *Viejas* to *Mujeres de Dignidad*
(From Old Maids to Dignified Women)

The women likewise discover valuable aspects of their femininity and come to understand more of what it means to be dignified women (*mujeres dignas*).[27] The term *vieja* is often a derogatory term that men use for their wives, which means, "old woman" or "old maid." Beneath such words, men often communicate messages that contribute to inferiority complexes that lead to low self-esteem. A woman living in a family dominated by patriarchy, either of her spouse or her father, is seldom appreciated for who she is as a human being. More often than not, she is valued more for her functional contributions to the house (cleaning, cooking, raising the children) than for her human, personal, and sexual identity. She is often respected for her role as mother, lover, wife, maid, and servant, but very often the woman herself does not realize that one of the most fundamental and essential aspects of her life has been buried: her femininity. As one woman said:

> Many times there are women who are very submissive and can't think for themselves but are dependent on everything their spouses tell them . . . they put up with all of this and keep things inside, and they experience a type of trauma or impotence in the face of what they can achieve in the world . . . the Encounter helps them rehabilitate themselves.[28]

For such women, one of the most liberating aspects of the retreat is discovering a set of relationships in which they can share the pains and hopes of their lives in a safe way. As noted previously, the retreats are segregated between men and women, and part of the reason for this, they say, is because many Mexican women tend to feel less comfortable being completely honest when men are present. They feel more comfortable expressing themselves freely when they are around other women. As the women share more of themselves on the retreat, they begin to realize they are not alone in their struggles. In the process, they begin to redefine how they identify themselves. Rather than with respect to who they are as wives, mothers, slaves, workers, servants, and cooks, they see themselves as women in their own right. As some begin to accept themselves for who they are, they become more capable of reaching out to others. "I am much calmer now . . . I feel more confident, more myself. I would like other women to feel what I feel, to feel the same joys I feel now but never had before the Encounter."[29] Not infrequently, this new identity that women discover can cause tensions in relationships with other men who feel threatened by such changes, but nonetheless the retreat often marks a new moment of freedom and empowerment for these women. Women begin to define themselves not as a man's property or a man's *vieja,* but as a dignified person and/or an equal partner to her husband.

The retreat helps these immigrants create new frameworks for understanding reality and new horizons of interpretation, particularly amidst their pain of personal, social, economic, and political exclusion. As the process of intellectual conversion leads to the restructuring of the way men and women immigrants think of themselves, they begin to see their lives no longer through the lens of the dominant culture, which often intensifies their sense of inferiority, shame, and alienation, but through the lens of the Gospel. Properly understood, this means they begin to see themselves not as society often views them, that is, as instruments of cheap labor, but as God sees them: dignified, valued, and loved human beings.

From Functional Illiteracy to Internalized Wisdom

About 4 percent of the men and 8 percent of the women of the program are illiterate. They often believe they are useless because they are poor, because they work at jobs nobody else wants, because they have brown skin in a white society, because they are living in the country illegally, and because of many other factors. Many of these immigrants stop their formal education at the third grade, which is when many of them started working in the fields in Mexico. Their illiteracy often compounds their feelings of inadequacy, and mainstream U.S. society often reinforces the message that they are inferior people with an inferior mind.

The retreat appeals to another kind of learning. They are asked to consider how the deepest truths are not simply those learned in books but those that are internalized in their lives, that is, those truths that are those appropriated by experience and integrated into their own hearts. One team member told the following story, which I quote at length because of its significance:

> My husband can't read or write, and he got called to give a talk on one of the retreats. I had to give the same talk on the women's retreat, so I rewrote my talk, revised it in light of his vocabulary, and taped it on a tape recorder. He would then listen to me as I read it to him, to help train his eyes how to read so he could follow the words. When he had to give the talk, he got up there, the people prayed over him, and he had all the confidence in the world. He used a ruler to follow the script we had prepared, and he would follow what was written line by line. At one point, he made the mistake of looking up, and he lost his place. He was terrified. He suddenly feared that these people were going to know that he did not know how to read. But he paused, took a drink of water, and then looked at everyone and said, 'you know, I want to tell all you all something . . . I'm illiterate and do not know how to read and write . . . it has taken me two retreats to get the courage to come up here and give this talk, but that is OK, because now the rest of my talk is going to come from my heart.[30]

Following this candid admission, this immigrant said that three or four people came up to him and said, "Your honesty helped me come forward and talk to you . . . the truth is I can't read or write either . . . but you helped me believe that if you can do it, so can I." The public confession of his illiteracy liberated the others to accept their own and yet still see their own potential to make meaningful contributions to the Church and the community.

In the process of intellectual conversion, these immigrants begin to realize that, in God's economy, the poor are called, the broken are healed, and the oppressed are empowered. They begin to reference their lives not by society's standards but by Christ's standards. They begin to note the fact that Jesus was a poor, humble immigrant laborer, yet in essence he was more dignified than the rich and powerful of this world.

This ongoing process of intellectual growth allows the Scriptures to interpret their lives while their very lives bring new meaning out of the Scriptures.[31] Scriptures become a new way of deepening their understanding of reality, and their reality becomes the context through which they read the Scriptures. Not only do they interpret the Scriptures, but they also allow the Scriptures to interpret their lives.[32] The Gospel provides a new way of understanding reality and a new way of understanding their own lives.

In summary, the process of intellectual conversion for these immigrants entails the reexamination of long-held ideas and attitudes that shape the way they understand themselves and their world and how these attitudes influence the way they respond to reality.[33] Some began to redefine themselves not as low-class migrant workers, but as dignified members of God's family. Still others said they started to see the world not simply as an evil forum where the devil reigns but as a world that is constantly being renewed and transformed by God's grace. This new prism of understanding enabled them to clarify their values and reorganize the priorities of their lives. For them, intellectual conversion responds to the heart's desire for the truth, the truth that frees and liberates.[34]

PERSONAL MORAL CONVERSION
THROUGH THE EXPERIENCE OF THE GOOD

In the mind of many immigrants who live on the margins of society in the United States, the hope for a better life always looms large on the horizon. The struggle to make ends meet and attain a more comfortable standard of living leads many immigrants to work day and night and direct their energies to work alone. Most immigrants view life as a matter of survival. They work to live and live to work, but seldom do they perceive a deeper purpose behind their lives, their struggles, and their daily toil. "Before the retreat," Roberto said, "life was very routine. I lived in order to survive . . . but this Encounter has helped me reconstruct my entire outlook on life."[35]

As noted in chapter 2, many immigrants find their lives in moral disarray when they come on the weekend. Patterns of infidelity, abuse, alcoholism, and drugs wreak havoc on many of their relationships, which often intensify their disorientation, confusion, and frustration. On the retreat, many are confronted with their relational problems stemming from their own destructive choices. Some expressed that the retreat enabled them to confront their lack of moral responsibility in various areas of their lives.

Because the retreat provides these immigrants with an opportunity to find a new center for their lives, they can develop new reference points from which they evaluate and reevaluate their world, their relationships, and their own lives. Reflecting on the impact of the weekend on his own growth and development, Julio noted, "The Encounter was, more than anything else, an encounter with myself."[36] Many immigrants expressed how they moved from powerlessness to empowerment, from self-centered lives to Christ-centered lives, and from being immigrants to being missionaries.

From Powerlessness to Empowerment

Deep within the Mexican immigrant psyche, partially because of the historical influence of the Spanish conquest, and partially because of the cultural of poverty, many live out of a deep sense of existential resignation. Before the retreat, their spirituality, according to them, is characterized by a certain theological fatalism, a passivity, an acceptance of the way things are. While there is virtue in their unquestioned faith in divine providence, more often than not they spoke about their prior faith as if it were a painkiller, or a giant Tylenol, which numbed their pain but also numbed the totality of their heart and kept them from discovering the depths and potentialities of their lives. Such a faith, according to them, often led them to believe that they are not agents of their own destiny, yet alone active agents in the building of God's kingdom on earth.

As a result of the retreat, many immigrants spoke about moving from a place of powerlessness to a place of empowerment. Part of the way this shift happens in Coachella is simply through people discovering their own inherent gifts. For a lot of people these talents lay dormant and were untapped. Some discovered that the process of evangelization, which intensifies their spirituality, is the process of bringing these talents to birth and orienting them toward the common good, for building up the body of Christ.

Personal, moral conversion begins to dawn for them when they start to realize they have something to say, something to offer, and something to contribute.

Often those immigrants who are illiterate have the most difficulty believing that they have something important to give. True empowerment happens as they discover that they too have a role to play in the life of the Church, and their own talents are necessary for the good of the community. The retreat, therefore, initiates a process whereby they change from a passive, resigned faith in God's providence to a dynamic, empowered faith in God's providence that enables them to become co-creators with God, powerful instruments of grace, and dignified human beings. "It is an incredibly beautiful thing," said María, "to think that God is using me in all my ignorance."[37]

From Self-Centered to Christ-Centered

The retreat also enabled some immigrants to become less focused on work, money, and material goods and more focused on relationships, especially their relationship with God. Some expressed a desire for greater honesty, fidelity, and integrity in their relationships and to leave behind destructive patterns that have damaged the most important relationships in their lives. Many expressed how a new relationship with Jesus Christ has grounded and centered their lives and begun to mold and shape them into new patterns of behavior. Prior to the retreat, many said that God was not the center of their lives and had very little influence on their daily decisions. After the retreat, many begin to restructure their understanding of what is truly important, according to the norms of the Gospel and a life of faith in Christ.

As their spirituality grows, many immigrants express a greater desire to take on the mind and heart of Christ and follow him as a disciple. Many indicated that they were not interested in simply fulfilling the canons of religious minimalism (such as religious obligations like attending Sunday Mass) but a desire to respond to the even greater, concrete demands of Christian discipleship, such as forgiveness, love of enemies, and the care of the poor.

For these immigrants, two of the most important characteristics of Christian discipleship are humility and generosity. Even within the Valley Missionary Program itself, there is a definite hierarchy, status, and position that a few leaders enjoy. Whether they are retreat directors, base community facilitators, music coordinators, or the presidents of the program, their positions of leadership and authority shape the organizational structure of the community. Yet within this community there are some internal controls as to how this leadership is exercised. Though these immigrants are as vulnerable as any to the human tendency

toward pride and authoritarianism, the community has a certain
sensus fidelium, which influences how these positions are lived
out. The members speak about Christian community as a community of equals rather than a society of social stratification.

The basis of this community of equals has its reference point not
in a pragmatic, administrative common sense (though it is this) but
in its reference to Christ, who himself is humble. Because of their
common spiritual experience on retreat, the community constantly
evaluates relationships and behavior with respect to the life of
Christ, and they categorically reject signs of pomposity and arrogance. Attitudes of superiority or inflated hierarchy are met with
disdain, suspicion, and rejection. Distinctions between rich and
poor, smart and illiterate, powerful or weak are firmly rejected as
contrary to the mind and heart of Christ. The presidents of the program, past and current, believe that leadership expresses itself by
getting down on their hands and knees and washing the feet of
others. Julio said, "when they washed my feet I felt that they were
doing all this because they loved me and wanted me to change and
leave my pride behind."[38]

For a people accustomed to responding to a series of *jefes*
(bosses) and to seeing themselves and others in terms of where
they stood in the social ladder of power and domination, this is
truly a liberating experience of a new social creation. In the words
of Pepe, "The washing of the feet was really a sacred thing for me
. . . I began to feel that through this person of Christ I became one
with the other people on the retreat."[39] Many came to realize that
the grounding of their deepest identity is not social status, family
background, or economic prosperity but rather in who they are before God and how they respond to the revelation of God in their
daily lives.

For these immigrants, humility, in all its gentleness, has incredible power. Candidates find humility such a compelling virtue because it is the team leaders who practice it. This is the real power
of the team leaders. Many of these immigrants already work in
some of the most menial, service-oriented jobs in society. To preach
humility to them often means baptizing their oppression and deepening it through a distortion of this Christian virtue. Many powerful people have already preached humility to them, only to subsequently abuse, manipulate, and exploit them. These immigrants

have discovered that humility can be genuine only if one already holds some degree of power and authority in a situation. They realize that preaching humility to the powerless is enslaving, while preaching humility to the empowered is liberating. When they see the team members as leaders serve them meals, wash their feet, and attend to their needs, they often restructure their understanding of legitimate power. Such personal, moral conversions affect the way they subsequently treat their spouses, their children, and their co-workers.

By and large, the Christian tradition has tended to see the process of conversion as moving from the sin of pride to the grace of humble submission. John the Baptist puts it this way: "Repent, and believe in the good news." Often this is interpreted as meaning, "Put aside your sinful pride and submit yourself to the will of the Father." At Coachella we see the process of conversion is the exact opposite. For those who have been so beaten down and dehumanized, the conversion process is not simply a movement from humble submission and arrogance but to a rightful pride and a sense of dignity that assures them that they too are children of God with a divine mission to accomplish. They repent not so much from arrogance, pride, and egotism as from the negative self-judgments and messages about their own humanity and self-worth. For them, John the Baptist might need to say "Respect yourself as God respects you: this is the good news!" As Virgilio Elizondo notes,

> Conversion is the great equalizer, for it calls everyone to the life and freedom of the children of God. Some will come down while others will be lifted up; some will discover doubts while others will arrive at new assurance; some will come to recognize their sinfulness while others will recognize their saintliness. Conversion brings about a blossoming of everything that is authentically human—the image and likeness of God.[40]

Many immigrants in the valley begin to define humility not as self-debasement but as self-acceptance. Humility means being no more—nor less—than they truly are. True humility is empowering in that it enables these immigrants to deal with other people not primarily according to their social or economic status but their human worth. They gradually begin to see themselves not as being less than other people of higher social and economic status, but as equally valued human beings before God in God's kingdom.

From Immigrants to Missionaries

The life of an immigrant can often be the life of a wanderer. Many are accustomed to moving from place to place, from town to town, and from Mexico to the United States. Such wandering can also take place with respect to the larger purpose of their lives. The retreat is often an occasion for these immigrants to realize that they have a larger calling in life than mere survival. Some immigrants expressed how the retreat helped them begin to move from a life of aimless wandering to a life of definitive goals and aspirations: As Alejandro said, "For me, the Encounter was about a personal transformation. . . . I was very confused, misdirected, and had no idea of where I was going . . . but through the retreat I discovered there is more to my life than surviving and that I have a very real mission in life."[41] Practically speaking, salvation for immigrants like Alejandro meant living life with conscious intentionality, habitual self-reflection, and decisive commitment.

When these immigrants begin to realize that they are not simply passive recipients of the grace of the Church but are active instruments in the coming of God's kingdom, they no longer see themselves as immigrants but as missionaries. Upward mobility means less in terms of material success and more in terms of a Christian calling. For them, to be missionary means bringing Christ's presence to their families, their friends, and their co-workers. In part, they express that they want to offer other people the same opportunity to live the Missionary Encounter retreat so that they too might know the joy of this liberating, transforming relationship with God in the Spirit.

Because they believe they have found something through the retreat that is greater than anything else they have experienced, they commit themselves to this mission by sacrificing their time, energy, and resources for the program. The discovery of such a treasure helps them realize that any life worth living is worth sacrificing for, even dying for. In their stories, this missionary desire expresses itself in heroic generosity. They say that they sacrifice precious time, sleep, and substantial portions of their income to be a part of something that has moral and spiritual value to them. Many tithe 10 percent of their income to the program. Even though most make only between $4,500 and $15,000, as missionaries, they sacrifice as much as $500 each to be able to give these retreats in Mexico and other places. They believe their sacrifices are important because they know they are instrumental in the transformation of other people's lives.

To be certain, some people who make the retreat show no signs of moral conversion. Others show it for a time but quickly relapse into the same destructive patterns that governed their lives before the retreat. But in many cases, moral conversion does emerge, and even amid periodic failures and struggles, they exhibit a restructuring of the moral fabric of their lives. Such conversion, they say, flows from the wells of the experience of divine acceptance and a deep desire to respond to that love. To them, moral conversion is not about adopting a rigid code of conduct based on arbitrary rules and regulations but a gradual conforming of their lives to the mind and heart of Christ. Moral conversion is not about a litany of rules and regulations that are preconditions to divine acceptance, any more than a person is about his or her skeleton. Rather, moral integrity emerges as they try to respond to the love they have received through their encounter with Christ. Because of the connection that these immigrants make between their actions and their relationship with God, morality taken out of the context of relationship of love with Jesus Christ totally loses its meaning and purpose.[42] Moral conversion is intrinsically related to spirituality because it speaks to being faithful to the basic structures and properties of the human heart.

RELIGIOUS CONVERSION THROUGH
THE EXPERIENCE OF FRIENDSHIP WITH GOD

Before coming on the retreat, many immigrants already have personal yet rudimentary notions of their faith. Most identify themselves as Catholic and Christian, at least in name, and they come with a basic notion of God. But many of these same people have had little formal evangelization, catechism, or spiritual formation. Frequently they see God as an emotionally distant, punishing Father and vigilant policeman. Though they acknowledge

God as all-powerful and all-knowing, they often feel this God is so far removed from their daily lives that they do not really believe such a God would dare to care about them. Few recognize any connection between a life of faith and their human development.

These immigrants often become accustomed to expressing their religious beliefs in mechanical, routine ways. Some do this through promises, masses, penances, and pilgrimages (*promesas, mandas y peregrinaciones*). While these practices have value in their own right, they sometimes consider these more as religious fire insurance policies than celebrations of a deep, loving, authentic, and transformative relationship with God.

Religious conversion is the most central transformative dimension that flows from the retreat. The retreat opens for the immigrant new possibilities in life that flow from new perceptions of God, which, in turn, redefines how they understand themselves and their relationship to the world. They describe how the love of God is mediated through their encounter with a community that concretely has communicated to them that they are valued, welcomed, and accepted. We see signs of religious conversion in the movement from a distant, impersonal God to a close, personal friend, from sacramental obligation to sacramental celebration and from being *desgraciado* (disgraced) to '*graciado*' (graced).

From a Distant, Impersonal God to a Close Personal Friend

Religious conversion for these immigrants is often an awakening to a friendship with God, who they call *Jesus Amigo*. They begin to realize that Christ knows them as friend, accompanies them as a true *compañero* (companion) and invites them to discover a new freedom in life. For them, transformation happens as they make a profound act of trust in God's offer of friendship in Jesus Christ. Religious conversion becomes the intensification of faith in Christ and the transformation of their lives through the restructuring of their core beliefs, values and priorities.

Many talked about an ability to understand their relationship with God in a radically new way. In the place of a punishing Father bent on retribution for their sins, they say they discover God as a loving and caring Father who accompanies them in a personal way.

Prisoners in their own land. At the border wall between Tijuana and San Diego, many immigrants look through the tantalizing bars of freedom. Finding themselves imprisoned in socio-economic misery, most simply come in the hopes of finding *una vida mas digna*, a more dignified life.

The U.S. Border Patrol guards the door into the United States. Here agents guard the border between Mexicali, Mexico, and Calexico, California.

Photo: Elsa Medina Castro

Since 1995, U.S. Border Control policies have pushed immigrants into dangerous, life-threatening territory in order to find a way into the United States.

Immigrants often have to contact coyote-smugglers to help them navigate the long, arduous trek through the perils of the desert and the rugged terrain of the mountains.

A new Normandy. After losing a battle to the natural elements, hundreds of undocumented immigrants are buried in this cemetery in Holtville, California. Many of the people who die along the U.S.-Mexican border remain unpublicized, unrecognized, unidentified, unburied, and unmourned.

A Way of the Cross. Along the triple fence in Tijuana, a painful reminder: Since 1995, an immigrant a day has died trying to cross the border.

Tomb of the Unknown Immigrants. This cross marks the edge of Mount Hope Cemetery near San Diego. Across the street, next to the train tracks, below a highway, are buried some unknown immigrants who died in their attempts to reach the United States. In the public eye, these Mexican immigrants who die often seemed like nothing in life, and, in the end, they appear as nothing in death, without even a simple cross to mark their graves.

The Valley Missionary, which is explicitly Catholic and Christian in approach, builds on the indigenous culture of ancient Mexico. This pyramid shrine, which resembles that of Teotihuacan near Mexico City, was built entirely by the donations and labor of immigrant Mexicans.

Guadalupe is central to the spirituality of these Mexican immigrants. In the story of Juan Diego and his encounter with Our Lady of Guadalupe, these immigrants see their own story of oppression, liberation, and empowerment.

The physical setting of the shrine shapes the spirituality of the people, and the immigrant's spirituality shapes the architecture of the Program. Throughout the Shrine, various elements of native and contemporary Mexican culture intermingle with classical symbols of Christianity, giving rise to a truly inculturated spirituality.

In contrast to the discrimination that many experience in daily life, the retreat is a profound moment of welcome and hospitality. Through rituals of welcome at the beginning of each meal, immigrants begin to experience God's universal welcome to all, especially to the marginalized, rejected, and poor of society.

At each meal, immigrant-candidates are given gifts from friends, family members, and the base communities. The unmerited nature of grace begins to become real to them when they experience that others love them.

The team spends eight weeks preparing for the retreat. Not only do they take time off work to participate in the retreat, but also team members pay $75 to work on the retreat.

Part of the retreat's power comes from its ability to incarnate the principles of the Gospel into the culture of the Mexican people.

The foot washing ritual marks an important moment of healing and purification. This ritual deepens their appreciation of God's acceptance of them and gives them a framework for understanding how Jesus lives and acts in the world.

The purpose of the retreat is to form Base Christian communities. After the weekend, communities like these meet on a weekly basis. Some have been meeting for twenty-five years or longer.

The fruit of the spirituality of these immigrants the joy of a people.

More than simply rescuing them in times of danger, they begin to understand their relationship with God more in terms of a provident Father who is always with them. As Lupe said, "God is not so distant anymore. I feel that He is near and that we don't live so far from each other. Now our relationship is much stronger. For me, God is Father, friend, and companion."[43]

In the course of the four days of the retreat, the candidates gradually begin to experience God as an intimate conversation partner. Whereas previously prayer meant repeating a structured series of words by memory, like the Our Father and Hail Mary, the retreat enables them to discover prayer as a way of developing an everyday relationship with God as friend. "When the guy from our table got up to pray," said Jose, "his prayer seemed so personal and sincere, like he didn't seem to care what anybody thought of it. It came straight from the heart and it was so genuine."[44] Many say they begin to see prayer as a way of speaking to a caring friend, which enables them to worry less about ultimate control over their lives and trust more God's ability to act within their historical experience.

God becomes personal to them especially in their encounter with Christ before the Blessed Sacrament. "Upon entering the room where the Blessed Sacrament was," said Miguel, "I had this really strong emotional reaction . . . like someone was telling me, 'Come, here. I am that friend whom you are looking for.' That moment really hit me, that moment that I came to know Jesus as a friend, and I will never forget it."[45] Even some who previously had no experience before the Blessed Sacrament said this time was the most important moment of the retreat.

Statements like these indicate an important shift in their religious consciousness. During the visit to the Blessed Sacrament, they experience a powerful release of diverse emotions including pain, sorrow, need, and spiritual desire. Some do not even know how to put words to their experience. Often they referred to a feeling, a sensation, or an awareness that Christ was coming to them at this moment and addressing them as a friend. "At the moment when we visited the Blessed Sacrament," said Antonio, "something entered my heart, not just my mind but something on the inside."[46] Such encounters show the shift in the way these immigrants related to the sacred.

From Sacramental Obligation to Sacramental Celebration

Many immigrants who make the retreat either do not attend Church at all or they go infrequently, at Christmas, Ash Wednesday, and *Semana Santa* (Holy Week). Those who do attend Catholic Masses regularly refer to their faith practices as routine and even boring, saying they do not experience such worship as meaningful or stimulating. Many find that the preaching fails to correlate with their daily lives or touch the deeper aspirations of their hearts.

Other factors kept them from getting more out of their Church experience: large, impersonal, English-only liturgies, the lack of Latino clergy, and the feeling of being aliens even within their own Catholic Church. Not surprisingly, defections of Hispanics from the Catholic Church are at an all-time high.[47] Some studies indicate that since the 1970s one of every five Hispanics who was raised Catholic has left the Church.[48]

In contrast, the retreat enabled many immigrants to experience a movement from sacramental obligation to sacramental celebration.[49] It enables them to discover something new within their ritual, religious practices. Through their new relationship with God, they come to a new appreciation of the sacraments like Baptism, Eucharist, and Reconciliation. Their understanding of these sacramental celebrations changes from ritual, magical moments to real encounters with the risen Lord. They begin to see Baptism as a real welcoming into God's own family, the Eucharist as participation in the Lord's own table of fellowship, and Reconciliation as a real encounter with God's unlimited and rehabilitating mercy. They experience these moments as celebrations not simply because of good music and movement, but because there is the inner joy of being welcomed, nourished, and healed. They discover in them the treasure of an important person who has invited them to the table, cancelled all their debts, and sent them off to begin a new life.

In addition to seeing something new in the sacraments of the Church, they begin to see life itself in a more sacramental way. They begin to see God at work in helping a friend fix a pickup truck, doing the dishes in the evening or changing the diapers of a crying baby. Rather than limiting God to formal moments of religious gatherings, they begin to see more of God's presence in the totality of their lives. In essence, the retreat enables them to come to a more profound catechism of the liturgy, a deeper understanding of the meaning of a purpose of the religious rituals of the Church, and a greater sense of God's activity in their daily lives.

From *Desgraciado* to *Graciado* (From Disgraced to Graced)

Religious conversion also begins to express itself through a movement from being a *desgraciado* (disgraced) to being *graciado* (graced). In Spanish, the word "desgraciado" is one of the most offensive words one can say about another person. It refers to a person who, because of their destructive choices, is a social reject, an outcast, a person cut off from the community—literally, a person without grace. Many of the people who come to the retreat feel that they have been *muy desgraciados*, not only because of their painful histories and social marginalization but also because of the growing awareness of their own sinful actions. Many feel their social exclusion and negative social stereotypes imposed on them only confirm that they are excluded from society and from God's grace. As Elsa said, "as Mexican immigrants, with little money in this country, we often feel like we are unwanted, unwelcome, and unloved. Sometimes we get the feeling that not even God loves us."[50]

The message of the retreat directly corresponds to the human sufferings of these immigrants, and the retreat becomes a place where God, literally, graces his people, where He changes them from being *desgraciado* to *graciado*. It is not the conviction of sin that leads them to repentance. Rather, it is the experience of the beauty and goodness of God and the community that enlightens the extent of their own inner darkness and need for healing. Repentance happens not because of the awareness of sin but because of the compelling experience of love. At the core of the experience of grace is the experience of love, and they say that it is this love that renews and regenerates them. They begin to understand grace as that process through which God puts love back into the world.

Through the process of religious conversion God becomes more personal, more palpably real, and more manifest in their lives, which enables many of the immigrants to want to live a better life and connect to other people on a more substantial and spiritual level. These immigrants expressed how they changed as a result of the discovery of a profound and intimate friendship with God, which enlarged their self-understanding and created friendships of mutuality, depth, and integrity. In essence, their relationship with

God is more personal, real, and intimate. Though many claimed to have prayed to God in moments of danger, now they relate to a God who reigns over the totality of their lives.

FROM DEATH TO LIFE:
THE PASCHAL MYSTERY IN COACHELLA

Though the retreat marks the beginning of a conversion process, it is clear that this conversion process continues long after the spiritual high of the weekend fades into the background. The retreat is a first step and a foundational step toward a greater transformation, but it is not the final step toward the re-creation of their lives. The base communities are meant to be the place where the ongoing transformation of their lives takes place, and for many it becomes one of the major contexts through which they continue to live out their lives of faith.

While the journey of immigration is a way of the cross, and the retreat an experience of resurrection, the spiritual transformation of these people becomes an ongoing Pentecost experience. As they experience the Spirit of God in the depths of their hearts, they become empowered to invite others into that same Spirit and become something new in the process. In the midst of their poverty, they discover the riches of friendship. In place of exploitation, they find dignity and self-worth. In place of utter disregard, they find care and compassion. In place of individualism, they find family and solidarity. And in the face of the fear of abandonment, they discover God's commitment to them and the experience of God's mercy. The experience of the Encounter brings about a great horizon shift, from a closed heart to an open heart, from a false self to a new self, from making oneself the center of one's world to making Christ and others the center of one's life.

More than just going from darkness to light, sin to grace, godlessness to godliness, irresponsibility to responsibility, these immigrants are undergoing a conversion that, in many ways, is far more basic and fundamental: Conversion means becoming a human being. It means moving from being an alien to belonging to a caring community, from being ridiculed and rejected to being valued and esteemed, but most of all, from an oppressed existence to a liberated one where they discover the graced dimensions of their humanity. In essence, the conversion process for these Mexican immigrants is about their participation in the paschal mystery, that is to say, a movement from death to life. Conversion is nothing less than a passage from a death-like, dehumanized existence in a foreign land to a new life of meaning, freedom, dignity, and belonging. For them, conversion is the process of becoming a new creation.

NOTES

1. *Cuando primero cruce la frontera, no tuve ni un problema. Brinque sobre la cerca y corrí, y el oficial no me vio. Mi hermano estaba conmigo, pero el no tuvo mucha suerte; a él lo agarraron en cuanto se brincó. Pues yo me quedé solo. No sabía que hacer, entonces pensé en hablarle a mi familia y decirles lo que estaba pasando. Yo no tenía dinero y pedí a la gente en las calles por un poco de cambio. Y esto es lo peor. A cada persona que le pedía por dinero, se volteaba, me rechazaban, me llamaban malos nombres y hasta me amenazaban con llamar a la migra, cuando yo solo quería comunicarme con mi familia! Yo sé lo que es vivir sin comer por tres días. Sé lo que es esconderse en el compartimiento de equipaje de un autobús. Y también sé lo que es pasar temperaturas heladas de las montanas. Pero el peor tipo de sufrimiento es experimentar rechazos, cuando la gente me trataba como basura, como si fuera un perro. Esto me hacia sentir totalmente humillado, como si no valía nada. Me sentía tan bajo como ningún ser humano puede sentirse en la tierra . . . y me sentía así muchas veces desde que vivo aquí en los Estados Unidos . . . Pero cuando vine a este retiro, toda mi perspectiva sobre la vida cambió. Nunca me habían tratado tan bien en mi vida o en ningún otro lugar. ¡Me sentía como un rey! Comencé a darme cuenta de algo que nunca antes sabía; que si valía algo, que soy valioso, que tengo un propósito en la vida, que realmente soy alguien para Dios, que en verdad si me importa a otra gente, que no estoy solo y que tengo una misión en la vida.* Mexican immigrant, interview by author, 21 January 2000, tape recording, Coachella, Calif.

2. In the past forty years, much fruitful reflection has been done in the area of Liberation theology. Some of the theologians who have done seminal and groundbreaking work in this area are Gustavo Gutiérrez, Jon Sobrino, Leonardo Boff, and others. They have pointed both a new method for doing theology and a new focus for the people for whom one does theology. Liberation theology has to do with liberation of the poor. The second Vatican Council and *Evangelii Nuntiandi* point to the fact that salvation has to do with the full development of the whole human person, culturally, socially, economically, educationally, politically, and spiritually. As should be abundantly clear from the previous chapters, social injustices shape, influence and cause many of the sufferings that are imposed upon the Mexican immigrant.

3. I am grateful to Simon Hendry, sj, for this insightful definition on spirituality.

4. See Bernard J. F. Lonergan, *Method in Theology* (Minneapolis: Winston/Seabury, 1972) and Donald L. Gelpi, *Committed Worship: A Sacramental Theology for Converting Christians.* Vol. 1 and 2 (Collegeville, Minn.: Liturgical Press, 1993).

5. *Simplemente, fue lo más bonita que he vivido.* Male candidate, interview by author, 16 November 1999, tape recording, Coachella, Calif.

6. *Antes del Encuentro pensé que no valgo nada, y a veces me cohibía de los demás. En el Encuentro, realicé que Dios estaba cerca en mi corazón y me eso dio confianza en mi mismo y me capacitó para ayudar a los demás.* Female team member, interview by author, 2 December 1999, tape recording, Coachella, Calif.

7. *A veces uno se olvida mandar dinero a la familia en México, y de repente se da cuenta de lo que esta haciendo y quien esta olvidando.* Male team member, interview by author, 24 April 2000, tape recording, Indio, Calif.

8. Quoted in English. Male team member, interview by author, 24 April 2000, tape recording, Indio, Calif.

9. *Después de ésta confesión, salí un nuevo hombre . . . ése corazón duro ya no estaba tan duro. Sentí el perdón de Dios y el amor de Dios en una manera concreta. Para mí fue una alegría después de eso y me dio poder para amar a los demás.* Male team member, interview by author, 2 December 1999, tape recording, Coachella, Calif.

10. *Soy más sensible a la belleza que me rodea, pero me afectan más los sufrimientos de los demás y el daño que hacemos a nuestro mundo.* Male candidate, interview by author, 16 November 1999, tape recording, Coachella, Calif.

11. For other heroic examples of pro-indigenous evangelization in the early years of evangelization of Mesoamerica, see Helen Rand Parish and Francis Sullivan, *Bartolome De Las Casas: The Only Way* (1992). See also Ricard, Robert. *The Spiritual Conquest of Mexico: An Essay on the Apostolate and Evangelizing Methods of the Mendicant Orders in New Spain, 1523–1572,* trans. Lesley Byrd Samspon (Berkeley: University of California Press, 1966).

12. *Durante la comida Mexicana empecé a recordar mis raíces y mi cultura. También me ayudó a recibir los mensajes . . . para mí, me ayudó recibir el mensaje. Me di cuenta que aunque éramos muy pobres monetariamente, teníamos una riqueza grande en cuanto a la unidad de nuestra familia y nuestra historia como Mexicanos.* Female team member, interview by author, 19 November 1999, tape recording, Coachella, Calif.

13. See http://www.vatican.va/archive/hist_councils/ii_vatican_council/documents/vat-ii_decl_19651028_nostra-aetate_en.html.

14. *Aquí anda la paz.* Female pilgrim, interview by author, 28 December 1995, untaped conversation, Coachella, Calif.

15. For a good description of the pluses and negatives of the Latino family, consult: Lionel Sosa, *The Americano Dream: How Latinos Can Achieve Success in Business and in Life.* (New York: Dutton, 1998).

16. *A mí me ayudó a cambiar la manera que críe a mis hijos. En lugar de regaños duros y palabras malas, empecé de hablarles con mas amor y cariño.* Female team member, interview by author, 12 November 1999, tape recording, Coachella, Calif.

17. *En mi familia tengo más relación con mis padres y más comunicación con ellos. Antes estaba un poquito divididos, pero después del Encuentro, estamos más cerca de Dios y más cerca como familia.* Female team member, interview by author, 13 November 1999, tape recording, Coachella, Calif.

18. *A mí lo que más me impresionó fue escuchar la plática sobre el amor de amistad, o sea, el amor que encontramos en la comunidad. Es lo que más me ha quedado y me ha ayudado entender lo que significa 'iglesia.'* Male team member, interview by author, 2 December 1999, tape recording, Coachella, Calif.

19. *Ni en nuestras propias familias hemos recibido tanto amor.* Male team member, interview by author, 2 December 1999, tape recording, Coachella, Calif.

20. *Si mi vecino plantó flores, yo plantaría mejores. No importa lo que hizo, trataría ga-narle, en respecto a su casa, su familia o su vida personal.* Male team member, interview by author, 2 December 1999, tape recording, Coachella, Calif.

21. *El vivir el Encuentro me ayudó bastante . . . conocí a mucha gente que me dió la mano y que me querían sin conocerme . . . me hizo pensar en muchas cosas. Pienso que lo más que uno sufre, lo más que le pega.* Female team member, interview by author, 19 November 1999, tape recording, Coachella, Calif.

22. From this perspective, it is quite the opposite of mainline, American culture: The group defines the individual, not the other way around.

23. For more on the common myths and misconceptions about machismo, see Alfredo Mirandé, *Hombre Y Machos: Masculinity and Latino Culture* (Boulder, Colo.: Westview Press, 1998).

24. For more on machismo, see David D. Gilmore, *Manhood in the Making: Cultural Concepts of Masculinity* (New Haven, Conn.: Yale University Press, 1990); Matthew C. Gutmann, *The Meanings of Macho: Being a Man in Mexico City.* (Berkeley: University of California Press, 1996).

25. *Antes del Encuentro era una persona que quería ser yo solo el jefe de la familia. Quería mandar, quería hacer todo y controlar a mi esposa y decirle lo que tenia que hacer y no hacer. Ésto causó muchas discusiones y nos enojábamos mucho y resultó en mucho rencor entre nosotros. No vivíamos a gusto . . . y había tiempos cuando nos íbamos a separar. El Encuentro facilitó un arrepentimiento de mi parte y me ayudó a pedir perdón. Pero (el machismo) no terminó de repente. A veces mi machismo no me deja y vuelvo a hacer lo mismo.* Male team member, interview by author, 18 November 1999, tape recording, Coachella, Calif.

26. *Me siento que estoy aprendiendo como ser un hombre de verdad y de saber la diferencia entre ser macho y ser hombre de verdad.* Male candidate, interview by author, 20 November 1999, tape recording, Coachella, Calif.

27. For more studies on Latino women, see the works of Pilar Aquino and Ida Maria Isasi-Diaz. In particular, see Ada María Isasi-Díaz and Yolanda Tarango, *Hispanic Women: Prophetic Voice in the Church* (San Francisco: Harper & Row, 1988) and M.P. Aquino, *Nuestro Clamor Por La Vida* (San Jose: DEI, 1992).

28. *Muchas veces hay mujeres que son muy sumisas y [piensan] que no son nada más que lo que dice el esposo . . . ellas aguantan todo eso, guardan las cosas por adentro, y experimentan un tipo de trauma o una impotencia sobre lo que se puede lograr en el mundo . . . el Encuentro les ayuda a recapacitarse. . . .* Female team member, interview by author, 19 November 1999, tape recording, Coachella, Calif.

29. *Tengo más calma. . . . Me siento más capacitada, más mi mismo. Quisiera que otras mujeres se sientan como sentí yo, que sientan las mismas alegrías que no había sentido antes del Encuentro.* Female team member, interview by author, 19 November 1999, tape recording, Coachella, Calif.

30. Communicated in English. Female team member, interview by author, 17 April 2000, tape recording, Coachella, Calif.

31. See Margaret Hebblethwaite, *Base Communities: An Introduction* (Mahwah, N.J.: Paulist, 1994) and Casiano Floristán, *La Comunidad Cristiana De Base* (San Antonio: Mexican American Cultural Center, 1976).

32. See Sandra Marie Schneiders, *The Revelatory Text: Interpreting the New Testament as Sacred Scripture*, 1st ed. (San Francisco: Harper & Row, 1991).

33. Donald Gelpi notes that intellectual conversion has to do with greater commitment to what is true and real. See Gelpi, *Committed Worship*, vol. 1, 17.

34. Gelpi defines intellectual conversion as "the decision to turn from an irresponsible and supine acquiescence in accepted beliefs to a commitment to validating one's personal beliefs within adequate frames of reference and in ongoing dialogue with other truth seekers." Gelpi, *Committed Worship*, vol. 1, 17.

35. *Antes del Encuentro, mi vida era rutinaria, vivía más por vivir . . . pero ese Encuentro me ha ayudado a reconstruir mi perspectiva de vida.* Male team member, interview by author, tape recording, 2 December 1999, Coachella, Calif.

36. *El Encuentro fue más que nada un encuentro conmigo mismo.* Male team member, interview by author, 2 December 1999, tape recording, Coachella, Calif.

37. *Es algo bien bonito, que Dios, con mi ignorancia, me está usando.* Female team member, interview by author, 18 November 1999, tape recording, Coachella, Calif.

38. *Cuando lavaron los pies me sentí como si estaban haciendo todo esto para que dejara atrás mi orgullo y cambiara mi vida.* Male team member, interview by author, 12 November 1999, tape recording, Coachella, Calif.

39. *El lavar de los pies pués es una cosa sagrada para mi . . . empecé de sentir que en Cristo somos unidos, unos a los otros."* Male team member, interview by author, 13 November 1999, tape recording, Coachella, Calif.

40. Virgil Elizondo, *Guadalupe: Mother of the New Creation* (Maryknoll, N.Y.: Orbis, 1997), 87.

41. *Para mí, el Encuentro fue una transformación, con respeto a mi persona . . . era yo una persona muy confundida, no tenía una finalidad, no tenía yo buenas ilusiones . . . pero por medio del Encuentro, descubrí la vida es más que sobrevivir y que tengo una misión concreta en esta vida.* Male candidate, interview by author, 16 November 1999, tape recording, Coachella, Calif.

42. Gelpi defines moral conversion as "the decision to turn from irresponsible selfishness to a commitment to measure the motives and consequences of personal choices against ethical norms and ideals that both lure the conscience to selfless choices and judge its relapses into irresponsible selfishness." Gelpi, *Committed Worship*, vol. 1, 17.

43. *Dios no esta muy lejos ahora. Me siento que él es más cerca y no vivimos tan lejos uno al otro. Ahora nuestra relación es más fuerte. Para mí, Dios es padre, amigo, and compañero.* Female candidate, interview by author, 12 November 1999, tape recording, Coachella, Calif.

44. *Cuando el muchacho de nuestra mesa se levantó a rezar, me pareció tan sincero y personal, como si no le importaba que pensaron los demás. Vino directo del corazón.* Male candidate, interview by author, 21 November 1999, tape recording, Coachella, Calif.

45. *Después de la plática de vida espiritual, nos decía que íbamos a visitar a una persona que siempre, siempre ha estado con nosotros. Yo me pregunté, ¿Quien será ésta persona? Al entrar ante el Santíssimo, mi emoción fué tan fuerte; sentí que alguien me decía, 'Ven, aquí estoy. Yo soy ese amigo que estás buscando.' Esto me impactó tanto, éste momento de haber conocido a Jesús como un amigo, y nunca lo he olvidado.* Male team member, interview by author, 2 December 1999, tape recording, Coachella, Calif.

46. *En éste momento que entramos el cuarto donde tenía el Santíssimo, algo entró mi corazón, no simplemente en la mente sino ya interno.* Male team member, interview by author, 12 November 1999, tape recording, Coachella, Calif.

47. Thomas Quigley of the United States Catholic Conference questions these figures when he says, "[T]he simple truth is that we don't really have good data, and there are reasons to believe . . . that we're dealing with considerable exaggeration on the part both of the promoters of the evangelical movements and of some of the Catholic Cassandras determined to sound the alarm as loud as possible." See Thomas Quigley, "An Overview: Myths about Latin America's Church," *Origins* 23 (1993): 366.

48. Andrew M. Greeley, "Defection among Hispanics," *America*, July 30, 1988, 61 and "Defection among Hispanics (Updated)." *America*, September 27, 1997, 12–13.

49. The sacraments are seven liturgical rites of the church that reveal the divine presence to strengthen those who believe and lead them to transformation in Christ. They are concrete means through which participants experience the paschal mystery of Christ and grow into the likeness of God. They function as windows to the sacred and as outward signs that communicate to believers the grace of God. The seven sacraments in the Roman Catholic Church are Baptism, Eucharist (Mass), Reconciliation, Confirmation, Matrimony, Holy Orders, and Anointing of the Sick. In addition to these sacraments, theologians also speak of "sacramentals," or "sacramentality," which are additional ways beyond the seven liturgical rituals through which God's presence is revealed. See Joseph L. Cunningham, "Sacrament," in *The New Dictionary of Theology*, ed. Joseph A. Komonchak, Mary Collins, and Dermot A. Lane (Collegeville, Minn.: Liturgical Press, 1991), 910–22; Gelpi, *Committed Worship*; Paul Philibert, "Human Development and Sacramental Transformation," *Worship* 65:6 (1991): 522–39; Paul Bernier, *Eucharist: Celebrating Its Rhythm in Our Lives* (Notre Dame, Ind.: Ave Maria Press); and Bernard J. Cooke, *Sacraments & Sacramentality* (Mystic, Conn.: Twenty-Third Publications, 1983).

50. *Como Mexicanos, con poco dinero en este país, nos sentimos a veces que nadie nos quiere y que no nos quieren en este país. A veces nos sentimos que ni Dios nos quiere.* Female team member, interview by author, 16 December 1999, tape recording, Coachella, Calif.

4

Corazón Florido— The Flowering of the Heart: The Dynamics of Inculturation and Mission

THE MESOAMERICAN STORY AND THE GUADALUPE STORY

As the spirituality of many immigrants takes root in daily life, many look to Our Lady of Guadalupe for insight, strength, and guidance. Our Lady of Guadalupe speaks profoundly to many Mexicans, especially immigrants. While there are many reasons for this, very often they see something in the Guadalupe story that resembles their own story. They often refer to Guadalupe as *nuestra madre* (our mother). To them, she is the one they often turn to in time of need. She is the one who hears their cries and afflictions. She is the one who helps them in their trials. No discussion of the spirituality of Mexican immigrants would be complete without an in-depth reflection of the Guadalupe story, which is described in the Nahuatl text called the *Nican Mopohua*. In the pages that follow we will look at the *Nican Mopohua* primarily as a theological document. While much discussion in recent years has gone into apparitionist and anti-apparitionist debates, we will focus primarily on the text itself and examine the intrinsic connections between the story of Juan Diego and the story of contemporary Mexican immigrants.[1]

Very often the story of Juan Diego and Guadalupe is deeply embedded in the spiritual consciousness of the Mexican people. As we look more closely at the *Nican Mopohua,* we can see some striking connections between the journey of Juan Diego and the journey of these immigrants. In this chapter, I will bring out the interrelation and mutuality of interpretation among the indigenous Mexican religious ethos, the Virgin of Guadalupe, and the people of Coachella. First, I will bring out some of the Mesoamerican ethos of these people by focusing on two key concepts: *atltepetl* and *corazón.* Secondly, I will discuss the birth of the Christian religion into the Mexican religious soul through the Guadalupe event. And finally, I will bring out how both the dynamics of the Mesoamerican ethos and Our Lady of Guadalupe are embedded in the spiritual life of those who belong to the Valley Missionary Program. These interrelationships also help us understand a significant dimension of this immigrant journey and Mexican immigrant spirituality. I will argue that the Guadalupe story reveals an important prototype for the converting, Mexican Christian, and the Coachella story deepens our understanding of the Guadalupe story. This mutuality of interpretation between the Guadalupe story and the Coachella story gives rise to a truly inculturated spirituality.

THE RELIGIOUS ETHOS OF MESOAMERICA: TWO CORE MESOAMERICAN SYMBOLS

Atltepetl: Fertile Center of the Divine Spirit

As we probe more deeply into the spirituality of these immigrants of the Valley Missionary Program, certain elements of their cultural history help us better understand their spirituality today. Two key Mesoamerican symbols, in particular, help us appreciate some of the indigenous elements that are intrinsic to their spiritual lives. While it is clearly Christian, the spirituality of the people of the Valley Missionary Program draws in part from the wells of pre-Hispanic concepts. The pyramid-shrine that these immigrants have built is one example of how their spirituality is still nourished by the memory of the past.

As we look back hundreds of years into the history of Mesoamerica, just before the time when the Spanish arrived on the shores of Mexico in the early part of the sixteenth century, we see a people who worked the fields and maintained a great connection to the earth. The people of Mesoamerica were an agricultural people with an agricultural mentality. The agricultural mentality is a worldview that developed in people who worked the earth, who observed the patterns of growth and regeneration, who knew the mystery of seeds, and who developed a kind of organic optimism in their lives. The earth taught them truths about life, and, in observing the patterns of agriculture, they also saw how things came to be and were regenerated. The agricultural mentality created in the people a spirit of hope, a hope that arises out of the knowledge of the mystery of the earth and its regenerative powers.

As noted anthropologist Alfredo López-Austin notes in his book *Tamoanchan, Tlalocan: Places of Mist*, one of the most central concepts in Aztec thought and culture is the *atltepetl*.[2] An *atltepetl* was a sacred mountain or pyramid, which translates literally as "water-mountain" or "water-hill."[3] *Atltepetls* functioned as sacred depositories and fertile centers of the divine spirit, which were pregnant with life-giving energy. Hope also emerged from the ability to participate in divine beauty, and the *atltepetl* represented such beauty.

Throughout Mesoamerica, the indigenous people believed that their ancestors lived in the *atltepetls*.[4] They believed their ancestors organized the interior of this mountain like a granary. In the *atltepetls* they housed the seeds of agriculture, and they stored the powers of the community in the form of spiritual seeds. Periodically, the gods, or the ancestors who lived in the mountains, dispensed these seeds into the world in response to ritual sacrifices, pilgrimages, prayers, and other sacred offerings of human beings. As a result of these sacred gestures, the patron God dispensed energy into the cosmos, and this energy gave life to plants, people, and things. The great pyramids of Teotihuacán outside of Mexico City are examples of *atltepetls*. Like the pyramid shrine in Coachella, these *atltepetls* are places where spiritual and cosmic renewal took place.

Corazón: Source of Life and Knowledge

For the Aztecs, the seeds and the powers inside the *atltepetl* were called *corazónes* or hearts.[5] In the Mesoamerican mind the heart was the vital center of the human being and the locus of true knowledge. When energy was dispensed from the *atltepetls*, it came forth in the form of a heart. The heart was the container of divine energy; it possessed a spiritual power that gave life to the world.[6] In Mesoamerican thought and culture the heart is the vital force that gives life, which originates from and eventually returns to the *atl-tepetl*.

This power and energy emanating from the *atltepetl* emerged in the form of hearts. Hearts contained the energy that gave things their nature and their dynamism to grow and mature. In these communities everything had a heart. The town had a heart. The plants had a heart. The sky had a heart. Oceans, rulers, and many other objects had hearts. The heart was one of the central notions of life. As the renowned anthropologist Davíd Carrasco notes, even the act of confessing sins, known as *neyolmelahualiztli*, is known as "the act of straightening the hearts."[7]

In the Aztec soul, flowers, songs, and mountains were sacred. The most beautiful thing to come out of the earth was flowers. Flowers, along with song, were the ultimate expression of truth, and only they could touch the infinite desires of the human heart:

> Eagerly does my heart yearn for flowers;
> I suffer with songs, yet I create them on earth
> Where might I find lovely flowers, lovely songs?
> Where might I, Cuacuauhtzin, find lovely flowers, lovely songs[8]

In the Mesoamerican mind, flowers and songs were the only way of expressing divine truth and touching the heart.

GUADALUPE: ROOTING CHRISTIANITY IN MESOAMERICAN SOIL

Tepeyac: A Christian *Atltepetl*

One of the most striking instances in which the notions of *atltepetl* and *corazón* appear is in the story of Juan Diego and the Virgin of Guadalupe. The *Nican Mopohua* provides a rich forum in which to view the relationship between Nahua-Aztec religion and Catholic, Christian faith.

The *Nican Mopohua* is a serious and carefully constructed narrative written by a Nahuatl scholar that cannot be adequately understood apart from the Mesoamerican concepts that are intrinsic to it

(See appendix for full text version of *Nican Mopohua*). The text tells the story of Juan Diego and the Virgin of Guadalupe through Nahuatl eyes, and by more closely examining this story we can gain even a greater appreciation of the importance of *atltepetl* and *corazón* in Mesoamerican thought and life. As Don Angel María Garibay notes,

> [*The Nican Mopohua*] is a masterpiece of Nahuatl literature. The language of the poem gives great emphasis to visual precision, elegance, beauty, sound, and symbolic meaning. Hence every detail and the way the details relate to one another are important to the communication. The language embodies the entire Nahuatl cosmovision, which was totally different from that of the Europeans.[9]

The setting for the story of Our Lady of Guadalupe and Juan Diego is just ten years after the Spanish conquest of Mexico. At the time, the native culture and a large part of the population were virtually destroyed. So deep and pervasive was the suffering of the native peoples that they simply wanted to die. Their warriors had been killed, their women raped, their cities destroyed, their temples burned, and now they heard their gods were false. The words of one Nahuatl poet expressed the sentiments of a people: "If you say our gods are dead, it is better that you allow us to die too."[10] At the hands of the Spanish conquerors, these Aztecs became foreigners in their own land.

In the midst of the agonies of these native people, the Guadalupe story speaks of the appearance of the Virgin Mary to a poor, native Indian named Juan Diego. Unlike the Virgins that the Spanish honored, this Virgin looked and dressed like a native Indian woman from the time of Juan Diego. Juan Diego and the Virgin meet for the first time in front of a mountain called Tepeyac, where native Indians also worshipped the Mesoamerican goddess Tonatzin.[11]

Juan Diego is drawn to the mountain because he hears the beautiful sound of birds singing. There Juan Diego meets the Virgin Mary who speaks to his heart and tells him to go to the bishop to request a temple be built at Tepeyac, where she could show all her love and compassion to all the inhabitants of the land. At first, the bishop does not believe Juan Diego. Feeling discouraged, dejected, and incompetent, he returns to the Virgin, who empowers him to return to the bishop. The bishop asks for a sign, and, after a detour of tending to a sick uncle named Juan Bernardino, Juan Diego meets the Virgin again, who gives him a sign for the bishop. The sign is beautiful Spanish flowers emerging out the sacred mountain of Tepeyac. But beyond the flowers, she imprinted herself miraculously on the cloak (*tilma*) of Juan Diego and healed Juan's dying uncle. In brief, the *Nican Mopohua* emerges from a painful context, is set before a mountain, describes a divine encounter and ends with empowerment and mission.[12]

As we look at the text in more detail, we can see that the notions of *atltepetl* and *corazón* are crucial to understanding what is happening in the Guadalupe narrative They also give us insight into understanding the spiritual transformation that happens in Coachella today. The story begins in 1531, when "there was in the surroundings a poor dignified campesino. His name was Juan Diego. (Nican Mopohua, no. 2, cited as NM, no. X, in the pages that follow). The first thing we learn is that the protagonist of this story is a poor agricultural farmer. He is an outsider, one who works on the margins of society, in the country, away from the town, in the fields. He is an agricultural person with an agricultural mentality.

When Juan Diego enters the scene, "It was still night." Night here is not only understood as physical darkness but also cultural darkness, and even the darkness of spiritual confusion. In the previous decade, Juan Diego had seen his culture fall from imperial dominance of the entire region to subservient slavery to the Spanish crown. Because of war and the diseases that the Spanish brought with them, the indigenous people of Mesoamerica went from 27 million to 1.2 million people in less than a century—a loss of 96 percent of their population![13] In the midst of a people in crisis, we meet Juan Diego in the narrative. As we meet him, we see a person with a heart in movement: "He was going in search of the things of God and of God's messages" (NM, no. 7).

In the Aztec mind, darkness was the prelude to a new day, a new creation. As it begins to dawn, Juan Diego arrives "at the side of the small hill, in the place called Tepeyac" (NM, no. 8). This hill is an *atltepetl*. He hears beautiful singing but, as of now, no flowers grow around the *atltepetls*, nor does he hear music there. Had the new religion of the conquistadors managed to kill the inner life, the ancestors, and the hearts, of the *atltepetls*?

Would they ever produce flowers and life again? Arguably, these questions echoed in Juan Diego's consciousness. Yet the beautiful singing of the birds called his attention, and the symbol of the sacred mountain still drew him closer to what was happening, as if to acknowledge the presence of his ancestors there.

Although the new religion ignored, and even destroyed the *atltepetls*, Juan Diego, in his heart, could not forget the sacred quality of the *atltepetl* at Tepeyac. This flowery mountain, this water-mountain, was the home of his ancestors, the source of divine power, the granary of the hearts that give life to the world. The text notes that when he arrived at the hill, it begins to dawn (NM, no. 8). That is to say, new enlightenment will emerge from the place from which his ancestors sought divine enlightenment as well.

When Juan Diego heard the music, it both disoriented and attracted him at the same time. The text states, "Juan Diego stopped and said to himself: 'By chance do I deserve this? Am I worthy of what I am hearing? Maybe I am dreaming? Maybe I only see this in my dreams? Where am I?'" (NM, no. 10). These questions point to the emergence of his Mesoamerican consciousness. Though he was on his way to catechism, it is not his Catholic consciousness, nor its teachings or dogmas, that he makes reference to. Instead, he makes references to the *atltepetl*: "Maybe I am in the land of my ancestors, of the elders, of our grandparents?" (NM, no. 11). He is conscious that the ancestors live in the hill, that their hearts are in Tepeyac, and that he is near the storehouse of divine energy. This divine energy seems to have invaded his whole self: "[Maybe I am] In the land of Flower, in the Earth of our flesh? Maybe over there inside of heaven?" (NM, no. 11).

Next, the text reads, "His gaze was fixed on the summit of the hill, toward the direction from which the sun arises: the beautiful celestial song was coming from there to here" (NM, no. 12). His experience at the *atltepetl* was nothing less than an encounter, or at least a prelude to, an encounter with the divine. In Juan Diego's mind, when the Virgin calls him, she calls him from the *atltepetl*, "From the summit of the hill" (NM, no. 13). From the hill he hears the Virgin's words, "Dignified Juan, dignified Juan Diego" (NM, no. 13). The Lady who calls is like a beautiful flower emerging out of the *atltepetl*, and her entire garment is adorned with flowery vines. In this narrative, flower and song are woven together in a new way in order to signal the advent of something new.

In the verse that follows there is a correlation between what Juan Diego sees on the hill (the *atltepetl*) and what he experiences in his heart (*corazón*): he "dared to go where he was being called" (NM, no. 14). He found himself before the sacred mountain, and the woman called him to climb up it. It was daring in that this mountain, this *atltepetl*, was also represented in the pyramid, and the only people who climbed the pyramids were priests. But still he ascends to the top of the hill, and in his heart he felt confident, assured, and happy (NM, no. 14–15). Aztec priests ascended the pyramid to offer human sacrifices, but he is ascending the hill not to offer sacrifice, but to receive life! He returns to the top of the hill on each encounter with the Virgin (NM, no. 34). Even when he tries to avoid his encounter with the Virgin, the hill figures prominently (NM, no. 7). The Virgin even descends from the hill as a great figure of divinity (NM, no. 69). She even instructs him to go to the top of the hill to cut flowers, which he does (NM, nos. 79–81). In doing so, he now becomes a participant in divine life. Even when he is sent to explain these events to the bishop, he is instructed to tell the bishop that he was "Sent to the top of the hill" to go to cut all the flowers, which he recounts (NM, nos. 87, 103). He explains that the top of the hill was not a place where flowers grow, because there are stones, thistles, cacti, thorns and mesquites (NM, no. 104). In the wake of the destruction, the *atltepetl* appeared dead, lifeless, and barren. But from the top of the hill, new life emerges. It is there that Juan Diego's vision was transformed: "As I was arriving at the top of the hill, my eyes became fixed: It was the Flowered Earth" (NM, no. 105). The barren hill, symbolic of the destroyed temple, has become a flowery mountain again. The whole notion of *atltepetl* permeates the Guadalupe narrative, and it culminates in the transformation of the barren hill into a sacred ground.

The religion that the Spaniards tried to destroy is brought back to life, but in a very new way. There was continuity with the ancestors and transformation into something new. A new religion emerged that satisfies the deepest yearnings of their hearts because they could now remain faithful to the ancestors' ways while transforming them in new, beautiful ways. In this encounter, the mestizo of Spanish flowers and Mesoamerican *atltepetl* become the forum through which the divine presence is revealed.

Juan Diego: An Encounter with the Divine Heart

The *Nican Mopohua* is a narrative that is also pregnant with notions of *corazón*. When Juan Diego walks by Tepeyac, something touches his heart. In the midst of familiar symbols, music, and singing, he hears the Lady say, "Know and be certain in your heart . . ." (NM, no. 21). Here we see an example of how the heart is the deepest form of communication, that which speaks to the inner-depths of a person, that which goes beyond simply rational knowledge and reaches into the core of who one is as a person. The heart is the center of Juan Diego's being, the receptacle of the spirit, and the place where divine revelation is accepted and appropriated into his life (NM, no. 109). For this reason, Juan Diego refers to the Lady as "My Owner and My Queen" (NM, no. 21). This sounds strange to modern ears, especially in an individualistic American culture concerned with personal freedom, which holds that no one has ultimate claim over one's life. However, in this context, ownership is not oppressive. Juan Diego refers to the Lady as his owner because she has touched his heart and therefore has access to his inner life. In other words, she owns him because she has claimed his heart through love.

When Juan Diego hears singing, and as he approaches the summit of the hill, the text says, "His heart was in no way disturbed, and in no way did he experience any fear, on the contrary, he felt very good, very happy" (NM, nos. 14, 78, 89). Knowledge in the heart stabilizes his life and puts him in harmony with the cosmic order. This heart knowledge is greater for him than notional knowledge. The deepest form of knowledge is internalized in the heart.

In contrast, the bishop expresses a curiosity of the mind but not an openness of the heart to the message Juan Diego brings, not untypical of those in authority (NM, no. 37). The bishop's close-mindedness is depressing for Juan Diego, who wants to avoid causing pain to the Virgin's heart (NM, nos. 41, 45, 72, 75). When the Virgin speaks to him, she does not speak in superficial

terms: She speaks to the core of who he is, which goes beyond title, talent, and social location (NM, no. 42). Nonetheless, the
bishop probes the message with his heart, revealing the heart's
dynamic searching quality (NM, no. 52). The heart was a place of
wisdom, a place where intuitions about life were comprehended
and the place from which one acted on one's desires: In the case
of his sick uncle," . . . [he] felt deeply in his heart that this was the
time and place of his death, that he would not be healed" (NM,
no. 56). In the case of the bishop, the divine manifestation is what
changes his heart, but such change brings some sadness because
there is remorse, dying, and letting go (NM, nos. 88, 108).

Guadalupe: The Flowering of Mexican Christianity

Viewed from Aztec eyes, Guadalupe emerged out of a flowering
atltepetl, from which she offered her heart to Juan Diego and anyone else who would hear her message. As we look at the image impressed on his *tilma*, which still exists today, we can continue to
gain new insights. Her folded hands are not about prayer, but
about offering something. She is offering her heart, what is deepest
within her. The heart becomes the locus for the most authentic encounter with the divine.

The Christian religion began to take root in native Mexican soil
with the encounter of Our Lady of Guadalupe and Juan Diego at
the flowering *atltepetl* of Tepeyac. This encounter and its subsequent development brought about a truly inculturated evangelization of the Mexican people. Through her and Juan Diego, the new
religion brought in from Europe would be mestisized with the native religions to give birth to the Mexican Christianity of today.
This story is still instrumental in the rebirth of contemporary Christian people.

THE ENCOUNTER RETREAT IN COACHELLA: THE GUADALUPE STORY AND THE GOSPEL STORY

To penetrate the fuller meaning, in theological terms, of what really
happens at Coachella, it is helpful to look at how the Christian
Gospel took root in Mexico through the Guadalupe event. Beyond
simply being an apparition, the Virgin was, as Virgil Elizondo says,

"an encounter."[14] The many layers of this encounter also structure a pedagogical approach for a transformative evangelization, one that begins with the sufferings and wounds of a people and offers them a salvation that begins here and now. This salvation entails the acceptance of the rejected, the welcoming of the unwanted, the cleansing of the soiled, the healing of the broken, and the uplifting of the downtrodden.

The pedagogical model of Coachella, in many ways, mirrors that of the Guadalupe story.[15] While Coachella is not simply a dramatization of the Guadalupe-Juan Diego encounter, it draws on key elements of the Guadalupe event to re-create an effective, inculturated evangelization program. Like Juan Diego, candidates experience transformation within the milieu of their language, symbols, and cultural context. In this model, Mexican immigrants do not break away from who they are, but rather they experience the freedom of being most authentically themselves in an environment that is most familiar to them. In addition, such an environment allows them to connect with their immediate and distant ancestral heritage. In keeping with one of the deepest elements of Mexican spirituality, these immigrants find a way to revere and respect the ways of the ancestors.[16] Though mainline, U.S. American culture is rapidly eroding this value, respect for ancestors is still a very deep element of Mexican spirituality.

One of the ways we can see how the Guadalupe event takes root in the spirituality of these people is through the architecture of the shrine. The entire setting is presided over by statues of Our Lady of Guadalupe and Juan Diego, who sit atop a modern *atltepetl*. As this shrine becomes the place where they experience tremendous spiritual renewal, it becomes a new, sacred *atltepetl*, a place of connection to divine life.

Rising above the pyramid is the cross of Jesus, which connects the pyramid to heaven, making it a real spiritual-cultural oasis in the midst of a foreign urban desert. Strikingly, no one has to explain the meaning of these Mesoamerican symbols to any of the participants. Like Juan Diego, they instinctively connect with it and are attracted to it. They immediately perceive it as the revealing mirror of their own innermost identity and their connection with the past. At the shrine, they know they are once again rooted in their native culture, where they truly experience a new heart. This is the place where Mexican immigrants connect with their ancestors while reaching out to new ways of life for the present and future. It is the place of continuity and transformation. This *atltepetl* shrine is a place from which the hearts of these immigrants are re-created and sent into the world.

In summary, the Guadalupe story and the Coachella story mutually interpret each other. Looking closely at the Guadalupe event helps us understand better what is happening in Coachella. Looking more closely at Coachella also generates new insight into the Guadalupe narrative as well.

La Virgen and the Team: A New Message, a New Way of Life

'Dignified Juan, dignified Juan Diego.' Then he dared to go to where he was being called. His heart was in no way disturbed, and in no way did he experience any fear; on the contrary, he felt very good, very happy.' (NM, nos. 13–14)

From the very beginning, *La Virgen* addresses Juan Diego by name. One of the reasons Juan Diego experienced no fear was because the Virgin appeared as one of his own people. She spoke his language and knew his religious symbols and affirmed them. She entered into tender conversation with him and believed in him even when he could not believe in himself. She was patient with him, never scolding and never threatening. Even when he felt totally inadequate, she trusted him with a great mission. Juan Diego, in turn, found himself totally re-created, ennobled, and dignified. In short, he saw himself—probably for the first time since the conquest—as a human being. He climbed to the top of the *atltepetl*, and, in the encounter with the Virgin, his heart became totally rehabilitated.

By analogy, the team at the retreat reveals a divine message to the candidates in the same way the Virgin revealed her message to Juan Diego. Like the Virgin of Guadalupe, the team members are active emissaries of God. They are bearers of the divine message and share with these immigrants a transforming word. They greet the candidates by name with beautiful music in the background, and they speak their language. The entire atmosphere throughout the retreat celebrates and affirms their religious traditions and puts them in continuity with all that they hold as sacred to them. Like the Virgin, the team is patient with the candidates, and there is no manipulation, no coercion, and no threatening words. Most of all, they are entrusted with an important mission. Through the patient dialogue of the talks, the dramatizations, the rituals, the base communities, the meals, and the prayers, the candidates gradually discover their own inner dignity, just as Juan Diego did through his conversations with the Virgin. Their educational, economic, or social status does not matter. Simply because they are human beings, they are worthy instruments of a divine calling. Socially, most of them are very much like Juan Diego, simple *campesinos* who work the land, who are at the bottom of the social scale, who are often bossed around, but seldom trusted with any kind of mission. This commissioning begins with intimate conversation and leads into their being sent forth as God's trusted messengers.

The very composure of the team members is startling. They are just like the candidates in every way. They have lived similar experiences, are dressed in similar clothing, and they speak the same language. However, like the Virgin, the team is so different from the candidates in their evident self-confidence, sincerity, simplicity, joy, and overall sense of well being. It is not stretching the truth to say that the candidates' first experience of the team is very much like an apparition. Seeing some of their own people so empowered, liberated, and alive is certainly different from anything they have seen before, and it scares them at first.

One of the most alluring aspects of Our Lady of Guadalupe is her serene and inviting *rostro y corazón* (her countenance and heart) through which her compassion becomes tangible to all who encounter her. In contrast to the empty and distant looks and fearful and mistrusting eyes of the candidates, the team members exhibit calm, inviting, and welcoming faces. The beautiful, tender, warm, friendly, and inviting eyes of the Virgin, in which Juan Diego saw himself reflected in an accepting and loving way, now come real to the candidates through the very eyes of the team. Like Juan Diego, such an experience of acceptance and welcome leads them gradually to the realization that they have come to a sacred site.

Juan Diego and the Candidates: Out of Darkness, a New Light

Because in reality I am one of those *campesinos*, a piece of rope, a small ladder, the excrement of people; I am a leaf; they order me around, lead me by force; and you, my most abandoned daughter, my Child, my Lady and my Queen, send me to a place where I do not belong. (NM, no. 40)

Analogously, the candidates coming to the retreat-Encounter show much in common with Juan Diego. They too are coming out of the darkness of fear, mistrust, deceit, and all the tragedies they have lived, but they are also coming in search of the things of God, even if some do so hesitantly. They come from the darkness of being in a strange and foreign land, as Juan Diego's land had been turned into a foreign place for him. The immigrants come from the darkness of not being appreciated for who they are, as Juan Diego's humanity was not appreciated by the new powers who considered the Indians as inferior, even subhuman, to the Spaniards. The immigrants come from the darkness of being condemned to a life of silent suffering with no choice but resignation or death, just as Juan Diego and his Indian brothers and sisters suffered silent exploitation and abuse.

When the immigrants come on the retreat, they arrive in the evening, the prelude to a new dawn. In every sense of the word, it is the beginning of a new day, a new life, and a new world. In a way, nothing will be changed, as nothing was changed for Juan Diego. In another and far deeper sense, however, everything changes. Once the divine heart has touched them, everything looks different, including the way they look at themselves. Their encounter with divine life enables them to pierce through the walls of false judgments and stereotypes and empowers them to see the world as it truly is and their lives as they really are before God. This was the great revelation that Juan Diego received: He saw himself not for what society said that he was, an inferior and illiterate Indian, but for who he really was as a dignified human being, chosen to be the special ambassador of the Mother of God.

Many indigenous people like Juan Diego had always thought that they were not good enough to be missionaries, especially because all the missionaries were foreigners. Even when the Spaniards came with the best of intentions, these foreign missionaries directly or indirectly reinforced the indigenous people's own low self-image and feelings of inferiority. Deep down, like the immigrants of Coachella, they came to believe that they were not good enough and not worthy enough to be missionaries.

At Coachella, however, the immigrants begin to see themselves, probably for the very first time, not according to the stereotypes of society which label as inferior, "alien," or "illegal," but as beautiful, intelligent human beings with unlimited talents for doing good. This is the beginning of their conversion and transformation: when they move from false images of self, based on shallow values of society and discover authentic notions of who they are, based on the knowledge that they are made in the image and likeness of God.

Bishop Juan Zumarraga and the Church:
A Listening Church, a Church of the Poor

[The Bishop said to Juan Diego,]
My son, you will have to come another time . . . (NM, no. 32)

Historically, some Church officials have been slow to listen to the cries of the poor. Though many exceptions do exist, some Church leaders even cite official policies that end up denying the poor of basic services such as the baptism of their infants or the burial of their loved ones. In addition, the immigrant poor often find it difficult to locate Catholic churches in the United States that are welcoming and familiar with their Mexican culture. Many churches lack the music, atmosphere, decorations, language, and religious festivals that are intrinsic to Mexican spirituality. The voices of many economically poor people who have left the Catholic Church give testimony to the neglect of Hispanic presence in the community today.[17]

Nonetheless, the poor are a principle source of revelation of divine life in society. It is not simply that the Church reaches out to the poor to convert immigrants, but it is the immigrants, because of their need for and closeness to God, who convert and enrich the Church.[18] Many Church leaders who come to Coachella undergo conversions similar to that of Bishop Zumarraga. "I've seen the early Church only twice in my life," said one priest from Guadalajara, "the first was in the Catacombs of Rome, and the second is here in Coachella."[19] Such conversions lead many priests and deacons to acknowledge the graced work of the program and their willingness to collaborate with the people in bringing the retreats to new places in the United States, Mexico, and beyond. In the process, these immigrants begin to experience within themselves that they are building up the new temple requested by Our Lady of Guadalupe and participating in the building up of the Kingdom of God.

TEPEYAC AND THE SHRINE:
A NEW CENTER, A NEW HOME

And when he arrived at the side of the small hill, which was named Tepeyac, it was already beginning to dawn. (NM, no. 8)

Tepeyac became the most sacred mountain of Mexico, the place from which divine protection and life flowed to the people.[20] It was the new *atltepetl*, that is, the new flowering mountain, from which Spanish roses bloomed. It also became the new depository of hearts, from which God's life and love touched the people. As we look at the image of Our Lady of Guadalupe, we see light emanating from behind her. Through her, Juan Diego experiences new light and life.

Coachella, with its pyramid–shrine surrounded by hills, flowers, and water, is like a new Tepeyac. Poetically speaking, in Coachella these immigrants receive new hearts. Like their ancestors from Teotihuacán, at this site they become deified, that is, they discover their divine blessing and potential. The *atltepetl* of Tepeyac–Coachella once again becomes the place from which the renewed hearts of the immigrants are released into the community. This shrine becomes a new place of pilgrimage that immigrants come to for consolation, prayer, and spiritual growth. It becomes a new center, a new home that offers real enlightenment and liberation to the people.

Flor y Canto: A Divine Message, a Human Medium

He heard singing on the summit of the hill . . . all over the place (the top of the hill) there were all kinds of exquisite flowers from Castile, open and flowering. (NM, no, 9, 81)

One of the most distinguishing elements of the Valley Missionary Program is the immediate and overwhelming experience of beauty, especially through the music and decorations. From the very first moments of the retreat until the last, flower and song, *flor y canto,* are the basic language of the retreat.

The harmonious beauty of flowers and music has always been a core ingredient of Mexican religion.[21] The Guadalupe event, faithful to the indigenous mindset, respects this way of communicating divine truth through beautiful music and exquisite flowers. The text of the Nican Mopohua is structured accordingly, beginning with music and ending with flowers (NM, nos. 9, 107). To the Mesoamerican Indians, the presence of music and flowers signals divine communication. Guadalupe respects the culture and religious ethos of the people. She wants to communicate divine love and compassion in a way that can be truly comprehended by the people, who at this time were not understood by those in power, especially religious power.

Our Lady of Guadalupe communicated her message, then, through mediums familiar to the religious language of the people. This inculturation is especially important because the first missionaries encountered many challenges in the early years, in part because of the abuses and corruption of the Spanish conquerors and in part because of their inability to understand the religious framework of the people. In contrast, Guadalupe reaches the religious consciousness of the people in ways they can understand. As Spanish flowers grow from the hill of Tepeyac, it is a sign that a new Christian spirituality ultimately does emerge, but it is not a Christianity that is limited merely to colonial religion. Rather, the flowers symbolize a new mestizo religion of Christianity planted in Mesoamerican soil. Even though the flowers come from Castile, they grow in what is now Mexican soil. A truly incarnated Christianity eventually flourishes out of the innermost depths of the native land, out of the native soul of the people. This great incarnational miracle of Tepeyac gives birth to what is today Mexican Christianity.

This same mestisizing dynamic takes place at Coachella. The retreat is rooted in the very ordinary language of the Mexican immigrant, from decorations, to music, to the humor, to the food, to the surroundings, to the major religious icons. The Coachella setting is equivalent to *flor y canto.* Most especially in the *mañanitas* ceremony, these immigrants are welcomed through song and greeted with flowers. As much as in the days of Juan Diego as today, these flowers and songs are charged with spiritual power. Through so many words, songs, gestures, and decorations on the retreat, the candidates experience the Word of God that brings a message of consolation, healing, liberation, and empowerment. They experience that authentic Christian faith does not destroy them but enriches them, ennobles them, and leads them to a new relationship with God and others.

The Tilma and a Spirituality of Conversion: An Initial Response, An Ongoing Challenge

> He unfolded his white mantle (and) . . . in that very moment she painted herself, the precious image . . . appeared. (NM, no. 107)

One of the enduring legacies of the Guadalupe story is the image impressed on the white mantle, or *tilma*, of Juan Diego. This image integrates into a symbolic whole his encounter with the Virgin and the promises she offered him. As an icon of divine revelation, the image brings together the symbols of his Mesoamerican heritage with the new revelation of God through the medium of the Virgin, pointing toward the Christian mystery. As the text states, when the bishop saw the image, he fell to his knees and was greatly astonished (NM, no.108). In the face of the revelation of divine mystery, the Bishop's life and many others' were changed. The *tilma* was a manifestation of the divine presence among them and an opportunity for conversion for those who encountered it.

As we have seen, the Missionary Encounter retreat is also a moment of profound revelation. The retreat is a profound moment of insight, of understanding, of encounter, in brief, of divine disclosure. The miracle exists not so much in the changing of a white garment to an icon of the Virgin, but the changing of a bruised and broken people into a reflection of the divine image. As the immigrants realize the value of their own culture and tradition, while at the same time are open to a new transformation of it through their encounter with the Gospel, they come to embrace and even celebrate their own spiritual expressions. In the process, they become convinced that they do not have to abandon their cultural world to become reborn in Christ.

While the *tilma* reflects the moment of initial encounter that these immigrants have on retreat, it also holds out to them the potential for continued conversion subsequent to this foundational event. For some, the conversion process starts off strongly after the initial propulsion of the retreat, but it wanes with time. Much more reflection and study should be dedicated to understanding why some experience initial conversion through a strong experience like the Encounter but do not continue after a period of time. It would be useful to study further why, after an initial experience of conversion, the ongoing transformation does not become integrated into the lives of some of these immigrants. Whatever the reason, the Encounter retreat, like the *tilma* of Juan Diego, remains a sign to these people of the ongoing presence of God among them, the spark that initiates their spiritual journey and a call to an ongoing conversion in Christ.

JUAN DIEGO AS PROTOTYPE OF CONVERTING MEXICAN-IMMIGRANT CHRISTIAN

Among the Mexican immigrants of the Coachella Valley, the story of Juan Diego and Our Lady of Guadalupe is an interpretive key to understanding the dynamics of their encounter with the divine, their experience of healing, and their call to mission. For this reason, and many others, John Paul II refers to Our Lady of Guadalupe as "an impressive example of perfectly inculturated evangelization."[22] In other words, the Guadalupe story is key to understanding this Mexican immigrant spirituality.

Juan Diego is the prototype of the poor, marginalized, and displaced Mexican who is rehabilitated and transformed through his encounter with God and his discovery of and commitment to his divine calling. He is a broken and humiliated human being. Yet in hearing the call from the Mother of God, he breaks through the shackles of his damaged self-image and eventually carries out her mandate. Juan Diego's life models the movement from nonbeing to being and from his dehumanizing life to the developmental blossoming of his human potential.

The story of Juan Diego, then, becomes the hermeneutical lens through which these Mexican immigrants understand the Gospel and live out their spirituality. Their knowledge of the Gospel becomes real to them through their encounter with God in Christ, and ultimately this encounter is something appropriated and experienced in the heart. As we examine closely the Guadalupe story, we see the story of the Gospel as well. As we reflect further on the Coachella story, we see both the Guadalupe story and the Gospel story. These three stories—Guadalupe, the Gospel, and Coachella—intermingle with each other and form the tapestry that reveals the rich spirituality of this group of immigrants.

Like the Guadalupe story, which continues to unfold new levels of meaning with each generation, the story of Coachella is one that is still being written. Many layers of meaning are still yet to be explored as we reflect on the rich spirituality of these immigrants. With each new layer we see yet another facet of the transforming, spiritual power of divine revelation among the crucified people of today.

Much more research is also needed in correlating the foundational religious experiences of these immigrants with those of their ancestors in faith. As we have seen, this faith community reveals many compelling stories about people who have been abused and ignored but are healed and uplifted through their encounter with God in Christ. From this encounter, these immigrants experience some of the perennial truths about human life and the Scriptures. Their particular stories are related to the more universal story of human beings in pilgrimage to God. In them we already see hints of the Exodus, the *Magnificat,* and the Paschal mystery. Like many other faithful people who have walked before them, these immigrants experience a real geographical and existential Passover, a physical and spiritual movement across a border of death and a new beginning in a valley of life.

NOTES

1. See D.A. Brading, *Mexican Phoenix: Our Lady of Guadalupe: Image and Tradition across Five Centuries* (Cambridge, UK: Cambridge University Press, 2001); Jacques Lafaye, *Quetzalcoatl et Guadalupe: La formation de la consicence nationale au Mexique 1531–1813* (Paris: Gallimard, 1976); and Stafford Poole, *Our Lady of Guadalupe: The Origins and Sources of a Mexican National Symbol, 1531–1797,* (Tucson: University of Arizona Press, 1995).

2. An *Atltepetl* was the most basic, provincial sociopolitical unit of Aztec society. It was a comprehensive term that commonly refers to the community, the people, the city, or the government. See Alfredo López Austin, *Tamoanchan, Tlalocan:*

Places of Mist, ed. Davíd Carrasco and Eduardo Matos Moctezuma, The Mesoamerican Worlds Series (Niwot, Colo.: University Press of Colorado, 1997).

3. *Atltepetl* is a *disfrasísmo*, which is a common language form used in Aztec culture that expresses the duality of life into one word or phrase. Through this literary technique, two metaphors joined together express one thought.

4. I am especially indebted to Davíd Carrasco for these penetrating insights.

5. While popular usage and to a great extent scholarly terminology has referred to the Nahua as the "Aztecs," this term can be a misleading one. First of all, the term Aztec applies to no one. The name comes from the root tribe Aztecah-Chicomoztoques from which the inhabitants of Tenochtitlán emigrated. When they left Aztlan, the inhabitants of the capital of the Nahua world in Tenochtitlán were called, properly speaking, the "Mexica." They were not the only tribe in Nahua society, but at the time of the arrival they were the most dominant and influential. There were other tribes that preceded them like the Olmecs, Chichimecs, and other tribes, as well as neighboring tribes such as the Mixtecs, Tarascans, and Tlaxcalans. Nevertheless, the Mexicas were the most powerful for the one hundred years prior to the arrival of the Spanish. Anthropologists, colonial historians and scholars of spirituality have sought to bring out the complexity of the Nahua world so as to better appreciate its richness, culture, and respective contribution. While aware of the problems of using the term "Aztec," I follow the example of Miguel León-Portilla and use the term Aztec to speak more generally about the tribes that inhabited Mexico around the time of the Spanish conquest.

6. As Davíd Carrasco notes, the human body has animistic entities related to the cosmic order. The first of these is located in the head and was called *tonalli*, which provided warmth, energy, courage, and growth within a person. The second animistic dimension of a person was located in the liver, called the *ihiyotl*, which provided passion, feeling, and other emanations. The third entity was the heart, known as *teyolia*, which was the place of equilibrium. The word *teyolia* comes from the Nahuatl word *yolia*, which means "he who animates," and *yol* or life. The heart was understood to be the center of understanding, comprehension, and vitality. And these hearts come from the ancestors, who release them from the *atltepetl* periodically in response to religious rituals. See Davíd Carrasco, *City of Sacrifice:The Aztec Empire and the Role of Violence in Civilization* (Boston: Beacon Press, 1999), 180.

7. Carrasco, *City of Sacrifice:The Aztec Empire and the Role of Violence in Civilization*, 180.

8. From MSS "Cantares Mexicanos" as cited in Miguel León-Portilla, *Aztec Thought and Culture: A Study of the Ancient Nahuatl Mind*, trans. Jack Emory Davis (Norman: University of Oklahoma Press, 1963), 76.

9. Quote cited in Virgil Elizondo, *Guadalupe: Mother of the New Creation* (Maryknoll, N.Y.: Orbis, 1997), 3.

10. León-Portilla, *Aztec Thought and Culture*, 183.

11. For more on the relationship between the Virgin of Guadalupe and the indigenous goddess Tonatzin, see Richard Nebel, *Santa María Tonantzin Virgen de Guadalupe*.

12. For textual commentaries on the *Nican Mopohua*, see Virgil Elizondo, *Guadalupe: Mother of the New Creation* (Maryknoll, N.Y.: Orbis, 1997) and *La Morenita:*

Evangelizer of the Americas (San Antonio: Mexican American Cultural Center, 1981). For an alternative translation of the *Nican Mopohua*, see Luis Lasso de la Vega and others, *The Story of Guadalupe: Luis Laso De La Vega's 'Huei Tlamahuiçoltica' of 1649*, (Stanford, Calif.: Stanford University Press, 1998).

13. For more information on these population statistics and Mesoamerica before, during and after the Spanish conquest, see Gary H. Gossen, "The Religions of Mesoamerica," in *The Legacy of Mesoamerica: History and Culture of a Native American Civilization*, ed. Robert M. Carmack, Janie Gasco, and Garry H. Gossen (Upper Saddle River, N.J.: Prentice Hall, 1996), 128.

14. Elizondo, *Guadalupe: Mother of the New Creation*, 38.

15. For the same reason, Pope John Paul II calls Our Lady of Guadalupe the "Star of the new and first evangelization" for the Americas and the world. John Paul II, *Ecclesia in America* (Washington, D.C.: United States Catholic Conference, 1999), no. 11.

16. José Luis Guerrero, *El Nican Mopohua: Un intento de exégesis* (Mexico City: Universidad Pontificia de México, 1996), 135.

17. See United States Catholic Conference, *Hispanic Ministry: Three Major Documents* (Washington, D.C.: United States Catholic Conference, 1995) and Andrew Greeley, "Defection among Hispanics (Updated)," *America*, September 27, 1997, 12–13.

18. I am grateful for Lydio Tomasi, former director of the Center for Migration Studies (CMS) and current editor of the *International Migration Review*, for this important insight. For more information on CMS, see www.cmsny.org.

19. Testimony of a priest from Guadalajara, date unknown, circa 1994.

20. For great discussion on the role of sacred mountains, see López-Austin, *Tamoanchan, Tlalocan: Places of Mist*, 148–150.

21. León-Portilla, *Aztec Thought and Culture*, 74–79.

22. John Paul II, *Ecclesia in America*, no. 11. Address at the Opening of the Fourth General Conference of Latin American Bishops (October 12, 1992), 24: AAS 85 (1993), 826.

Afterword

Gustavo Gutierréz

There cannot be an authentic solidarity with the poor if one is not friends with them. Otherwise, one runs the risk of simply committing oneself to a culture, a social class, or a race. Without doubt, the poor belong to the categories that these terms legitimately speak about. Our intention is not, of course, to discard them; rather we seek to be aware of the danger of forgetting that behind the poor are concrete persons that know joys and sufferings, who know of marginalizations, but also know of hope.

The study of Daniel Groody comes from those moments shared with the Mexican immigrants, of having accompanied them in the lowest times of their lives, of the love he received from them and that which he knew how to give to them, of having been seated at their table, of having prayed together, of a common faith. It comes, in one word, from friendship. What emerges from this friendship is a reflection on the faith of these lives, lives of human beings whose dignity and rights are not recognized, who have suffered endless indignities, but who at the same time encounter in Christian faith an element of identity and hope.

We should not be surprised that the theological reflection which emerges from this experience revolves around death-life, as is beautifully expressed in the title of the book, *Border of Death, Valley of Life*. In effect, in the end, poverty means death, as said by some of the first missionaries of this continent: "the Indians die before their time." This premature and unjust death continues to be the fate of the poor today. Physical death by hunger, by sicknesses that they are not in the condition to confront, or by immigrating to places where they think they can find jobs and a more dignified life. Death also when they are marginalized because of their culture, the color of their skin, or their limited ability to handle the knowledge and technologies of contemporary society. The immigrant seeks to survive in the midst of the lack of work, mistreatment, the traps of the *coyote*, the threats of the Border Patrol, and exhausting and exploitative work.

Nevertheless, Daniel's work does not limit itself to an analysis of this real and crushing reality of suffering. There is no doubt that this reality marks the existence of those that are called, in biblical terms, "strangers in a foreign land." But one must not fall into the temptation of thinking that the lives of these immigrants are defined by their problems and pains. With great finesse, and a true realism, Daniel enables us to see that in the midst of this situation these immigrants know how to celebrate life and live moments of great joy—a joy that is not an escapism, even less an escapism in front of the hardships of their lives. The truth is, without this joy there is no human life worthy of that name. In the terrible yet beautifully poetic description that the prophet Joel makes of the devastation of his people, after pointing out the degree to which death and destruction had taken over them, at the end of the cruel image that he paints, he says "surely, joy withers away among the people" (Joel 1:12). The joy of the people was the last to fall, it resisted until the end; its extinction meant that nothing was left, except death; at this moment life withered away, exactly as the prophet said. Everything ended.

This is not the case of the immigrants that Daniel accompanies in his book. From their experience he explores a reality that he qualifies, with precision, from the "heart" (*corazón*). The heart, as pointed out by the well-known Mexican scholar Virgil Elizondo in the foreword, is central to Mexican life. The heart is, perhaps, one of the most central categories of this work. In coming to know the heart of these Mexican people, Daniel has come to understand the lives of these immigrants. In every day language the heart is seen as the center of the deepest feelings of a person; but it is at the same time the center of memory. If we go to the Latin roots we see that *corazón* (*cor*) belongs to the same family as *re-cor-dar*, to remember.

The great events of life register in the heart (from which comes the word "to record"). To learn from memory is to do this, and from this comes the expression, "by heart." A people without memory is a weak people, at the mercy at whatever is imposed on them, which is why the powerful of the world have tried to erase the memory of the oppressed and marginalized.

This is the heart of the people; it is not a fixation on the past but rather a memory that makes one free, capable of learning and assimilating without losing their identity. In the heart of the immigrant resides their faith and their hope in the God of life in whom they celebrate with joy and trust. There they encounter the balm that feeds their struggle for justice and dignity, and also their immense capacity to welcome others. Thanks to Daniel Groody for reminding us all of this, *con corazón*.

—Gustavo Gutierréz
Feast of Our Lady of Guadalupe

Appendix: *Nican Mopohua*[1]— The Guadalupe Story

(1) Here we recount in an orderly way how the ever Virgin Holy Mary, Mother of God, our Queen, appeared recently in a marvelous way at Tepeyac, which is called Guadalupe.[1]

SUMMARY

(2) First she allowed herself to be seen by a poor and dignified person whose name is Juan Diego; and then her precious image appeared in the presence of the new Bishop D. Fray Juan de Zumárraga. The many marvels that she has brought about are also told.

THE SITUATION OF THE CITY AND ITS INHABITANTS

(3) Ten years after the conquest of the city of Mexico, arrows and shields were put down, everywhere the inhabitants of the lake and the mountain had surrendered.

(4) Thus faith started; it gave its first buds; and it flowered in the knowledge of the One through Whom we live, the true God, Téotl.[2]

(5) Precisely in the year 1531, a few days after the beginning of December, there was in the surroundings a poor dignified campesino. His name was Juan Diego. It was said that his home was in Cuauhtitlan.[3]

(6) And in so far as the things of God, all that region belonged to Tlatelolco.[4]

FIRST ENCOUNTER WITH THE VIRGIN

(7) It was Saturday, when it was still night. He was going in search of the things of God and of God's messages. (8) And when he arrived at the side of the small hill, in the place called Tepeyac, it was already beginning to dawn.

(9) He heard singing on the summit of the hill: as if different precious birds were singing and their songs would alternate, as if the hill was answering them. Their song was most pleasing and very enjoyable, better than that of the Coyoltotol, or of the Tzinizcan or of the other precious birds that sing.[5]

(10) Juan Diego stopped and said to himself: "By chance do I deserve this? Am I worthy of what I am hearing? Maybe I am dreaming? Maybe I only see this in my dreams? Where am I? (11) Maybe I am in the Land of my ancestors, of the elders, of our grandparents? In the Land of Flower, in the Earth of our flesh? Maybe over there inside of heaven?"

(12) His gaze was fixed on the summit of the hill, toward the direction from which the sun arises: the beautiful celestial song was coming from there to here. (13) And when the song finally ceased, when everything was calm, he heard that he was being called from the summit of the hill. He heard: "dignified Juan, dignified Juan Diego."

(14) Then he dared to go to where he was being called. His heart was in no way disturbed, and in no way did he experience any fear, on the contrary, he felt very good, very happy.

(15) He went to the top of the hill and he saw a lady who was standing and who was calling him to come closer to her side. (16) When he arrived in her presence, he marveled at her perfect beauty. (17) Her clothing appeared like the sun and it gave forth rays.

(18) And the rock and the cliffs where she was standing, upon receiving the rays like arrows of light, appeared like precious emeralds, appeared like jewels; the earth glowed with the splendors of the rainbow. The mesquites, the cacti and the weeds that were all around appeared like feathers of the quetzal and this stems like turquoise; the branches, the foliage and even the thorns sparkled like gold.

(19) He bowed before her, heard her thought and word which were exceedingly recreative, very ennobling, alluring and producing love. (20) She said: "Listen, my most abandoned son, dignified Juan: where are you going?"

(21) And he answered: "My Owner and my Queen: I have to go to your house of Mexico-Tlatelolco, to follow the divine things which our priests, who are the images of Our Lord, give to us." (22) Then she conversed with him and unveiled her precious will. She said: "Know and be certain in your heart,[6] my most abandoned son, that I am the ever Virgin, Holy Mary, mother of the God of Great Truth, Téotl, of the One through Whom we Live, the Creator of Persons, the Owner of what is Near and Together, of the Lord of Heaven and Earth.[7]

(23) "I very much want and ardently desire that my hermitage[8] be erected in this place. In it I will show and give to all people all my love, my compassion, my help and my protection. (24) Because I am your merciful mother and the mother of all the nations that live on this earth who would love me, who would speak with me, who would search for me and who would place their confidence in me. (25) There I will hear their laments and remedy and cure all their miseries, misfortunes, and sorrows.

(26) "And for this merciful wish of mine to be realized, go there to the palace of the Bishop of Mexico, and you will tell him in what way I have sent you as messenger, so that you may make known to him how I very much desire that he build me a home right here, that he may erect my temple[9] on the plain. You will tell him carefully everything you have seen and admired and heard.

(27) "Be absolutely certain that I will be grateful and will repay you, and because of this I will make you joyful; I will give you happiness and you will earn much that will repay you for your trouble and your work in carrying out what I have entrusted to you. Look, my son the most abandoned one, you have heard my statement and my word; now do everything that relates to you."

(28) Then he bowed before her and said to her: "My Owner and my Queen, I am already on the way to make your statement and your word a reality. And now I depart from you, I your poor servant." Then he went down so as to make her commission a reality; he went straight to the road which leads directly to Mexico [City].

FIRST INTERVIEW WITH THE BISHOP

(29) Having entered the city, he went directly to the palace of the Bishop, who had just recently arrived as the Lord of the Priests; his name was Don Fray Juan de Zumárraga, a priest of Saint Francis. (30) As soon as he arrived, he tried to see him. He begged his servants, his attendants, to go speak to him. After a long time, they came to call him, telling him that the Lord Bishop had ordered him to come in. As soon as he entered, he prostrated himself and then knelt. (31) Immediately he presented, he revealed, the thought and the word of the Lady from Heaven and her will. And he also told him everything he had admired, seen and heard. When he (the Bishop) heard all his words, his message, it was as if he didn't give it much credibility. (32) He answered him and told him: "My son, you will have to come another time; I will calmly listen to you at another time. I still have to see, to examine carefully from the very beginning, the reason you have come, and your will and your wish. (33) He left very saddened because in no way whatsoever had her message been accomplished.

SECOND ENCOUNTER WITH THE VIRGIN

(34) The same day, he returned [to Tepeyac]. He came to the summit of the hill and found the Lady from Heaven: she was waiting in the very same spot where he had seen her the first time. (35) When he saw her, he prostrated himself before her, he fell upon the earth and said: "My Owner, My Matron, My Lady, the most abandoned of my Daughters, my Child, I went where you sent me to deliver your thought and your word. (36) With great difficulty I entered the place of the Lord of the priests; I saw him; before him I expressed your thought and word, just as you had or-

dered me. (37) He received me well and listened carefully. But by the way he answered me, as if his heart had not accepted it, [I know] he did not believe it. He told me: 'You will have to come another time, I will calmly listen to you at another time. I still have to see, to examine carefully from the very beginning the reason you have come, and your will and your wish.' (38) I saw perfectly, in the way he answered me, that he thinks that possibly I am just making it up that you want a temple to be built on this site, and possibly it is not your command.[10]

(39) "Hence, I very much beg you, my Owner, my Queen, my Child that you charge one of the more valuable nobles, a well-known person, one who is respected and esteemed, to come by and take your message and your word so that he may be believed. (40) Because in reality I am one of those campesinos, a piece of rope,[11] a small ladder,[12] the excrement of people; I am a leaf; they order me around, lead me by force;[13] and you, My most abandoned daughter, my Child, my Lady and my Queen, send me to a place where I do not belong.[14] (41) Forgive me, I will cause pain to your countenance and to your heart, I will displease you and fall under your wrath, my Lady and my Owner."[15]

(42) The ever venerated Virgin answered: "Listen, my most abandoned son, know well in your heart, that there are not a few of my servants and messengers to whom I could give the mandate of taking my thought and my word so that my will may be accomplished. But, it is absolutely necessary that you personally go and speak about this, and that precisely through your mediation and help, my wish and my desire be realized.[16] (43) I beg you very much, my most abandoned son, and with all my energy I command that precisely tomorrow you go again to see the Bishop. (44) In my name you will make him know, make him listen well to my wish and desire, so that he may make my wish a reality and build my temple. And tell him once again that I personally, the ever Virgin Mary, the Mother of the God Téotl, is the one who is sending you there."

(45) Juan Diego answered her: "My Owner, my Lady, my Child, I will not cause pain to your countenance and your heart. With a very good disposition of my heart, I will go; there I will go to tell him truthfully your thought and your word. In no way whatsoever will I fail to do it; it will not be painful for me to go. (46) I

will go to do your will. But it could well be that I will not be listened to; and if I am listened to, possibly I will not be believed. (47) Tomorrow in the afternoon, when the sun sets,[17] I will return your thought and word to you, what the Lord of the priests has answered me.

(48) "Now I take leave of you, my most abandoned daughter, my Child, my Matron, my Lady, now you rest a bit." Then he went to his home to rest.

SECOND INTERVIEW WITH THE BISHOP

(49) The next day, Sunday, when it was still night, when it was still dark, he left his home and went directly to Tlatelolco to learn about the things divine, and to answer roll-call so that afterwards he could see the Lord of the priests.

(50) Around ten in the morning, when they had gathered together and heard Mass and answered roll-call and the poor had been dispersed, Juan Diego went immediately to the house of the Lord Bishop.

(51) And when he arrived there, he made very effort to see him and with great difficulty he succeeded in seeing him. He knelt at his feet, he cried and became very sad as he was communicating and unveiling before him the thought and the word of the Lady from Heaven, hoping to be accepted as her messenger and believing that it was the will of the ever Virgin to have him build a dwelling in the place where she wanted it.

(52) But the Lord Bishop asked him many questions; he interrogated him as to where he saw her and all about her so as to satisfy his heart. And he told the Lord Bishop everything.

(53) But even though he told him everything, all about her figure, all that he had seen and admired, and how she had shown herself to be the lovable ever Virgin and admirable Mother of our Lord and our Savior Jesus Christ.[18] Yet, he still did not believe him.

(54) He [the Bishop] told him that he could not proceed on her wishes just on the basis of his word and message. A sign from her would be necessary for the Bishop to believe that he [Juan Diego] was indeed sent by the Lady from heaven. When Juan Diego heard this, he told the Bishop: "My Patron and my Lord, what is the sign that you want? [When I know, I can] go and ask the Lady from

Heaven, she who sent me here." The Bishop was impressed that he was so firm in the truth, that he did not doubt anything or hesitated in any way. He dismissed him.

(56) And when he [the Lord Bishop] had left, he sent some people from his household in whom he trusted, to follow him and observe where he went, what he saw, and with whom he was speaking. And so it was done. (57) And Juan Diego went directly down the road. His followers took the same route. Close to the bridge of Tepeyac, in the hillside, they lost sight of him; they kept looking for him everywhere, but they could not find him anyplace.

(58) Thus they returned infuriated and were angered at him because he frustrated their intentions. (59) In this state of mind, they went to inform the Lord Bishop, creating in him a bad attitude so that he would not believe him; they told him that he was only deceiving him; that he was only imagining what he was coming to say; that he was only dreaming; or that he had invented what he was coming to tell him. They agreed among themselves that if he were to come again, they would grab him and punish him harshly, so that he would not lie again or deceive the people.

JUAN DIEGO TAKES CARE OF HIS UNCLE

(60) On the next day, Monday, when Juan Diego was supposed to take something to be the sign by which he was to be believed, he did not return, because when he arrived home, one of his uncles named Juan Bernardino, had caught the small-pox and was in his last moments.

(61) First he went to call a doctor who helped him, but he could do no more because he [Juan Bernardino] was already gravely ill. (62) Through the night, his uncle begged him that while it was still dark, he should go to Tlatelolco to call a priest to come and hear his confession and prepare him well because he felt deeply in his heart that this was the time and place of his death, that he would not be healed.

THIRD ENCOUNTER WITH THE VIRGIN

(63) And on Tuesday, when it was still night, Juan Diego left his home to go to Tlatelolco to call a priest.

(64) And when he arrived at the side of Tepeyac hill at the point where the road leads out, on the side on which the sun sets, the side he was accustomed to take, he said: (65) "If I take this road, it is quite possible that the Lady will come to see me as before and will hold me back so that I may take the sign to the Lord of the priests as she had instructed me. (66) But first I must attend to our affliction and quickly call the priest. My uncle is agonizing and is waiting for him."

(67) He then went around the hill; he climbed through the middle; and he went to the other side, to the side of the sunrise, so as to arrive quickly into Mexico, and to avoid the Lady from heaven delaying him. (68) He thought that having taken this other route, he would not be seen by the one who cares for everyone.

(69) He saw her coming down from the top of the hill; and from there, where he had seen her before, she had been watching him. She came to him at the side of the hill, blocked his passage, and, standing in front of him said: "My most abandoned son, where are you going? In what direction are you going?"

(70) Did he become embarrassed a bit? Was he ashamed? Did he feel like running away? Was he fearful? He bowed before her, greeted her and said: "My child, my most abandoned daughter, my Lady, I hope you are happy, How did the dawn come upon you? Does your body feel all right, my Owner and my Child? (71) I am going to give great pain to your countenance and heart. You must know, my Child, that my uncle, a poor servant of yours, is in his final agony; a great illness has fallen upon him and because of it he will die.

(72) I am in a hurry to get to your house in Mexico, I am going to call one of the beloved of Our Lord, one of our priests, so that he may go and hear his confession him and prepare him. (73) Because for this have we been born, to await the moment of our death. (74) But if right now I am going to do this, I will quickly return here; I will come back to take your thought and your word. My Matron, and my Child, forgive me, have a little patience with me; I do not want to deceive you, my most abandoned Daughter, my Child. Tomorrow I will come quickly."

(75) After hearing of Juan Diego's discourse, the most pious Virgin answered: "Listen and hear well in your heart, my most abandoned son: that which scares you and troubles you is nothing; do

not let your countenance and heart be troubled; do not fear that sickness or any other sickness or anxiety. (76) Am I not here, your mother? Are you not under my shadow and my protection? Am I not your source of life? Are you not in the hollow of my mantle where I cross my arms? Who else do you need?[19] (77) Let nothing trouble you or cause you sorrow. Do not worry because of your uncle's sickness. He will not die of his present sickness. Be assured in your heart that he is already healed. (And as he learned later on, at that precise moment, his uncle was healed.)

(78) When Juan Diego heard the thought and word of the Lady from heaven, he was very much consoled; his heart became peaceful. He begged her to send him immediately to see the Lord of the priests to take him his sign, the thing that would bring about the fulfillment of her desire, so that he would be believed.

(79) Then the Lady from heaven sent him to climb to the top of the hill where he had seen her before. (80) She said to him: "Go up, my most abandoned son, to the top of the hill, and there, where you saw me and I gave you my instructions, there you will see many diverse flowers: cut them, gather them, put them together. Then come down here and bring them before me."

(81) Juan Diego climbed the hill and when he arrived at the top, he was deeply surprised. All over the place there were all kinds of exquisite flowers from Castille, open and flowering.[20] It was not a place for flowers, and likewise it was the time when the ice hardens upon the earth. (82) They were very fragrant, as if they were filled with fine pearls, filled with the morning dew. (83) He started to cut them, he gathered them; he placed them in the hollow of his mantle. (84) And the top of the hill was certainly not a place where flowers grew; there are only rocks, thistles, thorns, cactus, mesquites; and if small herbs grew there, during the month of December, they were all eaten up and wilted by the ice.

(85) Immediately he went down; he went to take to the Queen of Heaven the various flowers which he had cut. When she saw them, she took them with her small hands, and then he placed them in the hollow of his mantle.[21]

(86) And she told him: " My most abandoned son: these different flowers are the proof, the sign, that you will take to the Bishop. In my name tell him that he is to see in them what I want, and with this he should carry out my wish and my will.

(87) "And you, you are my ambassador; in you I place all my trust.[22] With all my strength [*energía*] I command you that only in the presence of the Bishop are you to open your mantle, and let him know and reveal to him what you are carrying. (88) You will recount everything well; you will tell him how I sent you to climb to the top of the hill to go cut the flowers, and all that you saw and admired. With this you will change the heart of the Lord of the priests so that he will do his part to build and erect my temple that I have asked him for.

(89) As soon as the Lady from Heaven had given him her command, he immediately took to the road which leads to Mexico. He was in a hurry and very happy; his heart felt very sure secure; he was carrying with great care what he knew would [bring about] a good end. He was very careful with that which he carried in the hollow of his mantle, less anything would fall out. He was enjoying the scent of the beautiful flowers.

THIRD INTERVIEW WITH THE BISHOP
AND THE APPARITION OF THE VIRGIN

(90) Upon arriving at the palace of the Bishop, he ran into the doorkeepers and the other servants of the King of the priests. He begged them to go tell him [the Bishop] that he wanted to see him; but none of them wanted to, they did not want to pay attention to him, both because it was still night and they knew him: he was the one who only bothered them and gave them long faces;[23] (91) and also because their fellow workers had told them how they had lost him from their sight when they had been following him. He waited for a very long time.[24] (92) When they saw that he had been standing with his head lowered[25] [very sad] for a long time, that he was waiting in vain for them to call him, and that it seemed that he carried something in the hollow of his mantle, they approached him to see what he had and satisfy their hearts.

(93) And when Juan Diego saw that it was impossible to hide from them what he was carrying, that he would be punished for this, that they would throw him out or mistreat him, he showed them just a little of the flowers.

(94) When they saw that they were all different flowers from Castille and that it was not the season for flowers, they were very

astonished, especially by the fact that they were in full bloom, so fresh, so fragrant, and very beautiful. (95) Three times they tried to grab some of them and take them from him, (96) but they could not do it because when they were about to grab them, they did not see any more real flowers, but only painted or embroidered ones, or flowers sewn in his mantle.[26]

(97) Immediately they went to tell the Lord Bishop what they had seen and that the poor little Indian who had already come many times wanted to see him, and that he had been waiting for a very long time. (98) Upon hearing this, the Lord Bishop realized that this meant the despicable man had the proof to convince him and bring about what he was coming to ask for.

(99) Immediately he ordered that he be brought in to see him. As soon as he [Juan Diego] entered, he knelt before him [the Bishop] as he had done before, and once again he told him everything he had seen and admired and also her message.

(100) He said to him: "My owner and my Lord, I have accomplished what you asked for, I went to tell my Matron, my Owner, the Lady from Heaven, Holy Mary, the precious mother of God Téotl, how you had asked me for a sign in order to believe me, so that you might build her temple where she is asking you to erect it. (101) And besides, I told her that I had given you my word that I would bring you a sign and a proof of her will that you want to receive from my hands. When she received your thought and your word, she accepted willingly what you asked for, a sign and a proof so that her desire and will may come about.

(102) "And today when it was still night, she sent me to come and see you once again. But I asked her for the sign and the proof of her will that you asked me for and that she had agreed to give it to me. Immediately she complied.

(103) She sent me to the top of the hill, where I had seen her before, so that there I might cut the flowers from Castille. After I had cut them, I took them to the bottom of the hill. And she, with her precious little hands, took them; she arranged them in the hollow of my mantle, so that I might bring them to you, and deliver them to you personally. (104) Even though I knew well that the top of the hill was not a place where flowers grow, that only stones, thistles, thorns, cactus and mesquites abound there, I was still neither surprised nor did I doubt. (105) As I was arriving at the top of the hill, my eyes became fixed: It was the Flowering Earth! It was covered

with all kinds of flowers from Castille, full of dew and shinning brilliantly. Immediately I went to cut them. (106) And she told me why I had to deliver them to you: so that you might see the sign you requested and that you believe in her will; and also so that the truth of my word and my message might be manifested. Here they are. Please receive them."

(107) He unfolded his white mantle, the mantle in whose hollow he had gathered the flowers he had cut, and at that instant the different flowers from Castille fell to the ground. In that very moment she painted herself, the precious image of the ever Virgin Holy Mary Mother of the God Téotl, appeared suddenly, just as she is today and is kept in her precious home, in her hermitage of Tepeyac, which is called Guadalupe.

CONVERSION OF THE BISHOP

(108) When the Lord Bishop saw her, he and all who accompanied him fell to their knees and were greatly astonished. They stood up to see her; they became saddened; their heart and their mind became very heavy.

(109) The Lord Bishop, with tears and sadness, prayed to her and begged her to forgive him for not having believed her will, her heart and her word.

(110) When he stood up, he untied the mantle from Juan Diego's neck, the mantle in which had appeared and was painted the Lady from Heaven. Then he took her and went to place her in his oratory.

THE CONSTRUCTION OF THE HERMITAGE

(111) Juan Diego spent one more day in the Bishop's home who had invited him [to stay]. And on the next day he said: "Let us go to see where it is the will of the Lady from Heaven that the hermitage be built."

(112) Immediately people were invited to construct and build it. And when Juan Diego showed where the Lady from Heaven had indicated that the hermitage should be built, he asked permission

to leave. (113) He wanted to go home to see his uncle Juan Bernardino, the one who had been in his final agony, whom he had left to go to Tlatelolco to call a priest to come, hear his confession, and prepare him well, and the one who the Lady from Heaven had said had been healed. But they did not let him go alone, they accompanied him to his home.

THE FOURTH APPARITION AND FIRST MIRACLE

(114) When they arrived, they saw his uncle who was well and with no pains. (115) He [Juan Bernardino] was very much surprised that his nephew was so well accompanied and honored, and he asked him why they were honoring him so much.

(116) He told him how when he had left him to go call a priest to come to hear his confession and prepare him well, the Queen of Heaven appeared to him over there, at Tepeyac, and sent him to Mexico to see the Lord Bishop so that he would build her a home at Tepeyac. (117) And she told him not to be troubled because his uncle was healed and he was very consoled.

(118) And the uncle said that this was true, that it was precisely then that she had healed him, and he had seen her exactly as she had shown herself to his nephew, and that she had told him that he had to go to Mexico to see the Bishop. (119) And [she told him] also that when he went to see the Bishop, he would reveal all that he had seen and would tell him in what a marvelous way she had healed him. And that he [the Bishop] would call and name that precious image, the ever Virgin Holy Mary of Guadalupe.

(120) They took Juan Bernardino to the Bishop so that he might speak and witness before him. (121) And, together with his nephew Juan Diego, the Bishop hosted them in his home for several days, until the hermitage of the Queen and Lady from Heaven was built at Tepeyac, where Juan Diego had seen her.

THE ENTIRE CITY BEFORE THE VIRGIN

(122) And the Lord Bishop transferred to the Major Church the precious image of the Queen and Lady from Heaven; he took her from

the oratory of his palace so that all might see and venerate her precious image.

(123) The entire city was deeply moved; they came to see and admire her precious image as something divine; they came to pray to her. (124) They admired very much how she had appeared as a divine marvel, because absolutely no one on earth had painted her precious image.

NOTES

1. Tepeyac was the sacred mountain site of the Goddess Tonantzin, which had been renamed by the Spaniards Guadalupe after Our Lady of Guadalupe of Extremadura, Patroness of Spanish re-conquista and of Cortez. Ancient sacred sites of the Indians were renamed with Spanish holy names. This was part of the strategy of the conquest: the religious subjugation of the native symbols of the sacred.

2. This was the Náhuatl designation for God while "True God" was that of the Spaniards.

3. Indicates he was from the city of the eagles, from the land of the ancestors and by saying he was from here, it was saying that he would be explaining the things of God (Siller, 60).

4. This was an ancient ceremonial center which had now become a center of Spanish evangelization and domination (Siller, 60).

5. Birds in Náhuatl thought indicate mediation between heaven and earth; the Coyoltotol was the symbol of great fecundity.

6. The heart is the active and dynamic center of the person, it is the symbolic place of ultimate understanding and certitude.

7. This litany of names is a most important revelation for they are the same names which were mentioned by the Náhuatl theologians in their dialogues with the Spanish theologians and which were discredited by the Spanish evangelizers. They appeared in the purest pre-conquest theology of the Náhuatls. She reestablishes the authenticity and veracity of these holy names.

8. Hermitage could refer to a home for the homeless, an orphanage, a hospice— all would have a very special meaning for a people who had been totally displaced and left homeless by the conquest.

9. Notice the progression from hermitage (home for the homeless), to a home (place of affectionate relationships), to a temple (the manifestation of the sacred). Thus, where everyone is welcomed *is* sacred earth.

10. In the presence of authority and those in power, the poor understand very well that they are not credible.

11. The rope that was tied around the Indians necks as they were chained and pulled around for forced labor.

12. The Indians were stepped on to climb the ladder of social and economic mobility.

13. The worst part of oppression and domination is that one actually begins to believe what those in authority say: that one is subhuman, inferior, incapable of dignified tasks, worthless, and a burden to society.

14. "I do not walk or put my foot upon" is the Nahuatl expression for a place where "I do not belong"—that is, where one is not wanted or allowed in.

15. This is a perfect example of the soul-crushing victimization of the victims of society. The disgraced and broken-poor are made to feel guilty for their situation of failure and misery and even worse, deserving of disgust and punishment.

16. Consistent with the Gospel and the beginnings of the Apostolic movement, it is precisely through the mediation of the "nothings of this world" (1 Corinthians 1), through the "stone rejected by the builders of this world." (Acts 4:11) that the Kingdom of God—the space where every human being will be recognized, valued, and loved—will irrupt into this world. In the Nican Mophua, the shelter, home, temple, which the Lady requests, is equivalent to the "Kingdom" in the Gospel stories. The abandoned of this world, act under the authority of God!

17. "In the afternoon when the sun sets" is the Nahuatl expression for the coming to an end of a stage or period of life and the expectation of something new which is about to begin. It is an expression of hope. Here it could easily mean "Tomorrow, hoping that something new will take place. . . ."

18. Note that it is Juan Diego that recognizes her as the Mother of Jesus Christ. She never mentions this in her conversations with him. It is he who makes the connection and thus announces to his people that the Mother of their *Nahuatl God Téotl* and the Mother of the *Spanish God Dios* is likewise the mother of the one and only savior of all, Jesus Christ.

19. Notice the five identifying statements—each one deepening and expanding the meaning of the previous one. Before she had identified herself as the Mother of God, now she introduces herself as the mother of Juan Diego and of the poor; *shadow* was the image-word meaning authority; *hollow of her mantle* meant tender service as the quality of true authority; *crossing of the arms* indicates the cross of sticks which produces fire out of which new divine life is born, Juan Diego is the first-born of the new creation; nothing else is needed (Siller, 83–84).

20. Note the constant insistence of "the top of the hill"—a contrast to the top of the pyramid-temple where the priests ascended to offer human sacrifices, now the new priests ascends to discover beautiful flowers in the place where he had first heard the heavenly music—a true place of divine–human encounter.

21. He brings the truth (flowers) to her; she touches them (confirms the truth) and places it under his care.

22. At this historical moment (unfortunately as even today) the Indian was considered to be unworthy of any trust, one who imagined things and easily lied and hence one who should be dominated and punished! (cf.: verses 31, 32, 37, 38, 46, 54, 56, 57, 58, 59); the Lady from heaven reverses this and brings out the ultimate and real truth about the poor and conquered Indian: the most trusted ambassador of heaven! The Indians who were declared unworthy of ordination by the Church, were to be the trusted ambassadors—spokespersons—of God.

23. Note the re-appearance of the phrase "while it was still night" which marks the moment at which the new creation is about to begin *but* those whose

livelihood and identity depends on the structures of the old creation, that is, the structures of domination, try to prevent it. The rise and liberation of the poor and the dominated of the world always bothers the structures of unjust domination and oppression.

24. The poor and undignified of the world are always made to wait.

25. Pre-conquest art.

26. Sewn in his mantle meant something had become part of one's innermost being.

Bibliography

Abbott, Walter M., ed. *The Documents of Vatican II*. Piscataway, N.J.: New Century Publishers, Inc., 1966.

Ainslie, Ricardo C. Cultural Mourning, Immigration, and Engagement: Vignettes from the Mexican Experience. In *Crossings: Mexican Immigration in Interdisciplinary Perspective*. Ed. Marcelo M. Suárez-Orozco, 283–300. Cambridge: Harvard University Press, 1998.

Albacete, Lorenzo. Secrets of the Confessional. *New York Times Magazine*, May 7, 2000, p. 120.

Alexander, Bobby C. Listening. *Journal of Religion and Culture*, Fall 1998: 175–87.

Alonzo, Joaquin M. El amor increado, en la devoción al corazón de Jesús, Es el 'esencial', el 'nocional' o el 'personal'. In *Collectanea theologica, al Joaquin Salaverri en el cincuentenario de su vida religiosa*, 461–84. Santander: Uniersidad Potificia Comillas, 1960.

Altemeyer, Bob, and Bruce Hunsberger. *Amazing Conversions: Why Some Turn to Faith & Others Abandon Religion*. Amherst, N.Y.: Prometheus Books, 1997.

Altheide, David L., and John M. Johnson. Counting Souls: A Study of Counseling at Evangelical Crusades. *Pacific Sociological Review* 20, no. 3 (1977): 323–48.

Andreas, Peter. The U.S. Immigration Control Offensive: Constructing an Image of Order on the Southwest Border. In *Crossings: Mexican Immigration in Interdisciplinary Perspective*. Ed. Marcelo M. Suárez-Orozco, 341–56. Cambridge: Harvard University Press, 1998.

Annerino, John. *Dead in Their Tracks: Crossing America's Desert Borderlands*. New York: Four Walls Eight Windows, 1999.

Anzaldúa, Gloria. *Borderlands: La Frontera = the New Mestiza*. San Francisco: Aunt Lute Books, 1987.

Aquino, María Pilar. *Our Cry for Life: Feminist Theology from Latin America*. Maryknoll, N.Y.: Orbis Books, 1993.

Arias, Mortimer. *Announcing the Reign of God: Evangelization and the Subversive Memory of Jesus.* Philadelphia, Pa.: Fortress Press, 1984.

Associated Press. Border Patrol Agent Who Sank Raft Carrying People to Resign. *Los Angeles Times,* December 12, 1999, sec. A, p. 14.

———. Immigrant Smugglers Use Youths as Guides. *San Antonio Express News,* February 2, 1999, sec. B, p. 2.

Attias, Jean Christophe. *De La Conversion.* Paris: Cerf, 1997.

Au, Wilkie. *By Way of the Heart.* New York/Mahwah, N.J.: Paulist Press, 1989.

Aubin, Paul. *Le problème de la "conversion."* Paris: Beauchesne, 1963.

Audinet, Jacques. *Le temps du métissage.* Paris: Les Editions de l'Atelier, 1999.

Avila, St. Teresa of. *The Collected Works of St. Teresa of Avila.* Trans. Kieran Kavanaugh and Otilio Rodriguez. vol. 1. Washington, D.C.: Institute of Carmelite Studies, 1976.

Baker, Susan González, Frank D. Bean, Augustin Escobar Latapi, and Sidney Weintraub. U.S. Immigration Policies and Trends: The Growing Importance of Migration from Mexico. In *Crossings: Mexican Immigration in Interdisciplinary Perspective.* Edited by Marcelo M. Suárez-Orozco, 80–105. Cambridge: Harvard University Press, 1998.

Bankston, William B., Jr. H. Hugh Floyd, and Craig J. Forsyth. Toward a General Model of the Process of Radical Conversion: An Interactionist Perspective on the Transformation of Self–Identity. *Qualitative Sociology* 4 (1981): 279–97.

Bañuelas, Arturo. *Mestizo Christianity: Theology from Latino Perspective.* Maryknoll, N.Y.: Orbis, 1995.

———. U.S. Hispanic Theology. *Missiology: An International Review* 20 (April 1992): 292.

Baptiste, D. A., Jr. Family Therapy with Hispanic Heritage Immigrant Families in Cultural Transition. *Contemporary Family Therapy* 9, no. 4 (winter 1987).

Bardy, Gustave. *La conversion au christianisme durant les premiers siècles.* Paris: Aubier, 1949.

Barnes, Fred. No Entry: The Republicans' Immigration War. *New Republic* 8 (November 1993).

Barrett, David B. *Evangelize!: A Historical Survey of the Concept.* Birmingham, Ala.: New Hope, 1987.

Baum, Gregory. *Religion and Alienation: A Theological Reading of Sociology.* New York: Paulist, 1975.

Bean, F. D., and M. Tienda. *The Hispanic Population of the United States.* New York: Russell Sage Foundation, 1990.

Becker, Howard S. Participant Observation and Interviewing: A Comparison. *Human Organization* 16 (1957): 28–32.

Beckford, James A. Accounting for Conversion. *British Journal of Sociology* 29 (1978): 249–62.

———. The Restoration of "Power" to the Sociology of Religion. *Sociological Analysis* 44 (1983): 11–33.

Behr-Sigel, Elisabeth. *The Place of the Heart: An Introduction to Orthodox Spirituality.* Torrance, Calif.: Oakwood, 1992.

Bellah, Robert N. *Beyond Belief.* New York: Harper, 1970.

———. et. al. *Habits of the Heart: Individualism and Commitment in American Life.* Berkeley: University of California Press, 1985.

Berger, Peter. *The Sacred Canopy: Elements of a Sociological Theory of Religion.* Garden City, N.Y.: Doubleday, 1967.

Berger, Peter, and Richard J. Neuhaus. *To Empower People.* Washington, D.C.: American Enterprise Institute, 1977.

Bernard, C. *Théologie Affective.* Paris: Cerf, 1984.

Blume, Michael A. Catholic Church Teachings and Documents Regarding Immigration: Theological Reflection on Immigration. In *Who Are My Sisters and Brothers?* Ed. Carleen Reck. Washington, D.C.: United States Catholic Conference, 1996.

Blumer, Herbert. *Symbolic Interactionism: Perspective and Method.* Englewood Cliffs, N.J.: Prentice-Hall, 1969.

Boelen, W. E. Marianne. Street Corner Society: Cornerville Revisited. *Journal of Contemporary Ethnography,* (April 1992): 11–51.

Boff, Leonardo. *Jesus Christ Liberator.* Maryknoll, N.Y.: Orbis, 1978.

———. *Trinity and Society.* Maryknoll, N.Y.: Orbis, 1986.

———. *Faith on the Edge: Religion and Marginalized Existence.* San Francisco: Harper & Row, 1989.

———. *St. Francis: A Model for Human Liberation.* New York: Crossroad, 1989.

———. *New Evangelization.* Maryknoll, N.Y.: Orbis, 1991.

———. *La estuctura pascual de la existencia humana. Mensaje* 347 (Marzo-Abril 1986): 78–81.

Bonino, J. Miguez. Love and Social Transformation in Liberation Theology. In *The Future of Liberation Theology: Essays in Honor of Gustavo Gutierrez.* Eed. Marc H. Ellis and Otto Maduro. Maryknoll, N.Y.: Orbis, 1989.

Boyack, Kenneth. *The New Catholic Evangelization.* Mahwah, N.J.: Paulist Press, 1992.

Brackley, Dean. *Divine Revolution: Salvation and Liberation in Catholic Thought,* 1996.

Brading, D. A. *Mexican Phoenix: Our Lady of Guadalupe: Image and Tradition across Five Centuries.* Cambridge, UK/New York: Cambridge University Press, 2001.

Briggs, Vernon M. *Immigration Policy and the American Labor Force.* Baltimore: Johns Hopkins, 1984.

Brereton, Virginia Lieson. *From Sin to Salvation: Stories of Women's Conversions, 1800 to Present.* Bloomington: Indiana University Press, 1991.

Brown, Raymond. *The Death of the Messiah: From Gethsemane to the Grave,* vol. 1. New York: Doubleday, 1993.

———. *The Churches the Apostles Left Behind.* New York/Mahwah, N.J.: Paulist Press, 1984.

Burton-Christie, Douglas. *The Word in the Desert: Scripture and the Quest for Holiness in Early Christian Monasticism.* New York: Oxford University Press, 1993.

Bustamante, Jorge A. *La inmigración indocumentada en los debates del congreso de los Estados Unidos.* México, D.F.: Centro Nacional de Información y Estadísticas del Trabajo, 1978.

———. *Cruzar La Línea: La migración de México a los Estados Unidos.* 1a. ed. México: Fondo de Cultura Económica, 1997.

Bustamante, Jorge A. and Wayne A. Cornelius. *Flujos migratorios Mexicanos hacia Estados Unidos.* 1a. ed. México, D.F.: Fondo de Cultura Económica, 1989.

Bustamante, Jorge A., Alberto H. Hernández, and Francisco A. Malagamba. *Estudios fronterizos México-Estados Unidos: Directorio general de investigadores, 1984.* 1a ed. Tijuana, BC: Centro de Estudios Fronterizos del Norte de México, 1984.

Bustamante, Jorge A., Clark Winton Reynolds, and A. Hinojosa Ojeda. *U.S.–Mexico Relations: Labor Market Interdependence.* Stanford, Calif.: Stanford University Press, 1992.

Butler, Dom Cuthbert, ed., St. Benedict's Rule for Monastaries. Collegeville, Minn.: Liturgical Press, 1935.

Bynum, C. Women's Stories, Women's Symbols: A Critique of Victor Turner's Theory of Liminalty. In *Anthropology and the Study of Religion.* Ed. Robert L. Moore and Frank E. Reynolds, 104–25. Chicago: Center for the Scientific Study of Religions, 1984.

Callahan, Annice. *Karl Rahner's Spirituality of the Pierced Heart: A Reinterpretation of Devotion to the Sacred Heart.* Lanham, Md.: University Press of America, 1985.

———. *Spiritualities of the Heart: Approaches to Personal Wholeness in Christian Tradition.* New York: Paulist Press, 1990.

Camarillo, Albert, *Latin Americans: Mexican Americans and Central Americans,* Encyclopedia of American Social History. New York: Scribner, 1993).

Capps, Donald, and James E. Dittes. *The Hunger of the Heart: Reflections on the Confessions of Augustine.* West Lafayette, Ind.: Society for the Scientific Study of Religion, 1990.

Cardenal, Ernesto. *The Gospel in Solentiname.* 4 vols. Maryknoll, N.Y.: Orbis, 1976–1982.

Carrasco, Davíd. *Religions of Mesoamerica: Cosmovision and Ceremonial Centers.* Religious Traditions of the World. San Francisco: Harper & Row, 1990.

———. *To Change Place: Aztec Ceremonial Landscapes.* Niwot, Colo.: University Press of Colorado, 1991.

———. *City of Sacrifice: The Aztec Empire and the Role of Violence in Civilization.* Boston: Beacon Press, 1999.

———, ed. *The Oxford Encyclopedia of Mesoamican Cultures.* New York: Oxford University Press, 2000.

Carrasco, Davíd, Lindsay Jones, and Scott Sessions. *Mesoamerica's Classic Heritage: From Teotihuacan to the Aztecs.* Boulder, Colo.: University Press of Colorado, 1999.

Chauvet, Fidel de Jesús. *El culto Guadalupano del Tepeyac.* Mexico City: Centro de Estudios Bernardino de Sahagún, 1978.

Chavez, Linda. *Out of the Barrio: Toward a New Politics of Hispanic Assimilation.* New York: Basic Books, 1991.

Chávez, Leo R., Estévan T. Flores, and Marta López Garza. Migrants and Settlers: A Comparison of Undocumented Mexicans and Central Americans in the United States. *Frontera Norte* 1, no. 1 (1989): 49–75.

Chesterton, G. K. *The Catholic Church and Conversion.* New York: Macmillan, 1926.

Christiano, Kevin J. *The Church and the New Immigrants,* Religion and the Social Order, Vatican II and U.S. Catholicism, vol. 2, 169–86.

Chupungco, Anscar J. *Cultural Adaptation of the Liturgy.* New York: Paulist Press, 1982.

———. *Liturgies of the Future: The Process and Methods of Inculturation.* New York: Paulist, 1989.

———. *Liturgical Inculturation: Sacramentals, Religiosity, and Catechesis.* Collegeville, Minn.: Liturgical Press, 1992.

Coatsworth, John H. Commentary on Enrique Dussel Peters' "Recent Structural Changes in Mexico's Economy: A Preliminary Analysis of Some Sources." In *Crossings: Mexican Immigration in Interdisciplinary Perspective.* Ed. Marcelo M. Suárez-Orozco, 75–78. Cambridge: Harvard University Press, 1998.

Cohen, I. Heart in Biblical Psychology. In *Essays Presented to Chief Rabbi Israel Brodie on the Occasion of His 70th Birthday,* 1, 41–57. London: Soncino Press, 1966.

Comoroff, Jean, and John Comaroff. *Of Revelation and Revolution,* vol. 1, 1991.

Conferencia General del Episcopado Latinoamericano (CELAM II: Medellín, Colombia, 1968). *Medellín Conference—Final Document. The Church in the Present-Day Transformation of Latin America in Light of the Council.* 2 vols. Bogotá: General Secretariat of CELAM, 1970–1973.

Conferencia General del Episcopado Latinoamericano (CELAM III: Puebla, Mexico, 1979). *Puebla Conference—Final Document. Visión pastoral de America Latina: Equipo de reflexión, departamentos y secciones de CELAM.* Bogotá: Consejo Episcopal Latinoamericano, 1978.

Conferencia General del Episcopado Latinoamericano (CELAM IV: Santo Domingo, Dominican Republic, 1992). *Documento de consulta: Nueva evangelización, promoción humana.* Bogotá: Consejo Episcopal Latinoamericano, 1991.

Conn, Walter E., ed. *Conversion, Perspectives on Personal and Social Transformation.* New York: Alba House, 1978.

———. *Christian Conversion: A Developmental Interpretation of Autonomy and Surrender.* New York: Paulist Press, 1986.

Connor, Kimberly Rae. *Conversions and Visions in the Writings of African-American Women.* Knoxville: University of Tennessee Press, 1994.

Conover, Ted. *Coyotes: A Journey through the Secret World of America's Illegal Aliens.* New York: Vintage Departures, 1987.

Conway, Flo, and Jim Siegelman. *Snapping: America's Epidemic of Sudden Personality Change.* Philadelphia: J.B. Lippincott, 1978.

Cooke, Bernard J. *Sacraments & Sacramentality.* Mystic, Conn.: Twenty-Third Publications, 1983.

Cormie, Lee. The Hermeneutical Privilege of the Oppressed: Liberation Theologies, Biblical Faith, and Marxist Sociology of Knowledge. *Proceedings of the Catholic Theological Society of America* 33 (1978): 155–81.

Cornelius, Wayne A. Appearances and Realities: Controlling Illegal Immigration in the United States. In *Temporary Workers or Future Citizens: Japanese and U.S. Migration Policies.* Ed. M. Weiner and T. Hanami, 114–44. London: Macmillan, 1997.

———. The Structural Embeddedness of Demand for Mexican Immigrant Labor: New Evidence from California. In *Crossings: Mexican Immigration in Interdisciplinary Perspective.* Ed. Marcelo M. Suárez-Orozco, 114–44. Cambridge: Harvard University Press, 1998.

Cunningham, Lawrence S., and Keith J. Egan. *Christian Spirituality: Themes from the Tradition.* New York: Paulist Press, 1996.

Cunningham, L. *The Catholic Faith: A Reader.* New York, Paulist Press, 1988.

———. *Thomas Merton, Spiritual Master:* The Essential Writings. New York, Paulist Press, 1992.

————. *Thomas Merton and the Monastic Vision*. Grand Rapids, Mich.: W. B. Eerdmans, 1999.

Cunningham, L. and J. Kelsay. *The Sacred Quest: An Invitation to the Study of Religion*. Upper Saddle River, N.J., Prentice Hall, 2002.

Cunningham, L. and J. Reich. *Culture and Values: A Survey of the Western Humanities*. Fort Worth, Holt Rinehart and Winston, 1990.

Cushman, Philip. The Self Besieged: Recruitment-Indoctrination Processes in Restrictive Groups. *Journal for the Theory of Social Behavior* 16 (1986): 1–32.

Danielou, Jean. *Prayer: The Mission of the Church*. Trans. David Louis Schlindler. Grand Rapids, Mich.: W. B. Eerdmans, 1996.

Dart, John. Immigrants Called 'Ripe Harvest Field' for Churches, *Los Angeles Times*, April 20, 1985, p.6.

Davis, Kenneth G. *Primero Dios: Alcoholics Anonymous and the Hispanic Community*. Selingsgrove, Pa.: Susquehanna University Press, 1994.

de Fraine, Jean, and Albert Vanhoye. Heart. In *Dictionary of Biblical Theology*. Ed. Xavier Leon-Defour, 200–202. Paris: Desclée, 1967.

de La Potterie, Ignace. "Le christ, comme figure de révélation d'apres S. Jean." In *Revelation de Dieu et langage des hommes*, 51–76. Paris: Les Éditions du Cerf, 1972.

de Sales, St. Francis. *Introduction to the Devout Life*. Trans. John K. Ryan. New York: Bantam Doubleday Dell, 1989.

De Vos, George A. *Social Cohesion and Alienation: Minorities in the United States and Japan*. Boulder, Colo.: Westview Press, 1992.

Deck, Allan Figueroa, S.J. "Fundamentalism and the Hispanic Catholic." *America*, January 26, 1985, 64–66.

————. *The Second Wave*. New York: Paulist Press, 1989.

————, ed. *Frontiers of Hispanic Theology in the United States*. Maryknoll, N.Y.: Orbis, 1992.

————. "Latino Religion and the Struggle for Justice: Evangelization as Conversion." *Journal of Hispanic/Latino Theology* 4/3 (February 1997): 28–41.

————. *The Worldview, Values and Religion of Mexican Immigrants in Orange County Today.*, Santa Ana, Calif.: Second Lives, A South Coast Repitrory Publications, 1983.

————. *A Christian Perspective on the Reality of Illegal Immigration*. Social Thought, The 1978 O'Grady Award Winner, Fall 1978, National Conference of Catholic Charities, Washington, D.C.

Demousteir, Calvez. The Disturbing Subject: Option for the Poor. *Studies in the Spirituality of Jesuits*, March 1989.

Diaz del Castillo, Bernal. *The Bernal Diaz Chronicles: The True Story of the Conquest of Mexico*. Garden City, N.Y.: Doubleday, 1957.

Díaz-Stevens, Ana María. *Oxcart Catholicism on Fifth Avenue: The Impact of the Puerto Rican Migration Upon the Archdiocese of New York*. Notre Dame Studies in American Catholicism. Notre Dame, Ind.: University of Notre Dame Press, 1993.

Dolan, Jay, ed. *The American Catholic Parish: A History from 1850 to the Present*. New York: Paulist, 1987.

————. *Transforming Parish Ministry: The Changing Roles of Catholic Clergy, Laity, and Women Religious*. New York: Crossroad, 1989.

———. *The American Catholic Experience: A History from Colonial Times to the Present.* Garden City, N.Y.: Image Books, 1985.

Dolan, Jay P., and Allan Figueroa Deck, eds. *Hispanic Catholic Culture in the U.S.: Issues and Concerns.* The Notre Dame History of Hispanic Catholics in the U.S. Notre Dame, Ind.: University of Notre Dame Press, 1994.

Dolan, Jay P., and Gilberto Hinojosa, eds. *Mexican Americans and the Catholic Church, 1900–1965.* The Notre Dame History of Hispanic Catholics in the U.S. Notre Dame, Ind.: University of Notre Dame Press, 1994.

Donahue, John R. *The Gospel in Parable: Metaphor, Narrative, and Theology in the Synoptic Gospels.* Philadelphia: Fortress Press, 1988.

Donovan, Vincent J. *Christianity Rediscovered: An Epistle From the Masai.* Maryknoll, N.Y.: Orbis, 1978.

Door, Donal. Option for the Poor: Its Biblical Basis. In *Spirituality and Justice.* Maryknoll, N.Y.: Orbis, 1986.

———. *Spirituality and Justice.* Maryknoll, N.Y.: Orbis, 1986.

Doorley, Mark J. *The Place of the Heart in Lonergan's Ethics: The Role of Feelings in the Ethical Intentionality Analysis of Bernard Lonergan.* Lanham, Md.: University Press of America, 1996.

Doran, Robert M. *Psychic Conversion and Theological Foundations: Toward a Reorientation of the Human Sciences.* Chico, Calif.: Scholars Press, 1981.

Doran, Robert M., and Fredrick E. Crowe, eds. *Collected Works of Bernard Lonergan.* Toronto: University of Toronto Press, 1988.

Dow, James. Universal Aspects of Symbolic Healing: A Theoretical Synthesis. *American Anthropologist* 88 (1986): 56–69.

Downey, Michael. *Understanding Christian Spirituality.* New York: Paulist Press, 1997.

———. *Hope Begins Where Hope Begins.* Maryknoll, N.Y., Orbis Books, 1998.

———. *Altogether Gift: A Trinitarian Spirituality.* Maryknoll, N.Y.: Orbis Books, 2000.

———. *A Blessed Weakness: The Spirit of Jean Vanier and L'Arche.* San Francisco, Harper & Row, 1986.

Dreyer, Elizabeth A. *The Cross in the Christian Tradition: From Paul to Bonaventure* (New York: Paulist Press), 2001.

Driscoll, Michael. Friendship. In *The New Dictionary of Catholic Spirituality.* Ed. Michael Downey, 423–29. Collegeville, Minn.: Liturgical Press, 1993.

Driskill, Joseph D. Habits of the Head and Heart: Elders and Contemporary Spirituality. *Impact*, 31 (1993): 16–26.

Dulles, Avery. *Models of the Church.* Expanded edition. New York: Doubleday, 1987.

———. "Fundamental Theology and the Dynamics of Conversion." *Thomist* 45/2 (April 1981): 175–93.

Duneier, Mitchell. *Slim's Table.* Chicago: University of Chicago Press, 1992.

Dunne, Tad. *Lonergan and Spirituality: Toward a Spiritual Integration.* Chicago: Loyola University Press, 1985.

Durrwell, F. X. *The Resurrection, a Biblical Study.* New York: Sheed and Ward, 1960.

———. *In the Redeeming Christ.* New York: Sheed and Ward, 1963.

Durand, Jorge and Massey, Douglas, S. *Miracles on the Border, Retablos of Mexican Immigrants to the United States.* University of Arizona Press, 1995.

Edwards, Denis. *What Are They Saying about Salvation?* New York: Paulist Press, 1986.

Edwards, Tilden. *Spiritual Friend.* New York: Paulist Press, 1980.

Eigo, Francis A., ed. *The Human Experience of Conversion: Persons and Structures in Transformation.* Villanova, Pa.: Villanova University Press, 1987.

Elizondo, Virgil. *Guadalupe: Mother of the New Creation.* Maryknoll, N.Y.: Orbis, 1997.

———. *The Future Is Mestizo: Life Where Cultures Meet.* Oak Park, Ill.: Meyer-Stone Books, 1988.

———. I Forgive But I Do Not Forget. In *Beyond Borders: Writings of Virgilio Elizondo and Friends.* Ed. Timothy Matovina, 208–16. Maryknoll, N.Y.: Orbis, 2000.

———. Our Lady of Guadalupe as a Cultural Symbol: "The Power of the Powerless." In *Liturgy and Cultural Religious Traditions.* Ed. Herman Schmidt and David Power, 25–33. New York: Seabury, 1977.

———. Métissage, violence culturelle, annonce de l'Évangile: La dimension interculturelle de l'Évangélisation. Ph.D. diss., Institut Cátolique, 1978.

———. *La Morenita: Evangelizer of the Amercias.* San Antonio: Mexican American Cultural Center, 1981.

———. *Galilean Journey: The Mexican-American Promise.* Maryknoll, N.Y.: Orbis, 1983.

———. *Way of the Cross: The Passion of Christ in the Americas.* Maryknoll, N.Y.: Orbis, 1992.

Ellingwood, Ken, H.G. Reza, and James Rainey. At Least 7 Migrants Perish in Cold. *Los Angeles Times*, April 3, 1999, sec. A, p. 1.

Emerson, Robert M., Rachel I. Fretz, and Linda L. Shaw. *Writing Ethnographic Fieldnotes.* Chicago: University of Chicago Press, 1995.

Epstein, Semour. The Implications of Cognitive-Experiential Self-Theory for Research in Social Psychology and Personality. *Journal for the Theory of Social Behavior* 15 (1985): 283–310.

Erikson, Kai T. "A Comment on Disguised Observation in Sociology." *Social Problems* 14, no. 4 (Spring 1967): 366–73.

Espín, Orlando O. Immigration,Territory, and Globalization: Theological Reflections. *Journal of Hispanic/Latino Theology* 7:3 (February 2000): 46–59.

———. Grace and Humanness. In *We Are a People.* Ed. Roberto Goizueta. Philadelphia: Fortress Press, 1992.

———. *The Faith of the People: Theological Reflections of the People.* Maryknoll, N.Y.: Orbis, 1997.

———. Popular Religion as an Epistemology (of Suffering). *Journal of Hispanic/Latino Theology* 2:2 (November 1994): 55–78.

Espín, Orlando, and Miguel Díaz. *From the Heart of Our People: Latino/a Explorations in Systematic Theology.* Maryknoll, N.Y.: Orbis, 1999.

Fastiggi, Robert. *The Conversion of Mind and Heart.* Atlanta: Scholars Press, 1990.

Falicov, Celia Jaes, McGoldrick, M., John K. Pearce, and J. Giordano, eds. *Mexican Families, Ethnicity and Family Therapy Center.* New York: The Guilford Press, 1982.

Fernández, Eduardo C. *La Cosecha: Harvesting Contemporary United States Hispanic Theology (1972–1998).* Collegeville, Minn.: Liturgical Press, 2000.

Fielding, Nigel G., and Jane L. Fielding. *Linking Data*, vol. 4. Qualitative Research Methods Series. Sage Publications: Beverly Hills, 1986.

Finney, John, M. A Theory of Religious Commitment. *Sociological Analysis* 39 (1978): 19–35.

Fitzpatrick, Joseph P., S.J. *Catholic Responses to Hispanic Newcomers*, Sociological Focus, Fordham University, vol. 23, no.3, August 1990.

Flatten, Mark. Tensions Heat Up Along Border. *East Valley Tribune*, May 27, 2000, sec. A, p. 1, 6.

Fowler, James. *Stages of Faith: The Psychology of Human Development and the Quest for Meaning*. San Francisco: Harper & Row, 1981.

Fragomeni, Richard. "Conversion." In *The New Dictionary of Catholic Spirituality*. Ed. Michael Downey, 230–35. Collegeville, Minn.: The Liturgical Press, 1993.

Fragoso Castanares, Alberto. Vida del beato Juan Diego. *Histórica: Organo del Centro de Estudios Guadalupanos* 2 (June 1991).

Frankl, Viktor. *Man's Search for Meaning*. Rev. ed. Trans. Ilse Lasch. New York: Simon and Schuster, 1962.

Freire, Paulo. *Pedagogy of the Oppressed*. Trans. M.B. Ramos. New York: Seabury Press, 1970.

Galarza, Ernesto, Herman E. Gallegos, and Julian Samora. *Mexican-Americans in the Southwest*. Santa Barbara, Calif.: McNally and Loftin, 1969.

Gallagher, Eugene V. *Expectation and Experience: Explaining Religious Conversion*. Ventures in Religion, vol. 3. Atlanta, Ga.: Scholars Press, 1990.

Gamio, Manuel. *Mexican Immigration to the United States; a Study of Human Migration and Adjustment*. New York: Dover Publications, 1971.

García-Rivera, Alejandro. *St. Martin De Porres: The "Little Stories" and the Semiotics of Culture*. Maryknoll, N.Y.: Orbis, 1995.

———. *The Community of the Beautiful: A Theological Aesthetics*. Collegeville, Minn.: Liturgical Press, 1999.

———. *Jesus, Mary, and Joseph Were Illegal Immigrants*. U. S. Catholic: Gray Matters, April 1995.

Garfinkel, Harold. *Studies in Ethnomethodology*. Englewood Cliffs, N.J.: Prentice-Hall, 1967.

Garrett, William R. Troublesome Transcendence: The Supernatural in the Scientific Study of Religion. *Sociological Analysis* 35 (1974): 167–80.

Geffré, C. *Le christianisme au risque de l'interpretation. Essais d'herméneutique théologique*. Paris: Ed. de Cerf, 1983.

Gelpi, Donald L. *Charism and Sacrament: A Theology of Christian Conversion*. New York: Paulist Press, 1976.

———. The Converting Jesuit. In *Studies in the Spirituality of Jesuits*, 18/1. St. Louis: Institute of Jesuit Sources, 1986.

———. The Converting Catechumen. *Lumen Vitae* 42, no. 401–415 (1987).

———. Religious Conversion: A New Way of Being. In *The Human Experience of Conversion: Persons and Structures in Transformation*. Ed. Francis A. Eigo. Villanova, Pa.: Villanova University Press, 1987.

———. Conversion: Beyond the Impasses of Individualism. In *Beyond Individualism*. Ed. Donald J. Gelpi. Notre Dame, Ind.: University of Notre Dame Press, 1989.

———. *Committed Worship: A Sacramental Theology for Converting Christians.* 2 vols. Collegeville, Minn.: Liturgical Press, 1993.

———. *The Conversion Experience.* New York/Mahwah, N.J.: Paulist, 1998.

———. Incarnate Excellence: Jonathan Edwards and an American Theological Aesthetic. *Religion and the Arts,* 2, no. 4 (1998): 443–66.

Giago, Tim A. Spirituality Comes from the Heart, Not from a Book. *American Indian Religions: An Interdisciplinary Journal* 1 (Winter 1994): 97–98.

Gilmore, David D. *Manhood in the Making: Cultural Concepts of Masculinity.* New Haven, Conn.: Yale University Press, 1990.

Goizueta, Roberto. U.S. Hispanic Popular Catholicism as Theopoetics. Ed. Ada María Isasi-Díaz and Fernando F. Segovia, 280–6. Minneapolis: Fortress Press, 1996.

———. Fiesta: Life in the Subjunctive. In *From the Heart of Our People: Latino/a Explorations in Systematic Theology.* Ed. Orlando Espín and Miguel Díaz, 84–99. Maryknoll, N.Y.: Orbis, 1999.

———. Liberation Theology, Influence on Spirituality. In *The New Dictionary of Catholic Spirituality.* Edited by Michael Downey, 597–600. Collegeville, Minn.: Liturgical Press, 1993.

———. *Caminemos Con Jesús: Toward a Hispanic/Latino Theology of Accompaniment.* Maryknoll, N.Y.: Orbis, 1995.

Goleman, Daniel. *Emotional Intelligence.* New York: Bantam Books, 1995.

Gonzales-Faus, Juan Ignacio. *La humanidad nueva—ensayo de Cristologia.* Madrid: EAPSA, 1975.

González, Roberto O., and Michael LaVelle. *The Hispanic Catholic in the United States.* Hispanic American Pastoral Investigations, vol. 1. New York: Northeast Catholic Pastoral Center for Hispanics, 1985.

Gordon, David F. Dying to Self: Self-Control through Self-Abandonment. *Sociological Analysis* 45 (1984): 41–56.

Gossen, Gary H., Robert M. Carmack, and Janine Gasco. *The Legacy of Mesoamerica: History and Culture of a Native American Civilization.* Upper Saddle River, N.J.: Prentice Hall, 1996.

Gottwald, Norman K., ed. *The Bible and Liberation: Political and Social Hermeneutics.* Maryknoll, N.Y.: Orbis, 1983.

Gould, Roger L. *Transformations: Growth and Change in Adult Life.* New York: Simon and Schuster, 1978.

Greeley, Andrew. *The Catholic Myth.* New York: Collier Books, 1990.

———. Defection among Hispanics. *America,* July 30, 1988, 61–62.

———. Defection among Hispanics (Updated). *America,* September 27, 1997, 12–13.

———. *The American Catholic: A Social Portrait.* New York: Basic Books, 1977.

———. *Parish, Priest and People.* Chicago: Thomas More Press, 1981.

———. *American Catholics Since the Council: An Unauthorized Report.* Chicago, Ill.: Thomas More Press, 1985.

———. Theology and Sociology: On Validating David Tracy. *Journal of the American Academy of Religion* 59, no. 4 (Winter 1991): 643–52.

Gregson, Vernon, ed. *The Desires of the Human Heart: An Introduction to the Theology of Bernard Lonergan.* New York: Paulist Press, 1988.

Greil, Arthur L., and David R. Rudy. Social Cocoons: Encapsulation and Identity Transformation Organizations. *Sociological Inquiry* 54 (1984): 260–78.

Griffin, E. *Turning: Reflections on the Experience of Conversion*. Garden City: Doubleday, 1982.

Griswold del Castillo, Richard and Richard A. Garcia. *César Chávez: A Triumph of Spirit, The Oklahoma Western Biographies, vol. 2*. Norman, Okla: University of Oklahoma Press, 1995

Groll, Douglas R. Proposition 187: Catalyst for Reflection on Our Immigrant Identity as an Impetus for Mission. *Concordia Journal*. April 1996, 164–77.

Groody, Daniel. Discernment, Desire and Decision-Making in the Life of Ignatius of Loyola. Berkeley, Calif.: Jesuit School of Theology, 1999.

Guerrero, Jose Louis G. *El Nican Mopohua: Un intento de exégesis*. Mexico City: Universidad Pontificia de México, 1996.

Gutiérrez, Gustavo. *A Theology of Liberation: History, Politics and Salvation*. Maryknoll, N.Y.: Orbis, 1973.

———. *The Power of the Poor in History*. Maryknoll, N.Y.: Orbis, 1983.

———. *We Drink from Our Own Wells*. Maryknoll, N.Y.: Orbis, 1984.

———. *On Job: God-Talk and the Suffering of the Innocent*. Maryknoll, N.Y.: Orbis, 1987.

———. *The God of Life*. Maryknoll, N.Y.: Orbis, 1991.

Gutmann, Matthew C. *The Meanings of Macho: Being a Man in Mexico City*. Berkeley: University of California Press, 1996.

Hammersley, Martyn, and Paul Atkinson. *Ethnography: Principles in Practice*. 2d. ed. London: Routledge, 1995.

Handlin, Oscar. *The Uprooted*. Boston: Little, Brown, 1951.

Hanson, Paul D. *The People Called: The Growth of Community in the Bible*. San Francisco: Harper & Row, 1986.

Happel, Stephen, and James J. Walter. *Conversion and Discipleship: A Christian Foundation*. Philadelphia: Fortress Press, 1986.

Harding, Susan F. Convicted by the Holy Spirit: The Rhetoric of Fundamental Baptist Conversion. *American Ethnology* 14 (1987): 167–81.

Häring, Bernard. *Evangelization Today*. New York: Crossroad, 1990.

Haughton, Rosemary. *The Transformation of Man: A Study of Conversion and Community*. London: G. Chapman, 1967.

Hayes-Bautista, David E., Aída Hurtado, R. Burciaga Valdez, and Anthony C.R. Hernandéz. *No Longer a Minority: Latinos and Social Policy in California*. Los Angeles: UCLA Chicano Studies Research Center, 1992.

Hebblethwaite, Margaret. *Base Communities: An Introduction*. Mahwah, N.J.: Paulist, 1994.

Hefner, Robert W. *Conversion to Christianity: Historical and Anthropological Perspectives on a Great Transformation*. Berkeley: University of California Press, 1993.

Heirich, Max. Change of Heart: A Test of Some Widely Held Theories about Religious Conversion. *American Journal of Sociology* 83 (1977): 653–80.

Hemrick, Eugene F., ed. *Strangers and Aliens No Longer: Part One, the Hispanic Presence in the Church in the United States*. Washington, D.C.: United States Catholic Conference, 1993.

Herrera-Sobek, María. *Northward Bound: The Mexican Immigrant Experience in Ballad and Song*. Bloomington: Indiana University Press, 1993.

Hervas Benet, Juan. *Los Cursillos De Cristiandad: Instrumento De Renovación Cristiana*. 6. ed. Madrid: Euramerica, 1965.

Hesburgh, Theodore. *The Theology of Catholic Action*. Notre Dame, Ind.: University of Notre Dame Press, 1946.

Himes, Kenneth R. The Rights of People Regarding Migration: A Perspective from Catholic Social Teaching. In *Who Are My Sisters and Brothers?* Ed. Carleen Reck. Washington, D.C.: United States Catholic Conference, 1996.

Hine, Virginia H. Bridge Burners: Commitment and Participation in a Religious Movement. *Sociological Analysis* 31 (1970): 61–66.

Hinojosa, Gilberto Miguel. *A Borderlands Town in Transition: Laredo, 1755–1870*. 1st ed. College Station: Texas A&M University Press, 1983.

Hoge, Dean R., Kenneth McGuire, Bernard Stratman, and Alvin A. Illig. *Converts, Dropouts and Returnees: A Study of Religious Change among Catholics*. Washington, D.C.: United States Catholic Conference, 1981.

Houdek, Frank. *Guided by the Spirit: A Jesuit Perspective on Spiritual Direction*. Chicago: Loyola Press, 1996.

Houlden, J. L. Conversion. In *The Oxford Companion to the Bible*. Ed. B. Metzger and M. Coogan, 132–34. New York: Oxford University Press, 1993.

Isasi-Díaz, Ada María, and Yolanda Tarango. *Hispanic Women: Prophetic Voice in the Church*. San Francisco: Harper & Row, 1988.

Irarrázaval, Diego. *Inculturation: New Dawn of the Church in Latin America*. Maryknoll, N.Y.: Orbis, 2000.

James, William. *The Varieties of Religious Experience*. Garden City, N.Y.: Image Books, 1978.

Jameson, F. and M. Miyoahi, eds. *The Cultures of Globalization*. Durham, N.C.: Duke University Press, 1998.

John of the Cross. *The Collected Works of Saint John of the Cross*. Trans. Kieran Kavanaugh and Otilio Rodriguez. Rev. ed. Washington, D.C.: ICS Publications, 1991.

John Paul II, *Redemptor Hominis*. Washington, D.C.: United States Catholic Conference, 1979.

———. *On the Permanent Validity of the Church's Missionary Mandate*. Washington, D.C.: United States Catholic Conference, 1991.

———. *Ecclesia in America*. Washington, D.C.: United States Catholic Conference, January 22, 1999.

Johnson, Cedric B. *Christian Conversion: Biblical and Psychological Perspectives*. Grand Rapids, Mich.: Zondervan, 1982.

Jones, Wilfrid Lawson. *A Psychological Study of Religious Conversion*. London: Epworth Press (E. C. Barton), 1937.

Juster, Susan. "In a Different Voice:" Male and Female Narratives of Religious Conversion in Post–Revolutionary America. *American Quarterly* 41 (1989): 34–62.

Kanellos, Nicolás, ed. *The Hispanic-American Almanac*. Detroit: Gale Research, 1993.

Kanellos, Nicholás, and Claudio Esteva-Fabregat, eds. *Handbook of Hispanic Cultures in the United States: Sociology*. Ed. Félix Padilla. Houston: Arte Público Press, 1994.

Kanter, Rosabeth Moss. Commitment and Social Organization: A Study of Commitment Mechanisms in Utopian Communities. *American Sociological Review* 33 (1968): 499–517.

Kaufman, Debra Renee. Patriarchal Women: A Case Study of Newly Orthodox Jewish Women. *Symbolic Interaction* 12 (1989): 299–315.

Kavanaugh, John Francis. *Following Christ in a Consumer Society: The Spirituality of Cultural Resistance*. Maryknoll, N.Y.: Orbis, 1991.

Kennedy, William Bean, Alice Frazer Evans, and Robert A. Evans. *Pedagogy for the Non-Poor*. Maryknoll, N.Y.: Orbis, 1987.

King, A.B. ed., *Culture, Globalization and the World-System: Contemporary Conditions for the Representation of Identity*. Minneapolis: University of Minnesota Press, 1997.

Kirk, Jerome, and Mark L. Miller. *Reliability and Validity in Qualitative Research* Qualitative Research Methods Series, vol. 1. Beverly Hills, Calif.: Sage Publications, 1986.

Klockers, Carl B. Dirty Hands and Deviant Subjects. In *Deviance and Decency: Ethics of Research with Human Subjects*. Ed. Carl B. Klockers and Finbarr W. O'Connor. Beverly Hills, Calif.: Sage Publications, 1979.

Lafaye, Jacques. *Quetzalcoatl et Guadalupe: La formation de la consicence nationale au Mexique (1531–1813)*. Paris: Gallimard, 1976.

Lamb, Matthew L. The Challenge of Critical Theory. In *Sociology and Human Destiny*. Ed. Gregory Baum, 1980.

Lasso de la Vega, Luis, Lisa Sousa, Stafford Poole, James Lockhart, and Miguel Sánchez. *The Story of Guadalupe: Luis Laso de La Vega's 'Huei Tlamahuiçoltica' of 1649*. Stanford, Calif.: Stanford University Press, 1998.

Leclercq, J. L'amité dans les lettres au moyen age. *Revue du moyen âge latin* 1 (1945): 391–410.

Leech, Kenneth. *Soul Friend: A Study in Spirituality*. San Francisco: Harper & Row, 1980.

Leo, Richard A. Trial and Tribulations: Courts, Ethnography, and the Need for an Evidentiary Privilege for Academic Researchers. *The American Sociologist*, (spring 1995): 113–33.

Leonard, Bill J. Getting Saved in America: Conversion Event in a Pluralistic Culture."*Review and Expositor* 82 (1985): 111–27.

León-Portilla, Miguel. *Aztec Thought and Culture: A Study of the Ancient Nahuatl Mind*. Trans. Jack Emory Davis. Norman: University of Oklahoma Press, 1963.

———. Un acercamiento a los antiguos códices y los Tlahtolli, narrativa, discursos del mundo Náhuatl. In *Historia de la literatura periódo prehispánico*, 25–67. México, DF: Editorial Alhambra Mexicana S.A., 1989.

———. *The Aztec Image of Self and Society: An Introduction to Nahua Culture*. Edited by J.Jorge Klor de Alva. Salt Lake City, Utah: University of Utah Press, 1992.

———. *Broken Spears: The Aztec Account of the Conquest of Mexico*. Boston: Beacon Press, 1992.

———. Those Made Worthy of Divine Sacrifice: The Faith of Ancient Mexico. In *South and Meso American Native Spirituality: From the Cult of the Feathered Serpent to the Theology of Liberation*. Ed. Gary H. Gossen and Miguel León Portilla, 4, 41–64. New York: Crossroad, 1993.

———, ed. *Native Mesoamerican Spirituality*. New York: Paulist Press, 1980.

León Portilla, M. and A. Valeriano. *Tonantzin Guadalupe: pensamiento náhuatl y mensaje cristiano en el "Nican mopohua"*. México, Colegio Nacional: Fondo de Cultura Económica, 2000

León, Luis D. Metaphor and Place: The U.S.–Mexico Border as Center and Periphery in the Interpretation of Religion. *Journal of the American Academy of Religion* 67, no. 3 (1999).

Levy, Jacques E., and Cesar Chavez. *Cesar Chavez: Autobiography of La Causa.* 1st ed. New York: Norton, 1975.

Lewis, C. S. *Surprised by Joy: The Shape of My Early Life.* New York: Phoenix Press, 1986.

Lofink, Gerhard. *Jesus and Community.* New York: Paulist Press, 1984.

Lofink, Norbert F. *Option for the Poor.* Berkeley: BIBAL Press, 1987.

Lofland, John, and Lyn H. Lofland. *Analyzing Social Structures: A Guide to Qualitative Observations and Analysis.* San Francisco: Wadsworth, 1995.

Lofland, John, and Rodney Stark. Becoming a World-Saver: A Theory of Conversion to a Deviant Perspective. *American Sociological Review* 30 (1965): 862–75.

Lonergan, Bernard. *Theology in Its New Context: A Second Collection.* Ed. W.F.J. Ryan and B.J. Tyrell. London: Darton, Longman & Todd, 1974.

Lonergan, Bernard J. F. *Method in Theology.* Minneapolis: Winston/Seabury, 1972.

———. Theology and Praxis. *CTSA Proceedings* (1977): 1–17.

———. *A Third Collection.* New York: Paulist, 1985.

Long, Theodore E., and Jeffrey K. Hadden. Religious Conversion and the Concept of Socialization: Integrating the Brainwashing and Drift Models. *Journal for the Scientific Study of Religion* 22 (1983): 1–14.

López Austin, Alfredo. *Tamoanchan, Tlalocan: Places of Mist.* The Mesoamerican Worlds Series. Ed. David Carrasco and Eduardo Matos Moctezuma. Niwot, Colo.: University Press of Colorado, 1997.

Lutton, Wayne. *The Costs of Immigration.* Petoskey, Mich.: Social Contract Press, 1994.

M. Suárez-Orozco, Marcelo. *Crossings: Mexican Immigration in Interdisciplinary Perspective.* Cambridge: Harvard University Press, 1998.

Maciel, David, and María Herrera-Sobek. *Culture across Borders: Mexican Immigration & Popular Culture.* Tucson: University of Arizona Press, 1998.

Marcoux, Marcene. *Cursillo, Anatomy of a Movement: The Experience of Spiritual Renewal.* New York: Lambeth Press, 1982.

Marín, Gerardo, and Raymond J. Gamba. The Role of Expectations in Religious Conversions: The Case of Hispanic Catholics. *Review of Religious Research* 34 (June 1993): 357–71.

Marins, Jose, y Equipo. *Para vivir a Maria, madre de comunidades.* Buenos Aires: Editorial Guadalupe, 1989.

Marins, Jose, and Teolide Trevisan. *CEBS: La Iglesia En Pequeno.* Santiago: Paulinas, 1996.

Martin, David. *Tongues of Fire: The Explosion of Protestantism in Latin America.* Oxford, UK/Cambridge, Mass.: B. Blackwell, 1990.

Martinez O'Connor, Jose Diego. *Cursillos y circulos de estudios de Accion Catolica.* Almeria: Talleres de Graficas Guia, 1972.

Masson, J. La mission y la luminare de l'incarnation. *Nouvelle Revue Theologique* 98:10 (December 1976): 865–90.

Mateos, Juan, and L. Alonzo Schökel. Jesus y El Padre. In *Nuevo Testamento,* 736. Madrid: Ediciones Cristiandad, 1974.

Bibliography 171

Matovina, Timothy, ed. *Beyond Borders: Writings of Virgilio Elizondo and Friends.* Maryknoll, N.Y.: Orbis, 2000.

Mauricio y Jiménez, Gabriel. La santa imagen del Tepeyac: Lo que ahí está y no hemos visto. *Histórica: Organo del Centro de estudios Guadalupanos* 1 (March 1991).

May, Gerald G. *Will and Spirit: A Contemplative Psychology.* 1st ed. San Francisco: Harper & Row, 1983.

McCarthy, Kevin F., and Georges Vernez. *Immigration in a Changing Economy: California's Experience.* Santa Monica, Calif.: Rand, 1997.

McCracken, Grant David. *The Long Interview.* Qualitative Research Methods Series. vol. 13. Newbury Park, Calif.: Sage Publications, 1988.

McFague, Sallie. Conversion: Life on the Edge of the Raft. *Interpretation* 32 (1978): 255–68.

McGuire, Meredith. Discovering Religious Power. *Sociological Analysis* 44 (1983): 1–10.

Mendieta, E and S. Castro-Gómez, eds., *Teorías sin disciplina: Latinoamericanismo, poscolonialidad y globalización en debate.* México City: Editorial Porría, 1998.

Metz, Johannes Baptist. *Poverty of Spirit.* Rev. ed. New York: Paulist Press, 1998.

Mieth, Dietmar, and Lisa Sowle Cahill, eds. *Migrants and Refugees,* Concilium. Maryknoll, N.Y.: Orbis, 1993.

Miller, Greg. 6 Fleeing Border Patrol Fall into Ravine; 1 Killed. *Los Angeles Times,* January 22, 1996, sec. A, p. 3.

Mirandé, Alfredo. *Hombre Y Machos: Masculinity and Latino Culture.* Boulder, Colo.: Westview Press, 1998.

Montgomery, Robert L. The Spread of Religions and Macrosocial Relations. *Sociological Analysis* 52 (1991): 37–53.

Morales, Cecilio J. Jr., Hispanics and Other "Strangers," Implications of the new Pastoral of the U.S. Catholic Bishops, *Migration Today,* vol. XII, no. 1.

Morris, Rosemary Poole. *Transformation through the Gospel: Helping It Happen.* D. Min. diss., San Francisco Theological Seminary, 1988.

Muller, Jean-Marie, and Jean Kalman. *César Chavez: Un Combat Non-Violent.* Paris: Fayard/Le Cerf, 1977.

Muldoon, James, ed. *Varieties of Religious Conversion in the Middle Ages.* Gainesville: University Press of Florida, 1997.

Muñoz, Ronaldo. *Dios de los Cristianos.* São Paolo: Edicones Paulinas, 1986.

Myers, Dowell. Dimensions of Economic Adapation by Mexican-Origin Men. In *Crossings: Mexican Immigration in Interdisciplinary Perspective.* Ed. Marcelo M. Suárez-Orozco, 158–200. Cambridge: Harvard University Press, 1998.

Nebel, Richard. *Santa María Tonantzin Virgen de Guadalupe: Continuidad y transformación religiosa en México.* México: Fundo de Cultura Económica, 1992.

Newman, J. *What Is Catholic Action?* Westminster, Md.: Newman, 1958.

Newport, Frank. "The Religious Switcher in the United States." *American Journal of Sociology* 44 (1979): 528–52.

Nicklesburg, George W. E. Resurrection (Early Judiasm and Christianity). In *The Anchor Bible Dictionary.* Ed. David Noel Freedman. New York: Doubleday, 1992.

Niebuhr, H. Richard. *Christ and Culture.* New York: Harper and Brothers, 1951.

Niggli, Josephina. *Mexican Village.* Albuquerque: University of New Mexico Press, 1994.

Nock, A. D. *Conversion: The Old and the New in Religion from Alexander the Great to Augustine of Hippo.* Baltimore: The Johns Hopkins University Press, 1933.

Nogues, Javier. Atltepetl. In *The Oxford Encyclopedia of Mesoamican Cultures.* Ed. David Carrasco. New York: Oxford University Press, 2000.

O'Connor, Anne-Marie. Conditions Turn More Perilous for Border Crossers. *Los Angeles Times,* January 16, 1999, sec. A, p. 1.

———. Study Finds Changes in Causes of Border Deaths. *Los Angeles Times,* August 12, 1997, sec. A, p. 3.

Oktavec, Eileen. *Answered Prayers, Miracles and Milagros Along the Border.* University of Arizona Press, 3rd printing, 1998.

Olson, James Stuart. *Catholic Immigrants in America,* Library of Congress, 1987.

O'Neill, W. R. and W. C. Spohn. Rights of Passage: The Ethics of Immigration and Refugee Policy. *Theological Studies* 59, no. 1 (1998): 84–106.

O'Rourke, David K. *A Process Called Conversion.* Garden City, N.Y.: Doubleday, 1985.

Orsi, Robert. *Thank You, St. Jude: Women's Devotion to the Patron Saint of Hopeless Causes.* New Haven: Yale University Press, 1996.

Paige, Harry W. *The Eye of the Heart: Portraits of Passionate Spirituality.* New York: Crossroad, 1989.

Pallares, Salvador. La aparición de la Virgen de Guadalupe. *Servir* 17, no. 93–94 (1981).

Paul VI. *Evangelii Nuntiandi: On Evangelization in the Modern World.* Washington, D.C.: United States Catholic Conference, 1976.

Pérez, Arturo, Consuelo Covarrubias, and Edward Foley. *Así Es: Historias De Espiritualidad Hispana.* Trans. Sarah C. Pruett and Elena Sánchez Mora. Collegeville, Minn.: Liturgical Press, 1994.

Perkins, Pheme. *Resurrection: New Testament Witness and Contemporary Reflection.* Garden City, N.Y.: Doubleday, 1984.

Perrin, Norman. *Rediscovering the Teaching of Jesus.* San Francisco: Harper & Row, 1976.

Perry, Tony, Josh Meyer, and Henry Weinstein. 7 Die as Truck Evading Border Agents Crashes. *Los Angeles Times,* April 7, 1996, sec. A, p. 1.

Peters, Enrique Dussel. Recent Structural Changes in Mexico's Economy: A Preliminary Analysis of Some Sources. In *Crossings: Mexican Immigration in Interdisciplinary Perspective.* Ed. Marcelo M. Suárez-Orozco, 54–74. Cambridge: Harvard University Press, 1998.

Philibert, Paul. Human Development and Sacramental Transformation. *Worship* 65:6 (1991): 522–39.

Piñeda, Ana María. Evangelization of the "New World": A New World Perspective. *Missiology* 20, no. 2 (1992).

Pontifical Council Cor Unum and Pontifical Council for the Pastoral Care of Migrants and Travelers. Refugees: A Challenge to Solidarity. *Origins* 22 (1992): 305–13.

Poole, Stafford. *Our Lady of Guadalupe: The Origins and Sources of a Mexican National Symbol, 1531–1797.* Tucson: University of Arizona Press, 1995.

Portes, A., and R. G. Rumbaut. *Immigrant America.* Los Angeles: University of California Press, 1990.

Preston, David L. Becoming a Zen Practitioner. *Sociological Analysis* 42 (1981): 47–55.

Quigley, Thomas. Overview: Myths about Latin America's Church. *Origins* 23 (1993): 366.

Rahner, Karl. *Dynamic Element in the Church*. New York: Herder & Herder, 1964.

———. *Foundations of Christian Faith: An Introduction to the Idea of Christianity*. New York: Crossroad, 1982.

Rambo, Lewis R. Education and Conversion. In *Christian Teaching*. Ed. Everet Ferguson. Abilene, Tex.: Abilene Christian University Press, 1981.

———. Charisma and Conversion. *Pastoral Psychology* 31 (1982): 96–108.

———. Conversion: Toward a Holistic Model of Religious Change. *Pastoral Psychology* 38 (1989): 47–63.

———. *Understanding Religious Conversion*. New Haven, Conn.: Yale University Press, 1993.

———. Theories of Conversion: Understanding and Interpreting Religious Change. *Social Compass* 46, no. 3 (1999): 259–71.

Rambo, Lewis R., and Lawrence A. Reh. Phenomenology of Conversion. In *Handbook on Conversion*. Ed. H. Newton Malony and Samuel Southard. Birmingham, Ala.: Religious Education Press, 1992.

Ramírez, Ricardo, ed. *Fiesta, Worship and Family*. San Antonio: Mexican American Cultural Center, 1981.

Rand Parish, Helen, and Francis Sullivan. *The Only Way*. New York: Paulist Press, 1991.

Ribero, Darcy. The Latin American People. In *1492–1992: The Voice of the Victims* Ed. Leonardo Boff and Virgil Elizondo, 1990. London: SCM Press, 1990.

Rievaulx, Aelred of. *Spiritual Friendship*. Kalamazoo, Mich.: Cistercian, 1997.

Rivera Herrera, Hugo D. *Presencia de Santa María de Guadalupe en el pueblo Mexicano*. Mexico City: Editorial Progreso, 1994.

Robbins, Thomas. Constructing Cultist "Mind Control." *Sociological Analysis* 45 (1984): 241–56.

Robinson, John A. T. *Honest to God*. Philadelphia: The Westminster Press, 1963.

Rodriguez, Jeanette. *Our Lady of Guadalupe: Faith and Empowerment among Mexican-American Women*. Austin, Texas: University of Texas Press, 1994.

Romero, Gilbert C. *Hispanic Devotional Theology: Tracing the Biblical Roots*. New York: Orbis, 1991.

Roozen, David A., William McKinney, and Jackson W. Carroll. *Varieties of Religious Presence: Mission in Public Life*. New York: Harper & Row, 1988.

Rosenberg, Morris. *The Logic of Survey Analysis*. New York: Basic Books, 1968.

Sales, Francis de, and Jane de Chantal. *Letters of Spiritual Direction*. New York: Paulist Press, 1988.

Salinas, Carlos. *Descubrimiento de un busto humano en los ojos de la Virgen de Guadalupe*. Mexico City: Editoial Tradición, 1980.

Samora, Julian. *Los Mojados: The Wetback Story*. Notre Dame, Ind.: University of Notre Dame Press, 1971.

———. *Minority Leadership in a Bi-Cultural Community*. San Francisco: R and E Research Associates, 1973.

Samora, Julian, Joe Bernal, and Albert Peña. *Gunpowder Justice: A Reassessment of the Texas Rangers*. Notre Dame, Ind.: University of Notre Dame Press, 1979.

Samora, Julian, and Charles de Young Elkus. *La Raza: Forgotten Americans; Papers, in Memory of Charles De Young Elkus.* Notre Dame, Ind.: University of Notre Dame Press, 1966.

Samora, Julian, Patricia Vandel Simon, Cordelia Candelaria, and Alberto L. Pulido. *A History of the Mexican-American People.* Rev. ed. Notre Dame, Ind.: University of Notre Dame Press, 1993.

Sánchez Jankowski, Martín. *Islands in the Street: Gangs and American Urban Society.* Berkeley: University of California Press, 1991.

Sánchez, Archbishop Roberto, Responding Pastorally to Sect Activity among Immigrants. *Origins* 19, no. 32 (January 11, 1990): 526–29.

Sandoval, Moisés. *On the Move: A History of the Hispanic Church in the United States.* Maryknoll, N.Y.: Orbis Books, 1990.

———. *El campesino hispano y las iglesias en los estados unidos.* Cristianismo y Sociedad, 96 (1988) 7–19.

Sanford, John. *Dreams and Healing.* New York: Paulist Press, 1978.

———. *Dreams: God's Forgotten Language.* San Francisco: Harper & Row, 1989.

Sanjek, Roger. *Fieldnotes: The Makings of Anthropology.* Ithaca, N.Y.: Cornell University Press, 1990.

Santos, John Phillip. *Places Left Unfinished at the Time of Creation.* New York: Viking, 1999.

Savaray, Louis M., Patricia H. Berne, and Strephon Kaplan Williams. *Dreams and Spiritual Growth.* Ramsey, N.J.: Paulist Press, 1984.

Sawicki, Marianne. Recognizing the Lord. *Theology Today* 44 (1988): 441–49.

Scherer, James A., and Stephen B. Bevans, eds. *New Directions in Mission and Evangelization 1: Basic Statements 1974–1991.* Maryknoll, N.Y.: Orbis, 1992.

———, eds. *New Directions in Mission and Evangelization 2: Theological Foundations.* Maryknoll, N.Y.: Orbis, 1994.

———, eds. *New Directions in Mission and Evangelization 3: Faith and Culture.* Maryknoll, N.Y.: Orbis, 1999.

Scheuring, Tom, Lyn Scheuring, and Marybeth Greene, eds. *The Poor and the Good News: A Call to Evangelize.* Mahwah, N.J.: Paulist Press, 1993.

Schillebeeckx, Edward. *Jesus: An Experiment in Christology.* New York: Crossroad, 1981.

Schlabach, Gerald. *And Who Is My Neighbor? Poverty, Privilege and the Gospel of Christ.* Scotsdale, Pa.: Herald Press, 1990.

Schneiders, Sandra. A Hermeneutical Approach to the Study of Christian Spirituality. *Christian Spirituality Bulletin* 2 (spring 1994): 9–14.

———. The Study of Christian Spirituality: Contours and Dynamics of a Discipline. *Christian Spirituality Bulletin* 6 (March 1998): 1, 3–12.

———. *Written That You May Believe: Encountering Jesus in the Fourth Gospel.* New York: Crossroad, 1999.

———. Theology and Spirituality: Strangers, Rivals, or Partners? *Horizons* 13 (Fall 1986): 253–74.

Schreiter, Robert J. *Constructing Local Theologies.* Maryknoll, N.Y.: Orbis, 1985.

Scotchmer, David G. Life of the Heart: A Maya Protestant Spirituality. In *South and Meso American Native Spirituality: From the Cult of the Feathered Serpent to the The-*

ology of Liberation. Ed. Gary H. Gossen and Miguel León Portilla, 4, 496–525. New York: Crossroad, 1993.

Segundo, Juan Louis. *The Historical Jesus of the Synoptics*. Maryknoll, N.Y.: Orbis, 1985.

Senior, Donald, and Carroll Stuhlmueller. *The Biblical Foundations for Mission*. Maryknoll, N.Y.: Orbis, 1983.

Sevilla, Bishop Carlos, s.j. *The Ethics of Immigration Reform*, Origins, April 16, 1998, vol. 27, no.43.

Shorter, Aylward. *Toward a Theology of Inculturation*. Maryknoll, N.Y.: Orbis, 1989.

Shuler, Philip L. The Meaning of the Term Gospel. In *The International Bible Commentary*, 1229. Collegeville, Minn.: Liturgical Press, 1998.

Sider, R. *Rich Christians in an Age of Hunger*. London: Hodder and Stoughton, 1977.

Siems, Larry, ed. *Between the Lines: Letters between Undocumented Mexican and Central American Immigrants and their Families and Friends*. Tucson: University of Arizona Press, 1992.

Siller Acuña, Clodomiro L. *Para Comprender El Mensaje De María De Guadalupe*. Buenos Aires: Editorial Guadalupe, 1989.

Simmonds, Robert B. Conversion or Addiction: Consequences of Joining a Jesus Movement Group. *American Behavioral Scientist* 20 (1977): 909–24.

Simon, Julian. *The Economic Consequences of Immigration*. Oxford: Basil Blackwell, 1989.

Smith, Jody. *The Image of Guadalupe: Myth or Miracle?* New York: Doubleday, 1984.

Smith, James P., and Barry Edmonston. *The New Americans: Economic, Demographic, and Fiscal Effects of Immigration*. Washington, D.C.: National Academy Press, 1997.

Smolich. Testing the Water: Jesuits Accompanying the Poor. *Studies in the Spirituality of Jesuits* (March 1992).

Snow, David. Further Thoughts on Social Networks and Movement Recruitment. *Sociology* 17 (1983): 112–20.

Snow, David A., Jr. Louis A. Zurcher, and Sheldon Ekland-Olson. Social Networks and Social Movements: A Microstructural Approach to Differential Recruitment. *American Sociological Review* 45 (1980): 787–801.

Snow, David A., and Cynthia L. Phillips. The Lofland-Stark Conversion Model: A Critical Reassessment. *Social Problems* 27 (1980): 430–47.

Sobrino, Jon. *Spirituality of Liberation: Toward Political Holiness*. 2d. ed. Maryknoll, N.Y.: Orbis, 1989.

———. *Jesus the Liberator*. Maryknoll, N.Y.: Orbis, 1993.

———. *Christology at the Crossroads*. Maryknoll, N.Y.: Orbis, 1994.

Sosa, Lionel. *The Americano Dream: How Latinos Can Achieve Success in Business and in Life*. New York: Penguin Group, 1998.

Spradley, J. P. *The Ethnographic Interview*. Austin, Tex.: Holt, Rinehart, and Winston, 1979.

Stackhouse, Jr., John G., Billy Graham and the Nature of Conversion: A Paradigm Case. *Studies in Religion/Sciences Religieuses* 21, no. 3 (1992): 337–50.

Stark, Rodney. *The Rise of Christianity: A Sociologist Reconsiders History*. Princeton, N.J.: Princeton University Press, 1996.

Stark, Rodney, and William Sims Bainbridge. Networks of Faith: Interpersonal Bonds and Recruitment to Cults and Sects. *American Journal of Sociology* 85 (1980): 1376–95.

Straus, Roger. Changing Oneself: Seekers and the Creative Transformation of Life Experience. In *Doing Social Life: The Qualitative Study of Human Interaction in Natural Settings*. New York: Wiley Interscience, 1976.

Straus, Roger A. Religious Conversion as a Personal and Collective Accomplishment. *Sociological Analysis* 40 (1979): 158–65.

———. The Social Psychology of Religious Experience: A Naturalistic Approach. *Sociological Analysis* 41 (1981): 57–67.

Stravinskas, Peter M.J. *Proselytism among Today's Immigrants: A Preliminary Report*. United States Catholic Conference: Bishops' Committee on Migration, 1987.

———. *Proselytism among Today's Immigrants, Pastoral Care of Migrants and Refugees*. Washington, D.C.: National Conference of Catholic Bishops, A Preliminary Report, February, 1987.

Sugirtharajah, R.S., ed. *Voices from the Margin: Interpreting the Bible in the Third World*. Maryknoll, N.Y.: Orbis, 1991.

Suro, Roberto. *Strangers among Us: How Latino Immigration Is Transforming America*. New York: Alfred A. Knopf Press, 1998.

Sylvest, Ed. *Nuestra Señora de Guadalupe, Mother of God*. Dallas: Southern Methodist University Press, 1992.

———. *Motifs of Franciscan Missionary Spirit in New Spain*. Washington, D.C.: Academy of American Franciscan History, 1975.

Tallon, Andrew. The Meaning of Heart Today: Reversing the Paradigm According to Levinas and Rahner. *Journal of Religious Studies* 11 (1983): 59–74.

Taylor, Brian. Conversion and Cognition: An Area for Empirical Study in the Microsociology of Religious Knowledge. *Social Compass* 23 (1976): 5–22.

———. Recollection and Membership: Converts' Talks and the Ratiocination of Commonality. *Sociology* 12 (1978): 316–24.

Taylor, Jeremy. *Dream Work: Techniques for Discovering the Creative Power in Dreams*. New York: Paulist Press, 1983.

Thérèse of Lisieux. *Story of a Soul*. Trans. John Clarke. Washington, D.C.: ICS Publications, 1972.

Times Wire Reports. Asleep on Tracks, 6 Immigrants Die. *Los Angeles Times*, October 13, 1998, sec. A, p. 10.

Tippett, A. R. Conversion as a Dynamic Process in Christian Mission. *Missiology: An International Review* 5 (1977): 203–21.

Tipton, Steven M. *Getting Saved from the Sixties: Moral Meaning in Conversion and Cultural Change*. Berkeley: University of California Press, 1982.

Todd, Emmanuel. *Le destin des immigres*. Paris: Seuil, 1994.

Tomasi, Silvano. Pastoral Action and the New Immigrants. *Origins* 21 (1992): 580–84.

———. *A Lesson from History: The Integration of Immigrants in the Pastoral Practice of the Church in the United States*. Center for Migration Studies Occasional Papers: Pastoral Series 7; A.

Topel, L. John. *The Way to Peace: Liberation through the Bible*. Maryknoll, N.Y.: Orbis, 1979.

Travisano, Richard V. Alternation and Conversion as Fundamentally Different Transformations. In *Social Psychology through Symbolic Interaction*. Ed. Gregory P. Stone and Harvey A. Faberman. Waltham, Mass.: Ginn-Blaisdell, 1970.

Turner, Victor. *Image and Pilgrimage in Christian Culture*. Oxford: Oxford University Press, 1978.

U.S. Bureau of Census. *Population Projections for States, by Age, Sex, Race, and Hispanic Origin: 1995–2050*. Washington, D.C.: Government Printing Office, 1996.

U.S. Immigration and Naturalization Service. *Building a Comprehensive Southwest Border Enforcement Strategy*. Washington, D.C.: Government Printing Office, 1996.

———. *Operation Gatekeeper: Two Years of Progress*. Washington, D.C.: Government Printing Office, 1996.

United States Catholic Conference. *A Pastoral Statement for Catholics on Biblical Fundamentalism*. Washington, D.C.: National Conference of Catholic Bishops, Bishops' Committee on Migration, 1987.

———. *The Hispanic Presence in the New Evangelization in the United States*. Washington, D.C.: National Conference of Catholic Bishops, 1996.

———. *Hispanic Ministry: Three Major Documents*. Washington, D.C.: United States Catholic Conference, 1995.

———. *Welcoming the Stranger among Us*. Washington, D.C.: United States Catholic Conference, 2000.

Vandenakker, John Paul. *Small Christian Communities and The Parish: An Ecclesiological Analysis of the North American Experience*. Kansas City: Sheed & Ward, 1994.

Vernez, Georges, and Kevin F. McCarthy. *The Costs of Immigration to Taxpayers: Analytical and Policy Issues*. Santa Monica, Calif.: Rand, 1996.

Vilar, J. Juan Diaz. *Somos Una Sola Iglesia/We Are One Church: Ten Themes for Reflection on the U.S. Bishops' Pastoral Letter "the Hispanic Presence: Hope and Commitment."* New York: Northeast Catholic Pastoral Center for Hispanics, 1984.

———. *Sectas: Un desafío a la nueva evangelización*. Mexico, D.F.: Dabar, 1993.

Wallis, Jim. *The Call to Conversion*. San Francisco: Harper & Row, 1981.

Ward, Benedicta. *The Sayings of the Desert Fathers*. Kalamazoo, Mich.: Cistercian Publications, 1975.

Watkin, Daniel J. 12 Illegal Immigrants are Found Dead in Desert. *New York Times*, 24 May 2001.

Weiss, Robert S. *Learning from Strangers: The Art and Method of Qualitative Interview Studies*. New York: Free Press, 1994.

Weller, Susan G., and Romney A. Kendall. *Systematic Data Collection*. Qualitative Research Methods Series, vol. 10. Newbury Park, Calif.: Sage Publications, 1988.

Whyte, William Foote. *Street Corner Society*. Chicago: University of Chicago Press, 1993.

Wilber, K. *Transformations of Consciousness: Conventional and Contemplative Perspectives on Development*. Boston: New Science Library, 1986.

Wilson, Stephen R. Becoming a Yogi: Resocialization and Deconditioning as Conversion Process. *Sociological Analysis* 45 (1984): 301–14.

Wink, Walter. *Naming the Powers*. Philadelphia: Fortress Press, 1983.

———. *Unmasking the Powers: The Invisible Forces That Determine Human Existence*. Philadelphia: Fortress Press, 1986.

———. *Engaging the Powers*. Philadelphia: Fortress Press, 1992.

Wittberg, Patricia. *The Rise and Fall of Catholic Religious Orders: A Social Movement Perspective*. SUNY Series in Religion, Culture, and Society. Ed. Wade Clark Roof. Albany, N.Y.: The State University of New York Press, 1994.

World Bank. *World Development Report*. Washington, D.C.: World Bank, 1995.

Wright, W. *Bond of Perfection: Jeanne De Chantal and François De Sales*. New York: Paulist Press, 1985.

Wuthnow, Robert. *"I Come Away Stronger": How Small Groups Are Shaping American Religion*. Grand Rapids, Mich.: Eerdmans, 1994.

———. *Sharing the Journey: Support Groups and America's New Quest for Community*. New York: Free Press, 1994.

———. *The Crisis in the Churches: Spiritual Malaise, Fiscal Woe*. New York: Oxford University Press, 1997.

———. *After Heaven: Spirituality in America since the 1950s*. Berkeley: University of California Press, 1998.

———. *Imitating Christ in the Age of "Whatever."* Princeton, N.J.: Institute for Youth Ministry, Princeton Theological Seminary, 1999.

Young, Wendy. United States Immigration and Refugee Policy: The Legal Framework. In *Who Are My Sisters and Brothers?* Ed. Carleen Reck. Washington, D.C.: United States Catholic Conference, 1996.

Ysaac, Walter L. *The Third World and Bernard Lonergan*. Manila, Philippines: Lonergan Center, 1986.

Zambrano, M. N. *¡No Más! Guía para la mujer golpeada*. Seattle: Seal Press, 1994.

Ziller, Robert C. A Helical Theory of Personal Change. *Journal for the Theory of Social Behavior* 1 (1971): 33–73.

Zitterberg, Hans L. Religious Conversion and Social Roles. *Sociology and Social Research* 36 (1952): 159–66.

Index

179

About the Author

Daniel G. Groody is currently an assistant professor of theology and the director of the Center for Latino Spirituality and Culture at the Institute for Latino Studies at the University of Notre Dame. A Catholic priest and a member of the Congregation of the Holy Cross, he has spent many years working in Latin America and along the U.S.–Mexican Border. He received a post-doctoral research fellowship from the University of Notre Dame and his Ph.D. from the Graduate Theological Union in theology and Christian spirituality. He also holds a Licentiate in Sacred Theology and Master of Divinity degrees from the Jesuit School of Theology at Berkeley, and a bachelors from the University of Notre Dame in the Great Books Program.

His Ph.D. dissertation is titled *Corazón y Conversión: The Dynamics of Mexican Immigration, Christian Spirituality, and Human Transformation.* He was the executive producer of the documentaries *Strangers No Longer* (produced for the United States Conference of Catholic Bishops) and *Dying to Live: A Migrant's Journey* (www.dyingtolive.nd.edu), which was accepted into various international film festivals, won national awards, and aired on PBS. In addition to being the executive director of special projects at Catholic Television of San Antonio, Texas, Groody is an adjunct faculty member at the Mexican American Cul-tural Center in San Antonio and Tepeyac Institute in El Paso, Texas.

Groody has lectured in the United States, Latin America, and Europe on issues related to Hispanic spirituality, immigration, and Our Lady of Guadalupe. He teaches courses in U.S. Latino spirituality and systematic theology and conducts retreats and missions nationally and internationally.